"Parents of teens may want to read *The Embrace* just to heed the warning signs."

—*Denver Rocky Mountain News*

"Jones provides a good overview of the facts, surrounding voyeuristic intensity."

—*Publishers Weekly*

"Readers will get some sense of the shadowy fantasy lives of 'kids fallen through life's crack.'"

—*Kirkus Reviews*

All She Wanted

"Aphrodite Jones finds herself deeply affected by the cases she covers. . . . The book grapples with sexual experimentation, murder, hate crimes, and the transgender movement. A page-turner."

—*Sun Sentinel* (Fort Lauderdale, Florida)

Della's Web

"This fragile family background has been compellingly documented by true crime writer Aphrodite Jones."

—*The New Yorker*

"The book sizzles . . . a gripping read."

—*Herald* (Lake Worth, Florida)

Also by Aphrodite Jones

Michael Jackson Conspiracy

Red Zone

The Embrace: A True Vampire Story

Della's Web

All She Wanted

Cruel Sacrifice*

The FBI Killer*

*Published by Pinnacle

APHRODITE JONES

A PERFECT HUSBAND

PINNACLE BOOKS
Kensington Publishing Corp.
http://www.kensingtonbooks.com

To the memory of:
Kathleen Hunt Peterson
Elizabeth Ratliff
Cherica Adams
Nicole Brown Simpson
and their surviving loved ones

Some names have been changed to protect the privacy of individuals connected to this story.

PINNACLE BOOKS are published by

Kensington Publishing Corp.
119 West 40th Street
New York, NY 10018

All Kensington Titles, Imprints, and Distributed Lines are available at special quantity discounts for bulk purchases for sales promotions, premiums, fund-raising, and educational or institutional use. Special book excerpts or customized printings can also be created to fit specific needs. For details, write or phone the office of the Kensington special sales manager: Kensington Publishing Corp., 119 West 40th Street, New York, NY 10018, attn: Special Sales Department, Phone: 1-800-221-2647.

Pinnacle and the P logo Reg. U.S. Pat. & TM Off.

ISBN-13: 978-0-7860-3250-1
ISBN-10: 0-7860-3250-2

First Printing: August 2004

10 9 8 7 6

Printed in the United States of America

AUTHOR'S NOTE

This work hopes to take the murder investigation of Kathleen Peterson and place it into a meaningful context, one that will make something good come out of such a cruel and unusual circumstance. This account attempts to go beyond the newspaper reports and TV sound bites. It is based on the memories of those interviewed, as well as my own observations, police reports, court transcripts, and other documents collected during my research.

The passages that are dramatized are based on the accounts of people who lived them. This is a true story, told in its entirety, using real names, dates, and places. However, the reader should note that for the purpose of narration, certain words and phrases have been placed into a dramatic context, not to improve on what interview subjects have said, but to make the transition from speech to print more fluent.

ACKNOWLEDGMENTS

During the time I spent in the Research Triangle and in Durham covering the trial and doing research for this book, I met a number of wonderful people, without whose help and encouragement I would never have been able to face this daunting task.

Members of the law enforcement community helped me understand the complexity of the Michael Peterson case. Among them, DA Jim Hardin, ADA Freda Black, ADA David Saacks, and Detective Art Holland. There were also members of the DA's staff who need to be credited for their assistance, as well as the staff of the clerk of the Superior Court in Durham, especially Angela Kelly, Myrtle Weaver, and MeLinda Stanley. I also must acknowledge Sheriff's Deputy Walter Dwayne McDougal, who treated me with respect and kindness, and court reporter Julie Chapin, who helped me sort through the most important transcripts of the jury trial.

Throughout this book, I often referred to members of the press, both the local and national media, without naming any names. I did this at the request of certain reporters who did not wish to be named, but I must give credit to the work by the journalists at the *Herald-Sun*, the *News & Observer*, and the *Independent Weekly*, who relentlessly covered this case for over two years, reporting brilliantly about courtroom happenings, some of whom pored over Peterson's unpublished manuscripts and dug into the history of the elusive Michael Peterson, a man people have come to call "murderer."

Michael Peterson did not grant any interviews for this book. Peterson allowed his attorneys to speak for him. To be clear, I was granted no formal interviews with Peterson's attorneys, but it has been my long-standing policy to discuss all aspects of the case—and of the lives of the people within it—that have become a matter of public record.

My deepest and most heartfelt appreciation goes to

Louis Flores, who, as a talented assistant, transcriber, and researcher, made this effort possible. I would also like to thank the following for their invaluable contributions: Caitlin Atwater, Fred Atwater, Amybeth Berner, Bruce Berner, Candace Zamperini, Peter Eichenberger, Joan Troy, Pamela Wallmann, the Piacenza family, Goldie Wallace, Woody Charcoal, and Robert Olason. I am also grateful to Lynn Lowry, who provided me with an understanding of the Internet voices on the *Court TV* message board, all of whom offered such valuable insights into the backdrop of this case. I am profoundly indebted to all of you for caring, for revealing the experiences and intimacies of your lives, and for allowing me to enter your personal universe.

I wish to thank Jeremie Ruby-Strauss, my editor at Kensington, who guided me through this process and believed in this book. And, as always, I am eternally grateful to my agents, Robert Gottlieb and Alex Glass, who had the strength and courage to see the big picture, to understand the significance of an American tragedy such as this.

Finally I want to thank my enthusiastic family and my truly great friends, but most of all, I wish to thank you, my dear readers, who have shown your appreciation and vital understanding of this type of work. I admire your keen smarts, and I need your support, more than you'll ever know.

Thanks are also due to Kevin Beggs, President, Lionsgate TV; Stephen Bulka, Lifetime Television; Henry Schleiff, President, Investigation Discovery; Jeanie Vink, Investigation Discovery; Lloyd Fales, NBC Peacock Productions; Michaela Hamilton, executive editor extraordinaire, Kensington Books.

"When ye see a cloud rise out of the west, straightaway, ye say, There cometh a shower. And so it is.

And when ye see the south wind blow, ye say, There will be heat, and so it cometh to pass.

Ye hypocrites, ye can discern the face of the sky and of the earth; but how is it that ye do not discern this time?

Yea, and why even of yourselves, judge ye not what is right?

When thou goest with thine adversary to the magistrate, as thou art in the way, give diligence that thou may be delivered from him, lest he hale thee to the judge, and the judge deliver thee to the officer, and the officer cast thee into prison.

I tell thee, thou shall not depart thence, till thou has paid the very last mite."

—Luke 12: 54–59

One

It was a balmy night in Durham, not a bit like winter, and Christmas was just around the corner, with all the holiday plans in place, when the Petersons decided to settle in for a cozy evening alone. Their Christmas tree was up, their presents for the kids had been bought, not yet wrapped, but that could wait. This particular Saturday night was a special evening for them. It was a time for Michael and Kathleen to celebrate, to bring the magic back to their marriage. The Petersons were tired of the social scene; they wanted things to be more simple. It was a relief for them to stay at home and just enjoy each other. They needed that. They talked about going on a second honeymoon in Bali, one of the places in the world where they spent their happiest times.

As they sipped champagne in their family room, watching *America's Sweethearts* on the TV, they held hands like two teenagers. The Petersons realized that as much as they loved each other, as much as they were devoted and supportive of one another, they seemed to have forgotten about romance. They each had become too busy with their own lives, each of them having full-time careers; then with all their other commitments, it seemed everyone else came first. This was especially true of their five kids, who had finally grown up but were ever-more demanding as college students.

The night before, Michael had taken Kathleen to a holiday bash thrown by one of the local newspapers—he was glad that she enjoyed it—they both delighted in the social whirlwind. But with more black-tie affairs soon to come, with an invitation to the governor's mansion for the following week, with Kathleen's new gown and evening shoes already lined up and waiting, Michael reminded his wife that they had to take time out for each other. Life was too short.

By the time the two had dinner and got themselves comfortable, Kathleen left all her cares behind. She relished her private time, especially since her days were filled with corporate meetings and presentations. Despite the fact that she was a wisp of a woman, tiny in height and frame, Kathleen was the type of woman who was larger than life. Not only was she regal and brilliant, a success in her work and a supporter of the arts, she was a woman of grace, someone whom many people looked up to.

But home alone with Michael, Kathleen was a different person altogether. With Michael, she could let go of her business persona, let her hair down, and confide whatever insecurities or troubles she might have on her mind. Around Michael, her signature pearls and business suits were gone. With him, she could let go of any pretenses. Even around her kids, Kathleen would wear sporty casual attire, but with Michael, it didn't matter what she wore. He loved her every day of her life, whether she was in a ball gown or in cheap comfortable clothes. That night, Kathleen had thrown on a navy sweatshirt with white sweatpants and was running around the house in clear flip-flop sandals. Kathleen didn't need to try to impress Michael—he wasn't only her husband, he was her best friend—and she loved him more than anyone could know.

A handsome man, ten years her senior, Michael Peterson was a very successful author when he married

Kathleen. And she was his dream wife, the woman he'd been searching for. Kathleen came from a place of strength and beauty; she was a glamorous woman, a real class act. With the advance from one of his books, Michael had bought the mansion they lived in. He afforded his wife the lifestyle most people only dream of—the elegant house on lavish acres in the heart of Durham, the Porsche, the BMWs, the Jaguar—the Petersons had it all. Having been on the *New York Times* list, Michael Peterson was a known entity in their small Southern city. People in Durham were aware of him; he dabbled in local politics and wrote columns for the local media, and his war-based novels were impressive, even if they were not always met with rave reviews.

On this special occasion, Michael and Kathleen were celebrating some good news. Peterson had sold the film rights to one of his most recent books, and the project looked like it was going to be a sure thing. Michael had reason to rejoice; he had been waiting a long time for his ship to come in. With Hollywood producers calling, he felt he had a shot at international acclaim. It was an answer to his prayers, really, because he knew Kathleen hadn't been herself lately. . . .

Michael wanted to bring that sparkle back into his wife's eyes. He understood that his wife had reasons to be nervous; her financial world was rocky, especially in the months following the 9/11 attack, when her company, Nortel Networks, was in trouble. But Michael wanted Kathleen to stop worrying so much. He was a complete charmer, he knew all the right things to say, all the right moves, and even though he realized that Kathleen was concerned about her future, that her company had already laid off so many people . . . he reminded Kathleen that she was a leader, a most prized employee, someone who could never be replaced.

Michael felt optimistic that Nortel would bounce

back, that the economic crash suffered by corporate America in the wake of 9/11 was only a temporary situation. A decorated war hero, Michael Peterson was more concerned about the terrorist attacks, the troops being sent abroad, and the threats of chemical warfare. Having fought as a U.S. Marine in Vietnam, Peterson had already lived through atrocities, through things like Agent Orange. He was concerned about the young men, the U.S. troops fighting battles overseas.

That was the type of person Peterson was, a very strong man, a man of conviction, a patriot. He was always concerned for his country, his fellow citizens, his friends and neighbors. People gravitated to Michael, they loved his worldly perspective; they were entertained by his sharp mind and brilliant wit. Michael's charismatic character was the reason Kathleen had fallen so head over heels in love with him. Not only was he a good-looking man, well mannered and well bred, Michael was also an excellent talker who provided a constant source of amusement, information, and guidance. Peterson was the type of man who was the rock, the keeper of the castle. For Kathleen, Michael was the man she could always count on. He was the soul mate who would be with her until her very last breath.

Beyond her executive position at Nortel Networks, Kathleen was one of those Martha Stewart types. She was used to working on projects at home, always cooking, decorating, making things happy and cheerful. The idea that Michael wanted to spend quiet time—romantic time—really made an impression on her. Michael had e-mailed her at work the day before and he was flirting. He told her how gorgeous she was, and said he wanted to work on their marriage. Between all the kids' needs, the keeping track of every household expense, the added burden of holiday spending, Michael reminded Kathleen that she needed to give more focus to him.

That was one thing about her husband, he was independent, but he always needed her. This was an important time for him. He had a major career move happening, and he wanted her support and input. Michael wanted to stop all the worrying and negative thoughts—it was time to focus on the positive, to smile about their good fortune and the bright lights of Hollywood that awaited them. Michael was ecstatic about the huge upturn his career was taking. It wouldn't be long now; after twenty-five years and all that writing, he would really cash in. Peterson had received $600,000 for one of his books already. And with the new movie deal, his name would finally be up there— right next to Tom Clancy and James Patterson—where it belonged.

It was only a matter of time.

That night, when Michael insisted that Kathleen forget about everyone else, Kathleen realized her husband was right. She needed to celebrate with him, to enjoy life for every moment it offered. If Michael was willing to bring their love life back, then she needed to do her part to keep her marriage intact. She needed to dote on her husband and let him brag to her. She needed to assure him that she believed in him fully, without doubt. And Kathleen did believe in Michael. She had always believed in Michael. He was her soul mate, a man she'd known for thirteen years. The two of them had been through everything and—in the end—all they really had was each other.

Still, no matter how much Michael wanted Kathleen to take a break from her endless worrying, Kathleen's job problems were still with her. She found her workload hard to escape. Even in the midst of their quiet Saturday night together, Kathleen would be interrupted by a call from

Canada. Instead of being able to fully relax, as she had promised herself, Kathleen had to break away from her romantic evening to receive e-mails from a Nortel coworker. But Kathleen wasn't going to let that bother her.

Even if the promise of Hollywood couldn't erase all the loss Kathleen had suffered, she wasn't going to let it show. Not on this night. Michael was well aware that Kathleen was firing her employees left and right, that she was working harder than ever for the same pay. He also knew that her stock options at Nortel had dropped over a million dollars. That million-dollar loss was her life's savings—and even though he tried to console her, reminding her it was only a loss on paper—the two of them had been through all that before. For Kathleen, that loss was real. Her blood and sweat had gone down the drain, and along with it, her plans for an early retirement.

Kathleen was determined to keep all that chatter in the back of her mind. She and Michael had been down that road so many times already. And he had a point: the worrying wasn't making anything any better. Kathleen realized that her work would always be there, that she could get back to it again in the morning. It suddenly dawned on her that the duty of being Michael's loving wife was all that really mattered. Kathleen decided that nothing unpleasant was going to spoil their evening. Nothing was going to stop her from being happy for her husband. On that given night, on Michael's big night to gloat, she wanted to put on a big smile and be loving. With all her heart, she wanted to help her husband succeed. . . .

Two

The Peterson mansion, once known as the John Buchanan House, was built in 1940 by a wealthy man who wanted a large stylish home that offered elegant areas for entertaining. Located in the posh suburb of Forest Hills, the mansion was, in certain respects, unusual. It was more modern, more upscale than many of the large old homes one might visit in the area. But at the same time, the Peterson house had all the high-end appointments—the traditional hardwood floors, the built-in bookshelves, the crystal chandeliers, the wide, sweeping spiral staircase—all the formal trappings evident in the homes of wealthy Southerners.

But the Peterson mansion was an enigma, because in a sense, the place seemed caught in between the old and the new worlds. Certain of the elements reminiscent of the old South were present, but others were distinctly missing, such as the traditional Corinthian columns and entryway parlors, things considered standard in old Southern homes. Oddly, there was something about the architecture that made the old house seem newer. There were large windows and outdoor patios, not real reminders of yesteryear. There were two worlds, it seemed, present in that old house, and perhaps the most symbolic reminders of that were the Petersons' two staircases. One was a sweeping oval shape, a centerpiece of the home, while the other lead down to the kitchen area, a more practical structure, hidden behind doors.

The home had a few multipurpose rooms, but they were split up in a strange way. There were two living rooms, with a foyer in between them. And then there were two entryways to the house. One was a more casual back door, often left unlocked. The other was the formal entrance off Cedar Street, which no one really used. It was more or less for show. Reminiscent of an earlier age, the Peterson house had some other strange features. There was a buzzer in the formal dining room that had once been used to page servants. And, like in the days of old plantations, there were bathrooms in the basement that had been built so that servants would not share the toilets used by their white homeowner employees.

In a sense, to look at it with an untrained eye, the Peterson home was a place that seemed cobbled together, almost like a patchwork gone astray. But the Peterson home was purposely built in that strange fashion, it rambled on, with its many separate wings downstairs, its five huge fireplaces, and its six sets of bedroom suites upstairs. Not that it wasn't beautiful. The home was gorgeous, with all its nooks and crannies, all its rooms set off with glazed hardwood floors, fourteen-foot ceilings, and elaborate crown moldings.

But then the interior decor of the house was another contradiction. Among the Petersons' typical Americana antiques were prized rare items, pieces supposedly from the Ming Dynasty. Mixed in with their contemporary green and black marble furnishings were elaborate Oriental screens, gold carvings, and porcelain objects on pedestals. The Petersons' home had all kinds of bizarre elements. There were antique cars that were never driven. There was even an unused bomb shelter out in the back of the property, sitting discreetly off the garage at the end of the circular driveway.

Then there was Michael Peterson's personal office and library, an unusually large space, very masculine, very imposing, which enjoyed its own private wing off the main entryway. Distinctly different from the rest of the mansion, Michael's office was heavy and dark, covered in a series of dark redwood panels. With such a massive amount of dark wood, Peterson's office, at times, seemed ominous. It was certainly not an inviting place. If anything, his office was intimidating. It was understood that Michael Peterson didn't want people in there. That was his writing place, his sacred ground.

At the other end of the house was the main living area, Kathleen's domain. An airy space filled with modern furniture, glass tabletops and leather couches, it was white, light, and cheerful. The eat-in kitchen was alive with lush green plants, colorful gadgets, ornate Asian bowls, and a collection of gourmet cookbooks. This part of the house showed off Kathleen's Mother-Earth style. She was clearly a good homemaker. She filled the place with floral designs, oak baskets, beautiful pottery, and vivid art prints.

The Petersons were certainly eclectic, and their home reflected varied tastes. Michael and Kathleen never seemed to care that their style didn't fit with the traditional color schemes or home furnishings of their neighbors. If the Petersons' trappings seemed unusual, that was by design. The Petersons liked the idea that their home reflected a global sensibility. There were the many artifacts Michael collected from his bygone eras—from places like Germany and Japan. There were American quilts that belonged to Kathleen and her first husband, Fred. Other pieces of Americana belonged to Michael and his first wife, Patricia. There were also the items Michael collected from his friend, Liz Ratliff. They were sentimental things, rare chests of drawers, old crafted lamps, and a great tapestry that hung above the winding spiral staircase.

There were so many ornate pieces of art, so many rare things—it would be difficult for anyone to keep track of it all. In one corner would be a large carved Chinese warrior figure dating back thousands of years; in another spot, simple blue-colored steins, marked handmade, from Germany. The Petersons had so many different histories in the family, their collection of home furnishings presented a large cross section of the world. There was no theme.

The Petersons didn't live in such a way that seemed quite pulled together. There was nothing about the home that seemed indicative of the Southern region in which they dwelled. No interior decorator would have condoned the ornate, rather garish Oriental artifacts strewn everywhere. But then, the Petersons were not concerned with the mixed image their home might portray. They weren't the types who wanted a perfect home, pulled neatly together by a decorator's touch. Quite the contrary. They were unusual folks, Michael and Kathleen, who had both traveled the globe extensively. They knew about fine living, and they liked to do things their way.

In fact, the Petersons didn't even employ a regular housekeeper. Kathleen did most of the housework herself. Of course it was a lot for her to handle. For so many years, she not only took care of Michael, but she had her daughter, Caitlin, whom she had custody of from her previous marriage, as well as Michael's four children, Todd, Clayton, Margaret, and Martha. Growing up in that house, the mix of kids were like another version of the Brady Bunch. There were the typical fights and jealousies, the sibling rivalries to be expected, but with Michael and Kathleen's constant love and devotion, the kids seemed to be turning out pretty well.

By the time the Petersons were living on their own, Michael and Kathleen finally having their own private "nest," the only person working for the Petersons was their maintenance man, Clyde. Mainly he took care of the yard and lawn furniture, little things like that. Clyde had worked for the family for years, doing odd jobs around the house. But as far as the rest of the chores and responsibilities of the home, with the children gone, Michael and Kathleen were able to manage the upkeep of the house alone.

Being a very private person, Michael was opposed to having any extra people underfoot. He was content, helping Kathleen with house chores when necessary. That suited his needs. Perhaps Michael thought paid servants were a waste of money. Perhaps he was a guy with a sense of humility. Whatever the reason, Michael felt he could tend to his own home maintenance.

As for Kathleen, she made it clear that she enjoyed taking care of things on the domestic front. It was her way to keep her house a home. Even if it took her hours to dust all the artifacts in the huge mansion, Kathleen was happy to do it. She didn't mind polishing silver; she didn't mind having to clean so many bathrooms. And then there were certain areas Kathleen never had to worry about—Michael's office, for example, was a place he meticulously kept clean and neat. And his other work areas were maintained the same way. Whether it be his workout gym or his car garage, Michael made sure to keep up his own end of the bargain, happy to take care of his own space.

For both of them, the house seemed to be one of their greatest joys. Michael and Kathleen loved entertaining. They often had neighborhood parties and the Peterson home was a place where everyone was made to feel comfortable. Kathleen, who spent most of her time in the kitchen, would serve countless meals, sometimes formally, in the grand dining room; other times she would opt for family style, from her granite countertops that served as eating spaces alongside her stove.

Kathleen's kitchen, like so many other kitchens, provided the main source of life in the home, with its informal dining area and large wood-burning fireplace. Her kitchen, with its adjoining family room, was a place for people to kick up their heels and relax. Being a hostess was a pleasure for Kathleen. She loved filling her home with people on the weekends, whether she was working with her kids on school projects in the living area, sipping champagne by the fire with a handful of dinner guests, or preparing simple meals, homemade goodies, for her neighbors and friends.

That was where the Petersons were, Kathleen's kitchen, on Saturday night, December 8, 2001. It was in the early part of their special evening together and Michael and Kathleen were just finishing a light dinner when their son Todd unexpectedly happened to drop by. Todd was the only one of the five children who still lived in the Durham area. It wasn't that unusual for him to pop over to the house, but that particular evening he was in his own world, and he was not very interested in what was going on in his parents' lives.

Todd hadn't meant to disturb them. He told Michael and Kathleen that he was on his way to a party with his new friend, Christina, who knocked on the door about a half hour later. A pretty girl, whom Todd formally introduced, Christina didn't have much to say. Todd seemed to be in a rush. He said he wanted to find something in his room, then he'd be ready to take off. The Petersons tried to exchange some pleasantries with Christina, but she seemed distracted.

Since Michael and Kathleen were about to watch their

rental video of the film *America's Sweethearts,* they decided not to pay too much attention to Todd and his girl. After all, he was a grown man with a life of his own. Over the years, they had met so many girls who'd been interested in Todd, but they had learned, the hard way, not to intrude into Todd's personal life. Their eldest son, Clayton, had been a handful. Now Todd seemed to be the more unsettled of their two boys. He was quite a catch—Todd was a *GQ*-type, the kind that girls went gaga over. Yet he seemed to have trouble finding satisfaction in life, despite being tall, muscular, and handsome.

Kathleen had given up trying to figure Todd out. Their son Clayton had gotten his act together; he had graduated first in his class from college and had found love with a kindhearted girl. But Todd, well, he seemed to have so much wasted talent. Kathleen had spent years worrying about Todd, trying to help him figure out a career, trying to encourage him in relationships. But all of her efforts seemed futile.

It was no wonder, then, that Kathleen didn't feel the need to make a fuss about Todd's comings and goings. He and Christina seemed to be on edge, itching to get out of there. Perhaps Todd's date realized they were intruding.

Whatever the case, Kathleen decided not to devote too much energy to Todd that night. It was important that nothing interfere with her private time. Kathleen needed the romance back with her husband. She needed to be in the comfort of his strong arms.

Three

On December 9, 2001, just after 2:40 in the morning, a frantic man dialed a 9-1-1 operator to report an emergency. The caller was breathing heavily as he told a Durham, North Carolina, emergency operator that his wife had an accident at their Cedar Street home. The caller was bordering on hysteria. His wife, he said, had fallen down the stairs. She had an accident, he reported, his wife was not conscious . . . but she was still breathing.

9-1-1 Operator: Okay. How many stairs did she fall down?
Caller: What? Huh?
9-1-1 Operator: How many stairs?
Caller: Stairs?
9-1-1 Operator: How many stairs?
Caller: Ah . . . Oh . . .
9-1-1 Operator: Calm down, sir. Calm down.

The caller seemed confused. He kept repeating that his wife wasn't conscious. He wanted an emergency crew to come over immediately. He had already given the address. But the operator wanted the man to calm down. She could hardly understand him, his voice was so shrill and his breathing so loud. The emergency operator assured him that an ambulance had already been dispatched, that she just wanted to ask him some questions.

    9-1-1 Operator: Calm down, sir. Calm down. How many stairs did she fall down?
    Caller: Oh, fifteen, twenty. I don't know. Please get somebody here right away. Please!
    9-1-1 Operator: Sir, somebody else is dispatching the ambulance.
    Caller: It's in Forest Hills, okay? Please! Please!
    9-1-1- Operator: Okay. Is she awake now? Hello? Hello?

But the phone was going dead. The 9-1-1 operator could hear the caller in the background yelling, "Oh, God!" Then their connection was lost. The operator dialed Engine 5, Medic 5, to be sure that an emergency crew was enroute. She spoke directly to the rescue team, asking them to copy the address on Cedar Street. Then just as she was completing her radio call, repeating that an unconscious female had fallen down a flight of stairs, a second emergency 9-1-1 call came in.

    9-1-1 Operator: Durham 911, where is your emergency?
    Caller: Where are they? Why is she not breathing? Please! Please, would you hurry up!

The caller could hear static through the phone. There was the sound of radio operators and in the background someone yelling "Code 5!" With each passing second, the caller was getting more frantic. Time was standing still.

    Caller: Can you hear me?
    9-1-1 Operator: Sir! Sir! Calm down! They're on their way. Can you tell me for sure she's not breathing?

But the caller said nothing more.

9-1-1 Operator: Sir? Hello? Hello?

The phone had gone dead again. All that was left was a dial tone.

Eight minutes later, the paramedics, who had made a wrong turn in the wooded neighborhood, raced up the long driveway on Cedar Street. All the lights were on in the house. They rushed in and found the victim of the fall, a forty-eight-year-old white female, without any pulse. Durham Police Department Officers McDowell and Figueroa were the next to arrive on the scene. Within minutes, Corporal McDowell asked communications to notify the Crime Investigation Department. The emergency medical services team hadn't even attempted to revive the woman's heart beat; it was clear that the woman was deceased. Police at the scene tried to identify the male there, the person who made the 9-1-1 call, but the gentleman was so hysterical and upset, he was just crying out of control.

Officer Figueroa, who had arrived at 2:50 A.M., observed that the victim, Kathleen Hunt Atwater Peterson, lay at the bottom of the backstairs with her head tilted up against the stairwell. Beside her were a pair of male athletic shoes, white socks, and a pair of clear-gel flip-flop sandals. Under her head was a blood-soaked roll of paper towels.

At 3:07 A.M., Durham Investigator Dan George arrived and made his way around the fire trucks and patrol cars, approaching the back entryway to the residence. Investigator George deliberately walked through the back door, trying to stay clear of the victim. Dan George spoke with Officer Figueroa about securing the residence. It was such a huge place, they would need plenty of backup. He noted that there was blood on the walls and on several steps leading up the stairway and was assured that the Crime Investigation Department (CID) were on their way.

He didn't want to stay long. He wanted to wait for the Crime Scene Investigation teams. Dan George felt there was foul play . . . and just as the police investigator began backing out of the doorway, the kitchen door opened and Michael Peterson, dressed in shorts and a T-shirt, running barefoot, came rushing past him. Peterson was covered in blood from head to toe.

"Do you want me to see her again?" a male voice suddenly called out.

The voice was Todd's, coming from behind Michael. Todd was trying to console his dad. He was offering to check on Kathleen. Then, like lightning, Michael approached his wife, bent down over her, crying and moaning, and began to caress her. The officers present had no chance to prevent it.

It was awkward. The police needed to find a way to remove Michael Peterson from the body. Without being harsh, finally, after a few failed attempts, they decided to ask Todd, who somehow managed to move his dad away.

But the damage had been done.

The scene was contaminated.

Michael Peterson had transferred bloodstains from Kathleen's body to his own.

And, as if that weren't trouble enough, when Investigator Dan George accompanied Michael and Todd Peterson back toward the kitchen area, he was surprised to see a civilian standing there, a young lady whom he recognized. She was Christina Tomessetti, the daughter of one of his best friends, and he wondered what Christina was doing there, alone in the kitchen, just waiting by the sink. Christina told Dan George that she and Todd had

been at a party, that they had arrived at the house just
moments after the fire trucks had gotten there.

As the uniformed officers attempted to secure the
scene, two other civilians suddenly appeared out of
nowhere. They were Heather Whitson and Ben Maynard, other friends of Todd's, whom he apparently had
called for help. Todd knew they were in the neighborhood, all of them had just seen each other at the party,
and Todd had specifically asked Ben to bring Heather,
who was a medical resident at Duke University. Todd
hoped Heather could be of some type of assistance, to
his dad at least, if nothing else.

At first, when Heather and Ben had arrived on the
scene, the Durham police were refusing to let them
enter. But immediately, Todd appeared at the front
Cedar Street entrance, asserting that it was okay for his
friends to come in. He needed someone to check on his
dad. Todd insisted, and he wouldn't take no for an answer. The police, trying to walk on eggshells in the
midst of such family grief, didn't argue with Todd. They
permitted his friends to enter.

Todd took his friends around the front entrance of
the house, around the spiral staircase. The three walked
into the kitchen through the formal dining room, and
once there, Heather and Ben tried to console Mr. Peterson. But the man was so distraught over the loss of his
wife, there was nothing they could do or say. He was all
bloody, but he didn't really need any medical attention.
He was just in shock.

Peterson kept mumbling and crying. He couldn't believe his wife, Kathleen, was dead. He just didn't believe
it. He didn't know how he could live without Kathleen.
He didn't know how a thing like this could have happened. The two of them were having a few drinks. The
two of them were celebrating. The last thing he knew, he
had gone out to the pool area, and had taken the dogs

outside for a while. He thought Kathleen had gone upstairs to bed. He couldn't understand how something like this could have happened.

It was impossible to think that his Kathleen was gone. She was his life. . . .

For some time , Michael Peterson could not be convinced that Kathleen was dead. To appease his father, there was a point when Todd asked to see the body himself, and the uniformed officers let him approach.

When Todd knelt down, police used a flashlight to help him take a look at his stepmom. Without asking, Todd touched Kathleen's leg. There was no sign of life.

With the flashlight blaring, everyone in the room got a close-up view of Kathleen Peterson's head, which seemed to be propped up at the foot of the stairs. People were aghast at all the blood around Kathleen's body, all the blood staining her clothes.

They noticed bruises, and such a strange look of pain on her face. . . .

Four

Throughout the first hour, before the Crime Investigation Department arrived, Michael Peterson was basically doing as he pleased. Michael was walking around, dazed and confused, shaking back and forth, pacing, making circles around the kitchen. At one point, Mr. Peterson even managed to get to the kitchen sink, where he began to wash his hands, but one of the officers stopped him. Peterson was advised that the blood on his hands would have to remain.

A state medical examiner from Chapel Hill had been sent to investigate the scene as well. His initial findings: Kathleen Hunt Peterson appeared to have hit her head on the steps. The blood spatter in the stairwell appeared to support the scenario described by Kathleen's husband, Michael.

Mr. Peterson had admitted to putting paper towels under Kathleen's head. He also admitted to partially wiping up the blood in the stairwell with paper towels. The medical examiner with whom Mr. Peterson spoke, Dr. Kenneth Snell, only six months out of his residency, had handwritten a report that concluded that Mrs. Peterson had hit her head at least twice on the stairs, causing scalp lacerations and abrasions. His findings suggested that Mrs. Peterson's landing at the base of the stairs, on her back, was an accident.

When the medical examiner discussed his opinion with the Durham police, it was unclear whether they were going to wait to see what an autopsy might reveal. Some of the Durham police believed the fall was an accident; others weren't sure what they had.

Certain patrol officers, those who had first responded, couldn't quite match the scene with an accident. There was too much blood; it was incongruent with a fall. Still, none of the Durham police officers initially dispatched to the Peterson mansion had the authority to designate it a crime scene. They had to wait for a homicide detective.

In the meantime, Officer A. D. McCallop escorted Michael and Todd Peterson to the back patio, where he asked the man and his son to sit quietly. Michael and Todd were being kept under police guard, informally, until backup could arrive.

"What is this? Do I need to call a lawyer?" Michael Peterson wondered aloud.

No one answered him.

Michael Peterson was not going to be treated in any manner that was disrespectful. For years, Peterson had written columns criticizing the Durham Police Department. Now, suddenly, in his darkest hour, he began to get the feeling that the police were trying to turn the tables on him. He started making rumblings to his son. He thought he was being framed.

At that point, Todd became irate. He didn't understand why he and his dad were being held prisoners in their own home. Todd decided he wasn't about to keep quiet. He insisted that Ben Maynard join him outside, and Ben was permitted to do that. Todd and Ben spoke more softly; they continued to comfort Michael.

While outside on the patio with the three civilians, uniformed officers carried on with their notes. They spotted some type of spill next to a silver kettle out on the patio; it was some type of clear fluid. There was also a perfect drop of blood, which police photographed; it was on the slate porch, just outside the back door of the residence.

Then as the temperature began to drop outside, the uniformed officers agreed to take the three men back into the house. Michael and Todd were placed in Mr. Peterson's office, kept under guard. Ben Maynard was placed in the foyer. Heather and Christina had already been separated from the rest of the civilians, asked to wait in the den, asked not to talk to each other. The officer guarding them suggested that the young women try to get some sleep. It was going on 4:00 A.M., and everyone was tired. Heather did dose off for a while, glad to have some relief from all the heartache.

Between 4:15 and 5:00 A.M., Officer McCallop guarded Michael and Todd in the senior Peterson's office. Todd was refusing to cooperate. Todd would not follow orders. He felt he was being treated inappropriately, that the police had no authority to act in that manner. No one had done anything wrong in that house.

Michael promised Todd that it all would be over soon. The two of them just had to be patient. In an effort to take his mind off things, Michael decided to go check his computer. He mumbled something about Kathleen's e-mail and began surfing the Internet. It seemed like he was looking through his e-mail list.

Among the backup police who entered all the confusion surrounding Kathleen Peterson's death was Sergeant Terry Wilkins. A seasoned officer who knew the significance of each moment that ticked away, he knew he had to protect the integrity of the crime scene. All the Durham police officers who arrived at the scene did their best to make order out of the chaos. Yellow crime-scene tape was placed in front of both entrances; the female civilians were questioned. After Michael and

Todd each refused to make any statement, Wilkins made the decision to separate Michael Peterson from his son. It was a touchy-feely time for them, he understood, but nonetheless, he couldn't afford to allow Peterson, a man covered in blood, any more opportunity to create a story.

If indeed there was a crime, which was not yet official—Wilkins did not want anyone's perceptions of the situation to be changed or tainted.

When Detective Art Holland arrived and viewed the scene, he took a quick look inside and immediately classified it as a suspicious death. Holland would be calling CSI to process the area, but not without a search warrant. Once the warrant was under way, Detective Holland, now the official lead criminal investigator in the Peterson case, requested that the Durham PD set up a Mobile Command Post at the back side of the mansion, on Kent Street. Holland made calls way up the chain of command, to his major and his captains. Detective Holland, with twenty-two years of experience on the police force, was making sure that there was little room for error.

Because Michael Peterson was a well-known individual in the community, because the mounting case was sure to gain regional attention, high-ranking officers also volunteered to help out at the scene. The Durham police were taking no chances. They used all their power to keep the scene intact.

But Michael Peterson saw this heavy police presence as a witch-hunt. He always knew the day would come when the Durham police would attack him. He was completely outraged that they would use the unlikely occasion of his wife's death to make trouble for him. There was not one shred of evidence, not one thing that pointed to him as a suspect. And all of the family members knew that. In the hours surrounding Kathleen's death, and later through the private family grieving times, all through Kathleen's wake and funeral, the family was further upset about the way the Durham police were mistreating Michael.

The idea that Michael could have killed Kathleen was ludicrous. Even Kathleen's biological daughter, Caitlin Atwater, made public statements to defend Michael Peterson. He was such a great stepdad, such a great human being. He and her mom were soul mates. They were two peas in a pod; they never fought, never argued. There was nothing but mutual respect and love between them.

Michael understood his family's pain. He felt bad for his kids, who had to endure, not only the loss of their mother, but now, a public media spectacle. Michael assured his family that the police would find nothing to charge him with. Still, he was all the more grief-stricken, just sick to his stomach, to think that he would have to endure all this public scrutiny. He was overwhelmed by his loss and, at the same time, profoundly sorry that Kathleen had to be involved in the Durham PD's latest public scandal.

As he wallowed in sorrow, Peterson mused about why the Durham police had it out for him. He thought about all the columns he had written, bashing the cops, attacking them for not taking care of Durham's drug problems, for not addressing Durham's drive-by shootings. He thought about the column where he made a mistake and wrote that the Durham PD only solved 5 percent of all crimes. Peterson recalled that Police Chief Teresa Chambers had written to him personally, to let him know that he should be ashamed of himself for his shabby reporting. The Durham PD had a 47 percent clearance on homicides, the chief wrote, going down the list of her department's accomplishments.

Peterson realized that the police had been gunning for him from the moment they arrived at the house, and he would later explain that to his five kids. He wanted them to understand where all the suspicions were coming from. He wanted them to know that perhaps, because he'd been such an outspoken critic of law enforcement and local government, he had brought this witch-hunt upon himself.

Still, Peterson was annoyed, on the night of his wife's senseless death, that the police had taken the opportunity to crawl all over his home. They were all standing around, on guard, for an alleged crime that *wasn't* a crime. The Durham police were heartless. They were making the family's tragedy all the more difficult.

Michael would assure the family—among them his brothers, Kathleen's sisters, and all five children—that he had no doubt about being cleared of any wrongdoing. He didn't worry a bit that the police wanted to spend so much time searching. Michael said he knew that no murder weapon could be found, that eventually police would realize that there was no murder. The idea that the police had pulled warrants to search the house, Michael surmised, was their form of harassment, of revenge.

As far as Michael Peterson could tell, the police officials were setting up their CSI teams in order to grab the attention of the local media. Kathleen Peterson was a pillar of the community; her untimely death would be sure to hit the local news by Monday. If police could drum up some false charges, that would make for better press coverage. In the meantime, Peterson would remain calm.

As he sat alone in his office, waiting to be given his freedom, Peterson called his attorney friend, Kerry Sutton. He wanted her to come over to the house that same morning, to see if she could assert his constitutional rights. The idea that Kathleen's body was found, that he was grieving and was unable to be with his wife, was unnatural. Ms. Sutton, an adept attorney who had once been Michael Peterson's political campaign manager, made her way over to the mansion before 9:00 A.M.

When the police told her that she would not be allowed into the house, that she would not be permitted to see Mr. Peterson, Sutton called their bluff and insisted that they either arrest her client, Michael Peterson, or let the man go free. She was not about to see the esteemed Mr. Peterson being held against his will, not without evidence of his guilt. It was an outrage that this grieving man was being treated as a criminal.

Sutton and other attorneys would later explain that the fact was, Kathleen's fall down the stairs caused a lot of blood, and some of that blood had gotten on Michael because he had held Kathleen when he came upon her. Everyone who was at the scene had witnessed that.

As for all the police suspicions, the attorneys were convinced that there was not enough evidence to show probable cause.

Five

On Monday morning, the local papers in the Triangle area of North Carolina made their initial reports about Kathleen Peterson's death. She was the wife of Michael Peterson, who had run unsuccessfully for Durham's city council earlier that year. Durham Police media spokesman, Major Dwight Pettiford, told the press that police were still looking into Mrs. Peterson's death. Though the major wouldn't confirm the extent of the investigation, the local news reported that the Durham PD mobile substation on Kent Street had about a dozen police cars parked outside it.

The details of Kathleen Peterson's death would remain shrouded. Major Pettiford told reporters very little. He mentioned that Durham police were not sure whether anyone else was in the house with Michael and Kathleen during the early-morning hours of December 9, 2001. The police spokesman said they were waiting for a statement from Michael Peterson, who had not yet been interviewed because he was spending time with his family.

Regarding the extent of Kathleen Peterson's injuries, the Durham police could not comment. They were waiting for an autopsy report. Mrs. Peterson's body had been sent to the state medical examiner's office in Chapel Hill, and the preliminary results were not available.

Maureen Berry, a dear friend and neighbor to the Peterson family, told a local reporter that she had been awakened by a fire truck and an ambulance at about 2:30 on Sunday morning. Ms. Berry had gone over to the house to talk to Michael and his son Todd, and she learned of the sad news from Mr. Peterson himself. He said that he had been sitting out by the pool, that Kathleen had gone upstairs to bed, that when he went inside, he found his wife lying near the back stairway.

Everyone who knew Kathleen was devastated by the news. Kathleen had not only been a loving wife, mother, and stepmother, she was one of those people who lived life to the fullest. She was an intelligent, extremely capable woman, a woman who was blessed with so many attributes. There wasn't a soul who had a bad word to say about her. Kathleen was considered a giving human being, a model citizen.

Not only was she a top executive at Nortel Networks, Kathleen had a creative side, and was a patron of the arts who served on the board of the North Carolina Ballet and the Durham Arts Council. She was full of life. She and her husband threw annual parties for the American Dance Festival. Kathleen loved to dance.

The fact that Kathleen died in her lovely home was all the more upsetting to friends and family, who had attended Kathleen and Michael's wedding in that grand old mansion, just a short five years prior to her death. People recalled Kathleen's delight on that occasion. Throughout her wedding, she was glowing, dressed in formal white. People remembered that even as a lovely bride, Kathleen was helping out. Even in her wedding gown, the woman with stars in her eyes still acted as the proverbial hostess.

* * *

The same day that the news of Kathleen's death hit the local papers, her children, siblings, and other family members, including her eighty-year-old mother, were making their way to Durham in utter shock and disbelief. There had been no funeral arrangements announced. There was still an investigation taking place in the Peterson house, so Michael hadn't the time or energy to make any arrangements.

Michael was too distraught; he was concerned about trumped-up charges, and he had already placed calls to his brother Bill, an attorney, who was flying in from Reno, as well two other attorneys in the area. Michael was advised to sign a power of attorney over to his son Todd, and on that day, he did so. It was just a further precaution. He had no idea what to expect from the Durham officials.

Peterson knew one thing for sure: They had an ax to grind.

At 8:50 A.M., on that same Monday, December 10, 2001, Captain R. T. James arrived at Cedar Street to respond to demands being made by attorney Kerry Sutton. Captain James crossed the crime scene tape, which secured the outer perimeter of the property, and was looking for Sutton, who had been denied access to the scene by a patrol officer. Captain James was prepared to have a brief chat with Sutton about police securing the crime scene, but the young female attorney had disappeared before the captain arrived.

After receiving another call, Captain James returned back to the Cedar Street mansion, later entering the house at about 12:30 P.M. He took a tour of the residence, walking through all of the fourteen rooms, donning a pair of disposable boots to keep from disturbing any evidence in the house.

Mrs. Peterson's body had been removed by the medical examiner, but there was still a lot of blood in the stairway where her body had been found. Captain James offered to be of assistance to the officers searching the residence. He touched nothing while he was inside the house. After about a half hour, he left.

While inside the residence, Captain James made a specific trip to the second floor, by way of the front spiral staircase. He went to take another look at the door and wall leading down the back stairway. He observed a few blue stains running down the back-stairway wall. They appeared to be remnants of luminol, an enhancement chemical that allows experts to see blood distribution, stains not visible to the naked eye.

Six

Though Michael and Kathleen Peterson had only been married five years, they had lived together in the Cedar Street house for over a decade. The idea that they lived together unwed, especially with children from previous marriages, didn't always sit well with the more traditional members of Kathleen's family. . . . But that was all ancient history now.

The Monday after her death, by the time Kathleen's two sisters, Candace and Lori, had arrived at the Cedar Street house, things were looking dire. Kathleen's children were overcome with grief and shock. Not only did they no longer have their mother, but now their father was being blasted, made to look suspicious by the local news. Reporters were indicating that Michael Peterson might be facing some kind of possible charge, although they couldn't say he'd done anything to deserve it. No doubt, the media was making things more difficult for Kathleen's family.

Candace and Lori had driven the long ride to Durham together. The whole time, they were flabbergasted. Heading to North Carolina from Virginia, there was still a sense of disbelief about their older sister's death. Candace and Lori wanted to hold on to the idea that it was all a mistake, that Kathleen wasn't really gone. It was just too impossible to imagine. Kathleen was so healthy, so young. The three of them had just been on a trip to Paris together.

But as they pulled up on Cedar Street, Kathleen's sisters were confronted with yellow crime-scene tape surrounding the perimeter of the Peterson property. Suddenly Kathleen's death had become real. Through the family grapevine, Candace and Lori had heard that police search teams had been in the house. They heard that Michael was being targeted, but they really hadn't believed it, until they saw it with their own eyes.

Still, it was shocking to see the yellow crime tape. Candace and Lori, two beautiful, well-bred women, had never been involved in this kind of drama. They knew nothing of police and search warrants. They knew nothing about local politics, about the depths to which local officials might hold a grudge. With husbands and children of their own, with steady lives that were basically normal, they needed some answers. Here were police surrounding Kathleen's home. The police seemed to be holding the house hostage. Candace and Lori hoped that someone could tell them just exactly what was going on.

When Candace went to talk to some of the officers at the command post on Kent Street, she was informed that the other family members were across the street. She was directed over to the home of Maureen Berry, Michael and Kathleen's friend and neighbor, who had offered her house as a place for the family to meet. The police wouldn't give any other details. Candace wondered what, if anything, these officers were doing, sitting there, outside the Peterson property. But with no formal charge announced, with the police being so evasive and unfriendly, Candace didn't have the nerve to ask.

Candace felt put off by the number of police officers who were out there on Kent Street, just yards away from her sister's property. The police were polite, but they were not being cooperative at all. They would not allow Candace any access to the house, even though she needed to get Kathleen's clothes to prepare for her burial. Candace

was informed that no one would be permitted inside the
Peterson home at that time. She was told that most of the
family, including Todd, were over at the Berry residence.

When Candace went over to Maureen Berry's with Lori,
she was happy to be greeted by such a warm and caring
soul. Maureen Berry made her home comfortable and
inviting for the grieving family, having put out tea and coffee, and all the cakes and cookies brought by friends and
neighbors. Candace and Lori were anxious to talk to
Todd, who briefly explained what happened when he returned home early on Sunday morning. Todd's story
made Candace and Lori even more upset. They wanted
to hear about it directly from Michael. Todd had his
aunts follow him over to Kerry Sutton's residence, where
Michael and his two brothers were huddled. Lori waited
downstairs while Candace and Michael spoke privately.

Michael expressed his grief and sorrow, he was still in
shock, barely able to make a coherent sentence. He
looked like he aged overnight. Candace asked about all
the police tape and Michael explained the unfortunate
circumstance he had created with the local police. He had
antagonized them over the years, and now they were
doing anything they could to get even.

Later that day, soon after police turned the house back
over to Mr. Peterson, Michael escorted his two sisters-in-
law inside his home. He watched the women go over to
the stairwell, and Todd and Clayton were there, trying to
hold their father together. But when Lori broke down in
tears, when Candace couldn't bear looking at Kathleen's
blood anymore, Michael became truly shaken.

Candace needed to move away from the area. The stairwell was just too grim. She told Michael she wanted to
retrieve some of Kathleen's personal belongings in the
master suite. Kathleen had a special set of pearls, and Candace had been asked to find them, along with appropriate
clothing for Kathleen's burial.

As Candace calmed herself, going upstairs to collect her sister's wallet, her jewelry, all the essentials needed for the funeral, Michael stood there, weeping. Even for the sake of his sons, Michael was unable to control his grief. With Clayton and Todd in the background, Michael sobbed as he watched Candace looking through Kathleen's beautiful clothes. Candace decided that the brand-new gown and shoes Kathleen had purchased for the governor's gala would be what her sister would have chosen to wear.

Candace had some questions about Michael's plans for the funeral, but Michael was too distracted, too overwhelmed, to answer her. All Michael could think about were the children. His boys were being strong, they were holding up. But the girls would be another story. Caitlin, Margaret, and Martha were each on their way home, headed back from their respective colleges. Michael did not know how he would console them. For Caitlin, there would be no words to ease the pain. For Margaret and Martha, Kathleen was the only mother, really, they had ever known. Michael still could not believe that the love of his life was dead. It seemed surreal that Kathleen was not with him.

Candace realized Michael's dilemma, but she still wanted to talk to him about what happened. While her sister Lori was upstairs, still walking around the vast house in a daze, Candace followed Michael back down to the kitchen area, where she questioned him about Kathleen's death.

Michael had no answers. He had no explanation as to why Kathleen fell. All he knew was that they had been drinking. He said they were drinking heavily that night, but he and Kathleen always drank on weekends. There was nothing unusual about that.

Candace found herself trying to get Michael to say something, anything, but he was unable to function. Michael was distracted. He had enough difficulty dealing with Kathleen's death, and then he had these added problems with the police. As she made her way back toward the stairwell where Kathleen's accident occurred, Candace was trying to understand how Kathleen actually fell. There was such an awful lot of blood.

Candace decided to press Michael, hoping that he might have some clue as to why Kathleen would have fallen so hard.

"Do you have any idea?" she asked him. "I mean, how could this have happened?"

"I just don't know. I was outside," he said.

"But there's so much blood here. How do you think she fell?"

"I have no idea. I came up the stairs to get some towels. . . ." Michael's voice trailed off.

"But, Michael, was she on any pills or anything? How many stairs did she hit?"

"I don't know," he told her, "but I think . . . she fell down the whole staircase."

Candace could see that her questions had further rattled Michael. There was no sense in talking to him about the accident. He clearly was guessing at what might have happened, and there was no real point in that. Candace felt sorry for him. She decided she should try to keep practical and levelheaded about the matter. She knew her mother would be arriving the following day, and Candace just couldn't let her poor mother come to the house and see all that dark red stain. She started looking around the kitchen, looking around the laundry area, trying to find rags and cleaning solutions. But Candace wasn't dressed properly. She would have to return the next morning to start cleaning.

Michael had no objections to that idea. If Candace was willing to clean up the stairwell, that was a good thing. The police apparently had finished whatever photographs and testing they were going to do, and Michael certainly didn't want to be reminded of his wife's death. Having to continue to live in that house, all alone, was punishment enough.

The following day, Candace and Lori returned. Lori went upstairs to look through Kathleen's personal items again. Caitlin had arrived in Durham, and there were a few things of her mom's that she had asked for. They were trinkets, just things of sentimental value. Caitlin's aunt Lori had offered to fetch them, not wanting Caitlin to enter the house.

By the time Candace actually rolled her sleeves up, on Tuesday morning, when she actually had the Windex and the bowl of water and the paper towels in her hands, she began feeling very lonely in that big, old, quiet house. With Lori, Michael, and the boys nowhere in sight, it sure was a spooky place. Without Kathleen, without her music going, the house did not have much life left in it.

Candace realized that the job of removing Kathleen's blood wasn't going to be so simple. There was more blood than met the eye, and Candace had to find the strength to get through it.

As she began, the blood started to bother her. As she was cleaning, Candace realized this was the last of her sister's life. And the blood seemed to be everywhere. It seemed to be endless. Candace had scrubbed and scrubbed in one corner.

The blood wouldn't come off the stairs.

To try to get her mind off the horror of her task, Candace decided to move over to a wall inside the staircase, where Kathleen had hung a poster of a black cat. It was a famous print called *Le Chat Noir*, and Candace liked the piece of artwork. When she took a closer look at it, she noticed the corner of the black cat had blood on it. Candace decided that would be an easier place to work.

Candace got the Windex out and sprayed. She was using a rag, removing the blood from the cat poster into a bowl of water. Then all of a sudden, a streak of red blood came running down from the poster, running right down Candace's arm.

It was too much. Candace just couldn't bear it. Kathleen's blood had mixed in with the Windex and was running bright red again. With a shriek, Candace threw the rag and the Windex down. She broke into uncontrollable sobs. Lori was upstairs somewhere, but the house was too big for Lori to hear her. Candace wasn't the type who would want Lori to come and see her crying, especially since she was covered with blood.

Candace decided the best way to honor Kathleen was to concentrate on her sister's memory. She wanted to remember the good times. So Candace washed herself up and went to retrieve Lori, and the two of them headed back over to the Berry house across the street.

Just before she and Lori left, they saw Clayton and Todd using duct tape and a blanket to try to cover the stairwell area. The young men were trying to be helpful. Michael came down and had a look at the job they were doing. It seemed like his sons had the accident all covered. But after a few minutes, the blanket fell. Clayton and Todd tried again, but it was obvious that the duct tape wasn't going to hold up. Michael was dismayed to see that his sons' idea wasn't working.

Candace just couldn't spend any more time thinking about it. Caitlin, who had already arrived from New York, and her sisters needed their attention. And their mom would be arriving within hours. It would be a very long day. Candace and Lori felt they would have to put things into proper perspective. They both had hearts of gold. They were used to dealing with touchy situations. Michael had asked Candace to take care of the funeral for Kathleen. Her brother-in-law made it clear that he was in no shape to handle that, and Candace offered to take on the responsibility. Being a conscientious woman, Candace wanted to be sure that her sister had a proper burial. If

Michael couldn't do it, someone would have to pick up the slack.

Candace, however, was not from the deep South. She and her husband, Mark, lived in the DC area. Candace had only been to North Carolina on visits. She wasn't sure about the Southern traditions, about the way people in Durham expected things to be done. She was hoping that Michael would have set up the service at the church at least, that he would have organized some kind of banquet hall, or perhaps made some provisions for the two dozen people who were Kathleen's immediate family.

But Michael had always left the social arrangements to Kathleen. He was not used to dealing with that sort of thing. His only request was that Kathleen's funeral service be held at the Duke University Chapel, the neo-Gothic centerpiece of the university's West Campus. As for the wake, the burial, the flowers, the tea and cake, and even Kathleen's stone monument, Michael didn't have the heart to be involved.

All the grieving people in the world weren't going to bring his wife back to him. Whatever flowers, whatever country hams or biscuits people wanted to bring, whatever dinners people wanted to arrange, those were things for the living.

To Michael, everything was Kathleen. All he had was Kathleen. With her gone, he felt dead inside. There was nothing to look forward to—no Christmas, no New Year's Eve—and the people of Durham who were interested in the public grieving, the people who knew him and his wife because of their local reputation, and even their friends and family, were all just a blur.

Candace realized she'd have to handle things as best she could. She had her sister Lori there, who would help, and all the neighbors from Forest Hills had come forward, opening their homes, serving up meals, just filled with tears and sympathy. Candace had no way of knowing how many people would be attending Kathleen's wake, but from the sound of it, Kathleen had so many people who loved her, so many employees and friends, there could be hundreds. It would be impossible to tell how many folks might decide to attend the wake, especially with Kathleen's death being blasted all over the local news.

If nothing else, Candace was determined that the funeral would serve her sister's memory. She needed to do that for her sister. She needed to remain strong. Fighting back tears in her eyes, Candace wrote her sister a loving eulogy. That was another thing she had hoped Michael, the novelist, would have undertaken. But he hadn't. Michael was at such a loss for words, he couldn't put his grief on paper.

Candace wasn't sure about how she could handle all these people. Kathleen's children were devastated, her mom was sick at heart, and if that wasn't bad enough, Michael had become absolutely useless. He was basically hiding out in his house, refusing to face the world. Still, Candace knew that the family would manage, somehow, in the midst of such grief, to pull things together.

Unfortunately, there had been no advance planning on the part of Kathleen concerning her death. There was no cemetery plot chosen, there were no instructions about burial or cremation. And there was no last will and testament. Once the eulogy was written, Candace had to find the strength to look in the phone book and contact a funeral home. The rest of the family would be arriving, the arrangements needed to be in place. She wished Kathleen had left some instructions, something that would have reflected her own wishes, but nothing of that kind existed. Everything was falling on Candace's shoulders.

Once Candace contacted the local funeral director, however, things became a bit easier. The people at the funeral home were gracious and full of respect for Kathleen; they were full of remorse for the family. They were such nice folks, the people in Durham. It seemed everyone was so kindhearted in North Carolina. There was all that Southern charm, all that grace of yesteryear. And as Candace became more entrenched with the funeral arrangements, she almost completely forgot about her grief.

It was still a difficult time for her, the whole funeral and wake process—especially because she had no one in the family to run things by—but Candace had put off her own grieving, really, without even having realized it. The death investigation was clouding everyone's minds. The newspeople were snooping around. Their lives weren't private anymore. And then, Michael and his sons were so caught up in their anger at the police. They were furious that the Durham police were trying to make news out of Kathleen's death. In the Petersons' minds, it was all a publicity stunt by the Durham police, who had no regard for the family's feelings at all.

The Petersons were still outraged by the fact that the police had taken over their home. The police had spent almost two days executing their search warrants. In all those hours, in all the panic surrounding Kathleen's death, Michael and his sons had felt such outrage. The police were checking all of their cars, cops were rummaging through everything they owned. The Cedar Street mansion had been turned upside down, yet there wasn't anything to find.

With Michael finally free to move about the house again, Candace had made a point to go back to see him on Tuesday morning. By then, Candace and the rest of the family, including Caitlin, Margaret, and Martha, were all staying in Durham at the Washington Duke, a ritzy hotel on the Duke campus, not far from the Forest Hills home. Kathleen's family had been given a floor of suites there, compliments of the management, to make the first few nights of their suffering just a little less difficult.

It was a godsend, actually, that Kathleen's family was

tucked away at a hotel, because over on Cedar Street, Michael was so upset, so beside himself with grief, there was really no reasoning with him. Candace had gone to his home to talk to Michael about making the final funeral arrangements. A short while after she got there, Candace noticed a couple of maintenance workers had been let into the house. They had plywood and other supplies, and Candace figured that Michael had hired the workers to paint the area. She was grateful for that. She felt a fresh coat of new paint was probably a good way to handle the horrific stairway.

But much to her surprise, the workers weren't there to paint at all. As Candace looked on in disbelief, the men started setting up a photography shoot. They were working on backlighting. Candace couldn't understand it. She thought it was the strangest thing in the world.

Moments later, Michael explained that, unfortunately, the photography had to be done. Because the police were trying to frame him, it had been suggested that Michael take photos of the scene. Michael said he really couldn't rely on whatever the police had done the night of Kathleen's death. The police were being obnoxious; they had been out to get him from day one. Michael felt their work efforts would certainly be slanted; the police work would be heavily one-sided. Michael needed to protect himself.

Candace didn't quite like the idea of her sister's death scene being preserved and photographed, but she realized that Michael was innocent. If he felt he needed to do certain things, if he felt the police were harassing him, it might make sense that he have his own set of photos. She figured that Michael's brother Bill, an attorney, might have suggested it, just as a precaution.

As soon as the photos were taken, Candace was happy to see that the stairwell was being boarded up. Candace felt there was no need for any of the other people in Kathleen's life—certainly not her daughters—to ever have to look at something like that.

As it was, the police presence around the house was unnerving. The yellow tape was causing extra grief for the family. Things were hard enough on them already, with Kathleen gone so suddenly.

With all the drama going on in that house—amid the police, the tears, and the media beginning to call—at least the blood wouldn't be visible any longer.

Seven

It had been a typical winter day in New York, December 9, 2001, the day Caitlin received word that there were important messages for her from her sorority friends at Cornell. She had been out late the night before and had strolled in at noon after crashing at a girlfriend's house. She couldn't understand why she had so many messages waiting for her. She walked around her sorority house, looking to find one of her friends to figure out what was going on, when she came across her friend Becka, who took her into the piano room, looking very upset.

Caitlin could see her friend had been crying. Caitlin knew it was something serious, there was that bad feeling in the air. She started to think one of their friends had an accident. But Becka was refusing to tell her what the matter was. Her friend wanted Caitlin to wait for some other people. Even though Caitlin was becoming increasingly upset, Becka wouldn't talk. Then Caitlin finally looked her friend in the eye and pleaded with her.

"You can't do this to me," Caitlin said. "What's upsetting you so much? What's wrong?"

"I can't tell you. I have to wait."

"I don't understand. Why are you doing this? What is it?"

Caitlin was begging her friend to speak. After a long

pause, after what seemed an eternity, Becka finally knew
she would have to break the news.

"Caitlin, it's your mom."

"What about my mom?"

"Caitlin, she's gone. There's been an accident. She fell
down the stairs. Caitlin, your mom is dead."

Becka's words whirled in Caitlin's head. This was the
first time ever that the cheerful nineteen-year-old had
suffered a real loss in her life. She never knew death. She
never knew tragedy. Up until then, any bad news Caitlin
ever heard had been followed by a silver lining. But not
this time. This time, the news was completely final.

As Caitlin was trying to process it all, the grief counselors from Cornell arrived. When Caitlin looked over at
the counselors, who had grim looks on their faces, she
instantly broke down in tears. The counselors reiterated
what her friend had just told her, but by that time Caitlin
had tuned everyone out.

Caitlin and her mom were very close. They spoke on
the phone every day. They loved each other; they were
friends. Caitlin was Kathleen's treasure. Though she
worked hard not to play favorites, Kathleen's other
daughters were really Michael's girls, born in Germany
to another woman, Liz Ratliff, and the Ratliff girls had
a lot of issues. Even though they'd been "adopted" by
Michael when they were children, the girls maintained
their distance.

In the back of her mind, Kathleen always knew that
Margaret and Martha had never totally accepted her. As
much as Kathleen bent over backward for them, as
much as she and Michael had hoped the Ratliff girls
would adjust to their American apple-pie lifestyle, Margaret and Martha were never completely okay.

Kathleen did everything she could to treat Margaret
and Martha as equal daughters to Caitlin. She did everything she could to make the Ratliff girls feel as one with

the family, but there was always that separateness about them. Kathleen sometimes felt that perhaps, even though their mother died when they were just babies, the girls had never really gotten over that loss. For whatever the reason, no matter how hard she tried, Kathleen could never fill that gap. The Ratliff girls called her Mom, they loved her, but Kathleen knew she could never take the place of their true mother.

So it became natural for Kathleen and Caitlin to gravitate to each other, especially after all three girls had gone away to college, each to opposite ends of the country. Once they were all off on their own, so to speak, Caitlin had become Kathleen's special concern. Kathleen was able to confide more in Caitlin. The two of them shared a special bond together. They looked alike, they thought alike. They were as close as a mother and daughter could be, and Caitlin always knew that.

As the grief counselors continued to give Caitlin advice, letting her know that all her professors would be contacted, telling her that she didn't have to worry about her classes, promising that people at Cornell would always be there for her, Caitlin couldn't really listen. They were working on her plane ticket to return to Durham, they said, and they wanted her to know that she could call them anytime, that she could lean on them.

But Caitlin was numb.

She didn't want to talk anymore.

She ran up to her room to call her sisters, and was able to get Margaret on the phone. She and Margaret just kind of cried to each other, but they didn't have many words to say. Caitlin hung up after she realized she needed to call her father, Fred, who had been her background support throughout her life. Even though Caitlin's parents had been divorced for years, and even though Michael Peterson had taken on a father-figure role in her life, Caitlin had Fred Atwater. He was her real father, and he made sure they kept a loving relationship. To her credit, Kathleen had insisted that Caitlin remain close to her biological dad. Kathleen made sure that Caitlin had a good relationship with Fred. Regardless of her new family with Michael, she wanted Caitlin to remain close to her biological father.

When Caitlin dialed Fred, her father was anxious to get the call. He was on his cell phone. He told Caitlin he was already in the car, on his way up to Cornell to pick her up. He was driving there from Philadelphia, where he had been on a consulting job. He was dropping everything, and he didn't want his daughter getting on a plane by herself. He asked her to book him a hotel room and said he'd be there in a few hours.

Friends brought Caitlin little stuffed teddy bears and left them at her door. Her mom's death had been announced to her sorority, and they had canceled that Sunday's usual meeting, in honor of Kathleen. Girlfriends were sitting in her room, just watching her. People were bringing her food, but Caitlin wasn't really eating or moving. She wasn't functioning.

It wasn't until her ex-boyfriend stopped over that Caitlin really lost it. The two had a huge cry together; they still had a connection. But then Caitlin recalled him leaving, and the next thing she knew, her dad showed up. Everything was happening through a filter for her. She couldn't name a single person who had brought cake or coffee or a stuffed animal. With her dad there, Caitlin felt a bit safer for a while, but everything inside her just hurt. She felt lost. She didn't want her dad to go to his hotel room, even if only for a few hours, but then she realized she had to get a grip on herself.

The following morning, as Fred took his daughter back to Durham, in a very gentle way, he began to warn Caitlin. He wanted her to know that it was going to be a bad scene down there. Fred hadn't really told her all the details, but he mentioned that the house had police tape around it. He said that her mom's death was being reported in the news. He wanted Caitlin to brace herself.

By the time Caitlin's flight touched down in North Carolina, a few of her high-school friends had left messages on her cell phone. When Caitlin called some of them back, speaking to kids who knew her mom, all Caitlin did was cry.

Because she and her father had gone to Philadelphia first, to catch a flight from there, Caitlin hadn't landed until late on Monday evening. She and her dad had been met at the airport by his wife, Carol, and it was understood that, since the Atwaters would not be entirely comfortable with the Peterson clan, Caitlin would be dropped off to spend some time alone with them.

There had always been hard feelings between Fred Atwater and Michael Peterson. Kathleen had had a bitter divorce from Fred, and Michael knew that. Michael had been the man to rescue her from all her sorrow after Fred had filed for divorce. Fred had never been able to redeem himself to Michael, who never liked having Fred in the picture. Fred and Carol Atwater realized it would be best to drop Caitlin off with her siblings. They would remain nearby and available for anything the family needed. They wanted to respect Caitlin's grieving.

So Caitlin was the last of the Peterson household to enter Maureen Berry's house, the Monday after Kathleen's death, and everyone was there waiting for her. As Todd came outside to console her, escorting her out of Fred's car, Caitlin barely noticed the yellow crime tape around her home. She was in tears, but also in shock, and she fought to put up a good front, to wipe her tears away for a moment, only to have them come back all the more, the minute she and her sisters saw each other. As the girls hugged and cried, Clayton and Todd were at a loss for words. They wrapped their arms around all three girls.

But there was not much else anyone else could do.

At that point, Michael appeared. He wasn't crying, but he was all welled-up. When he saw Caitlin, he went into a deeper sorrow. Young Caitlin had Kathleen's mannerisms, Kathleen's features, Kathleen's body shape, which made his grief all the more painful. Seeing Caitlin seemed to be the most upsetting for Michael. He immediately took her upstairs, to one of the guest rooms, so he could speak with her in private.

With Michael looking across the street at their home, shedding tears, Caitlin began to think more about her mom. She wanted Michael to tell her about her mom's day on Saturday. She wanted to know every detail about what her mom had done. She wanted to hear what the last day of her mom's life was like. She asked Michael to give her every detail, about when they woke up, about what they ate, about how her mother was feeling. She just wanted to know everything.

Caitlin wasn't thinking about the yellow tape; she hadn't crossed that bridge at all. She just wanted to hear about her mom. She wanted to be assured that her mom was happy and in a good mood that last day. So Michael sat Caitlin down and told her all about how they spent their time.

On Saturday, her mom had gone to work for a little while in the morning, but then she had called him. Kathleen had decided to take the rest of the day off. They went to do Christmas shopping. He and Kathleen had gone to Costco. They had stocked up the house. They had bought a few Christmas gifts, some things for the house, some things for Caitlin and the other kids. Michael said Kathleen was excited about everyone coming home for Christmas. She had already put a few presents under the tree.

He said that he had gone to the gym in the afternoon, as always, and when he got home, the two of them had

cooked dinner together. Michael said they had been celebrating his book option, his movie deal. The two of them
had some champagne. They were just enjoying the
evening. They'd watched a film he'd rented. At some
point, Todd had dropped by. Everything was normal.
They'd been drinking and talking, and had they stayed
up late.

Caitlin knew about that routine. Michael and her
mom would spend evenings alone like that sometimes,
just having a quiet dinner, drinking wine, and getting
into deep conversations. Usually when they would stay
up after midnight, they would wind up outside at the
pool. They liked to end their nights out there, under the
stars, where Michael would smoke a pipe, and her mom
would sometimes sneak one or two cigarettes.

Michael explained that he was outside with one of
their dogs, he recalled that it was going on 2:00 A.M. He
said that because her mom had a phone conference in
the morning, she had gone upstairs to get some sleep.
He said that about twenty or thirty minutes after she'd
gone up to bed, he came inside and found her at the
bottom of the stairs.

As Michael told her of these events, Caitlin was increasingly upset. He was about to go into further details.
He began to say he'd called 9-1-1, but Caitlin didn't really want to hear about anything like that. She told him
she didn't want to know.

Caitlin had heard enough. She didn't need to know
about the kind of shape her mom was in when Michael
found her. With Michael becoming more distraught as
he spoke, Caitlin could see he was reliving the horror.
She started crying, as did Michael, and he gave her his
shoulder to comfort her. The two of them were sitting
on a twin bed in a guest room that looked over at their
beautiful home. After Michael hugged Caitlin for a
minute, he got up and went over to the window to stare

at the big, old, empty place. The sight of it made him more tearful.

"Does Mom have life insurance?" Caitlin asked, as an afterthought. "Does she have a will?"

"I don't know," he told her. "I mean, I have all kinds of life insurance policies that I've taken out. But I don't know that she had any."

"Well, does she have a will?" Caitlin wanted to know.

"I don't think she had one. I know we had once talked to Mr. Egan, he's your mom's friend, you know, the lawyer. It was sometime last year. I can't remember. I know she was supposed to get to it. But I don't think she ever wrote anything out."

She and Michael were rambling on about different things. They talked for about thirty minutes, jumping from one subject to the next, mostly talking about Kathleen, but also worrying about Margaret's birthday, which was, unfortunately, that very same day. And then, suddenly, before Caitlin had a chance to stop him, Michael brought up the unpleasant subject of the police.

"You know, they've been at the house for over a day," he said. "The police are calling it a suspicious death. They're blowing this into a big thing."

"I don't understand any of this," Caitlin told him. "It doesn't make any sense."

"Well, you know, it's because I was the last person to see her. Because I was the only one there. So, of course, they're looking at me."

"But why?"

"Who knows? I can't really tell you. The police have never liked me around here."

"But I don't understand why they would want to do this."

"You know, Caitlin, how much I loved your mother."

"Of course I know that."

"I would never do anything to hurt her."

"I know," Caitlin said, "you and Mom loved each other."

"It's the police," he said. "They're trying to make problems."

"Well, I think it's just crazy."

"It is," Michael assured her, "but we'll get through it."

Michael and Caitlin had no more time to waste on the subject. They had to think about the others. Everyone was downstairs waiting for them. There was a small cake someone had brought, just to acknowledge Margaret's birthday, and they felt they should at least go down and talk to her, and just be with the rest of the family.

Eight

The Petersons were never really a touchy-feely family. As they sat huddled together, some of them crying, it was an awkward time for them. No one was really saying much. There was nothing being discussed about the funeral. The family was just receiving callers, people from the neighborhood, mostly, who were stopping in with goodies, who had come to offer some support.

The family was overcome with grief, and with the added trouble the police were causing, turning their most solemn time into a public circus, they had nothing to say to anyone. At about 10:00 P.M., when the police phoned Michael Peterson to say that he could return to his home, everyone felt a sigh of relief. The officials had informed him that the search warrant was completed, that the yellow tape had been removed. The Petersons would be able to grieve in a place of comfort.

Michael and his sons were anxious to get back over there, but the girls had no desire to enter the house. There was still blood in the stairway. It was too sad, really, for the girls to face. The girls had a lovely hotel room on the Duke campus waiting for them, and they were happy to go straight there, to be in the midst of their aunts and uncles, their cousins, and their lovely grandmother, Veronica.

As for the adults, they were not allowing the children

to see the full extent of their grief. It was already too hard on the girls, who were so fragile, each in their own way. For Caitlin, Kathleen's baby, there was a sense of complete and utter devastation. For Margaret and Martha, two girls who had long-before suffered the loss of their biological mother, losing their stepmother was all the more dramatic.

Things were different for Todd and Clayton Peterson. They were older, already finished with college. They still had their biological mother, Patricia Peterson, who was a constant presense in their lives. Patricia lived in Europe, where she had raised her sons until they graduated from high school, and the boys visited with her often, each taking trips back and forth to Germany. Nonetheless, even Patricia's phone calls could offer little comfort regarding the loss of Kathleen. Sure, Patricia had played a significant role in raising her sons, and she had played a role in raising the Ratliff girls. In her many years of marriage to Michael, Patricia had an impact on the four children. Her boys were close to her, but they still could not be consoled. As for Margaret and Martha, who had left Germany as children, they had formed a bond to Kathleen that Patricia could never replace.

The Ratliff girls had a special type of relationship with Kathleen. No doubt Margaret and Martha remained distant at times, but that was more a consequence of having been orphaned. There was always a distance the two girls kept from outsiders. They referred to both Patricia and Kathleen as Mom, but they were removed, at some level, from both women. Even if the Ratliff girls shared a close relationship with Kathleen, in the final analysis, it was only their dad, Michael, whom they considered true family. It was Michael who had spent all his adult life doting on them.

In the months after they had been orphaned, Margaret and Martha had truly become his. For most of their lives, hardly a moment had gone by that Michael wasn't there for Margaret and Martha. Michael was their one shining light. In a way, Michael had become the Ratliffs' savior. Michael was their primary parent, always taking the girls with him, back and forth from Germany to North Carolina. Michael was the one who helped with the burial of the girls' mom, Elizabeth, after she had died tragically in Germany.

He meant everything to them, and the feeling was mutual. So, as much as Margaret and Martha were saddened about the loss of their stepmother, to the Ratliff girls, it was their legal guardian, Michael, who was their only true parent. It wasn't that Margaret and Martha didn't feel their own sense of loss about Kathleen, but it was also for their dad's sake that the Ratliff girls grieved. They knew how much he loved Kathleen.

Of course Kathleen Peterson had tried to be a good mother to the Ratliff girls. But it was complicated. Over the years, Kathleen had to deal with Michael's ex-wife making trouble. In the months following Elizabeth Ratliff's death, once Michael and Patricia had been designated guardians to Margaret and Martha, Patricia had agreed to leave Germany, to move back to North Carolina with Michael, really for the sake of the girls. For whatever reason, Michael convinced her that it would be easier to raise the four kids in the States. But Patricia had a hard time making that adjustment back to American life. Living in Durham was not what she had expected, and having to supervise four demanding children just made her life impossible. Michael would later tell Kathleen that Patricia had been making comments about how she really didn't want to raise the Ratliff girls. Michael reported that Patricia said she hadn't signed up for a second family.

Nonetheless, Patricia had tried. She had moved back to the States, returning to the home she and Michael still

owned in Durham. It was the home that she and Michael
had bought in their early days of marriage, when they
were young college kids, when their lives were carefree.
But life with four kids was a whole different ball game.
Michael was working in isolation, writing his novels, and
most of the everyday burdens fell on Patricia. And so,
returning back to North Carolina would wind up being
disastrous for her, and especially for her marriage. Patricia would never feel quite comfortable in the States.
Even though she was an American, she didn't really
adapt very well. Because of that, Michael wound up re-
treating into a friendship with Kathleen, the glamorous
divorcée who lived nearby.

In the beginning, when Michael and Kathleen were
only friends, when Caitlin and Margaret and Martha
were three grade-school kids, living as neighbors, playing happily together, everything seemed simple and
innocent. But then Patricia noticed that Michael was
spending more and more time with Kathleen. For
months, she tried to keep a blind eye; she basically stood
back and said nothing. But as Michael and Kathleen became more and more involved, Patricia found them
together to be near impossible.

Michael and Kathleen were falling deeply in love, and
Patricia couldn't help herself from feeling hateful. Naturally, she resented Michael and Kathleen's love affair,
especially as it became increasingly open. As things became more serious, as Michael was threatening to move
out of their house, Patricia decided she wasn't about to
make things easy for Kathleen. She was painfully aware
of how well Kathleen was getting along with Michael,
Margaret, and Martha, and Patricia was becoming out-
wardly nervous about losing her family.

Back in those days, Patricia was still trying to save her
marriage to Michael. Determined to maintain her status
as his wife, Patricia requested that Michael move back

with her to Germany. She had accepted a teaching position there, and would be taking their sons with her, whether he liked it or not. Patricia would suggest that Michael keep the house in Durham, that he rent it out as an investment property, but she insisted that North Carolina would no longer be her home. Michael would have to choose. If he wanted to live with his sons, he would have to leave the United States.

Patricia figured that since she and Michael had been happy back in Germany, they could rekindle their love there. They had many friends in that part of the world, Patricia having worked many years as a teacher for the Department of Defense. She knew Michael loved it there; he had written his first novel in Germany and adored European ways. Germany was a place of so many fond memories for Michael, a man who loved being an expatriate. And Patricia knew that.

The two of them had initially agreed to return to the states as a temporary fix. They felt the old Southern ways, the Southern hospitality, would make life more cushy for their larger family. But once she became a full-time teacher and a full-time mom in Durham, Patricia grew increasingly unsettled with the American ways of life. As Michael became more enamored with the ease of an American existence, Patricia felt that her sons would be best served growing up in Europe. As for the Ratliff girls, Patricia felt Michael should determine what the best upbringing for them would be. Their "adopted" girls were in grade school; Margaret and Martha would be able to withstand another move. If Michael wanted his sons in his life, he would have to take the girls away from America. Patricia felt the girls would flourish in Germany, where their biological mom, Liz, had wanted them to grow up. She believed that Michael would somehow agree.

But no one could have foreseen the love that Michael

would find with Kathleen. The love affair between Michael and Kathleen had started off slowly, with their girls being best friends. But as the two of them continued to see each other, they realized how much they really had in common. When their secret love affair was no longer hidden, Patricia was devastated. At first, she was hopeful that she could outlast Kathleen. Patricia was willing to do anything to keep Michael in her life, to make concessions about staying in America, to do whatever her husband might ask. But when Michael announced that he was going to move into Kathleen's house, just a few blocks away, telling Patricia that he had decided to live with Kathleen out of wedlock . . . Patricia could hardly stand it.

At first, Michael had this idea that Caitlin, Margaret, and Martha could live like sisters. They all seemed so happy together, and Kathleen was all for it. But that was too much of a leap for Patricia to make. In those early years, even though Patricia hardly showed it, she disliked Kathleen and her preppy daughter, Caitlin. Patricia refused to allow her sons to even visit Kathleen's home. As the tug-of-war for Michael continued, Patricia picked up and moved back to Germany, taking hers sons with her.

By shifting households, Patricia Peterson felt certain that she would force Michael back into her life. But to her surprise, Michael, who had gone back to give Germany a try for a few months, who had taken Margaret and Martha overseas to try to keep his family whole, had decided that there was no way he could make it work with Patricia. Instead, Michael had grown spiteful toward Patricia and her attempt to keep him away from Kathleen. It became even more clear, with all the miles and the Atlantic Ocean between them, that Kathleen was the only woman Michael loved. After only nine months, not being able to live apart from her, Michael returned to Kathleen. With his two daughters in tow, Michael Peterson would never move from his home base of North Carolina again.

Once Michael returned, Kathleen took on greater responsibilities for the Ratliff girls. Margaret and Martha were always closer to Michael, and Kathleen had her daughter, Caitlin, but Kathleen tried very hard to be a true mother to Margaret and Martha. Kathleen seemed to know how to handle the kids; she was fair with all three girls. She showed each of them the same unconditional love. The same love she had for Caitlin, she tried to bestow to Margaret and Martha. Kathleen only became the type of mother they needed.

As the girls grew up together, they blossomed under Kathleen's watchful eye. She encouraged them to become involved with sports; she guided them through their school projects. But Kathleen wasn't the type to take control of the girls. Martha and Margaret were still Michael's children. She tried to earn their admiration, and she understood that Michael was the person they loved best. It was okay that Michael was the mainstay for the Ratliff girls. Kathleen knew her place, and did everything possible to complete their lives.

It would take years, but Kathleen slowly earned the title of Mom. Through her nurturing and fairness, she had won them over. Margaret and Martha loved her. They considered themselves hers. Even though they stayed in touch with their "mom" Patricia, who would make annual summer visits to Durham, who would try to assert her own status with the girls, Margaret and Martha had developed a very unique relationship with Kathleen—one that was hardly penetrable.

Patricia, of course, would continue to operate from the sidelines. She would continue to resent Michael's true love of Kathleen. For a long time, Patricia tried to delay her divorce from Michael, but Kathleen had won Michael's heart. Kathleen stood by him, and had managed to live through his lengthy separation and divorce.

When Michael was finally free, the two of them moved out of Kathleen's Forest Hills home. They had purchased their storybook mansion on Cedar Street. At that point, Kathleen and Michael had been together for over five years. With their move into their very own home, with Michael publishing a new book and reaching a new height of success, the two decided they should marry. They loved each other, and they wanted to make everything official.

Michael was well on his way to becoming a famous author, and Kathleen was also becoming a success, climbing the corporate ladder at Nortel Networks. The two worked so well together, and once they were married, things were better than ever. Michael and Kathleen were really on top of the world. Their lifestyle felt so right. They had a love and respect that few couples ever knew. Their ties to the kids had become so strong that neither of them needed to worry about how Patricia might affect the family. When Michael's sons returned to Durham to begin looking at American universities, the boys fit right in. Kathleen treated Clayton and Todd with the utmost respect. After years of marriage, Kathleen was no longer concerned about doing anything that might make Michael balk. She no longer had to walk a fine line, no longer had to worry about causing ripples or waves with the children.

Certain bad feelings continued to exist between Patricia and Michael and Kathleen over the years, but once Clayton and Todd had decided to attend Duke University, to live back home with Michael, Patricia was good about letting Michael keep his boys close to his home. For their part, Clayton and Todd came to know what a good soul Kathleen was. . . . They held her in a separate place.

As the boys began to appreciate how gentle and respectful Kathleen was with them, as they shared stories about Kathleen's kind ways, their mother began to set her hard feelings aside. Michael and the children backed Kathleen one hundred percent, and eventually Patricia conceded that Kathleen had become a central figure in the Peterson family.

It had taken years, but Patricia had come to understand that Michael and Kathleen were entrenched with the children, that they all enjoyed having an American life. Michael was relieved about that. Michael admired Kathleen for seeming to have endless patience in the war that went on during the first few years of their relationship, but finally the whole situation with Patricia, all the fighting, all the struggle with the kids, was over. After so many years of working on things, of working things out, Michael and Kathleen had it all together. Their own relationship was tight. And their life with their patchwork family—their sons, their daughters—had become the ultimate and quintessential American dream.

Not that any of that mattered anymore.

Whatever family wounds there had been, whatever peace Patricia had made with Michael and Kathleen, was no longer relevant. Kathleen had died so quickly, so tragically. Her children, including Caitlin, regardless of having other parents in their lives, regardless of being young adults, would still have a hard time fending for themselves.

Everyone knew that Kathleen worked so hard to keep the Peterson household together. Everyone knew how much Kathleen had gone out of her way for her kids, making five-course family dinners, insisting that all of them sit together for her home-cooked meals But now with Kathleen's death, all any of them could feel was sorrow.

Kathleen was gone, and the Peterson kids would begin

to wonder how they would actually manage without her. They had that big house, and there were so many responsibilities to think about. It wasn't that they weren't willing . . . but they had all moved away. Except for Todd, they each had their separate lives in other parts of the country. The kids knew Michael would never be able to keep up such a big household by himself. The kids knew Kathleen had always taken on the family chores, the nitty-gritty work behind the scenes. Kathleen had always done all the social arrangements for the family get-togethers, she had always handled the shopping, the baking, all the extras that only a mom could do.

Now, with Michael all alone, of course, things would be different. Even the basics would be difficult for him. And the frills, the holiday gatherings and charity events, those things would be out of the question.

With Kathleen no longer there to run things, everyone felt ill at ease. Kathleen was the glue that held them all together. Even Michael, who was a fabulous dad to his children, who was loved and respected by all of them, would never be able to equal Kathleen. There was all the love she put into things, all the handmade care that Kathleen devoted to the family. Kathleen was a one-of-a-kind woman, a breadwinner, a supermom and homemaker. Michael would always be the first to tell people that.

Nine

"We stayed in this hotel room, and we were all talking about how sad we were," Caitlin recalled, speaking of the first night back in Durham with Margaret and Martha. "We hadn't seen each other in three months, and we all had those random stories that would pop into our heads about Mom."

The three sisters wanted to share anecdotes about happy times. They were leaning on their pillows, still distraught, but they needed to calm themselves down. Remembering happy things, the little mottoes Kathleen had, the way she advised them about boys, those were the types of things the girls wanted to talk about. But no matter how many stories they told about shopping sprees, no matter how many comments they would make about their experiences with Kathleen at home in Durham, or with Kathleen in faraway places, like Hong Kong, they still kept coming back to the subject of her shocking death, and about all the police suspicions. They resented the police for intruding into their private lives. They knew their dad had been a public figure in Durham. They knew that the death investigation was standard police procedure. But it still didn't seem fair.

"It's so crazy that they're doing this to our dad," Margaret complained.

"I don't understand why they're blowing things out of

proportion," Martha blurted. "They're trying to make a big deal about it for no reason."

"I wish they would just let it go," Caitlin said. "I wish they would just leave us alone."

The girls didn't want to talk about the news reports. They knew that Michael had been advised, by his lawyer friends, not to talk to the press. Kerry Sutton, the family friend who was initially representing him, had been angered by the circumstances. Sutton told local reporters that Michael Peterson had been treated like a criminal from the get-go, and because of the so-called police misconduct, Michael had decided to hire a criminal attorney. The girls were aware that their dad had called a top lawyer out of Chapel Hill. But they had no idea what Barry Winston, the attorney, was going to do for Michael. No charges had been filed; there was no foul play being reported.

The girls felt confident that the situation would work itself out. They knew their dad was innocent. There was no question in their minds. They would later make statements to the media to confirm their beliefs.

The following morning, as the girls woke up in their hotel room at the Washington Duke, the three of them were still in shock. They really wanted the whole world to go away. None of them wanted to get out of their beds. They were content to stay bunched together, the three of them just comforting each other. They felt upset, and wanted to grieve in their own quiet way. No throng of mourners, no amount of public accolades for their mom, was going to change the fact that they were confronting her death.

When they were asked by their aunts, Candace and Lori, to help run some errands, to help with funeral arrangements, they weren't really feeling up to it. But the flowers needed to be ordered, and their mom's cemetery plot needed to be chosen. It was all so depressing for the girls. Margaret and Martha were just beside themselves, but Caitlin felt these things had to be handled. Clayton and Todd were busy, holed up in the house with their dad. Caitlin told her sisters that they had no real choice.

The local news, meanwhile, was giving reports about the hazards and injuries that people suffered from stairway falls. One expert noted that in 2001 alone, over 1 million people across America had been treated in hospitals as a result of a slip in a stairway. The local news commented, in particular, about the Petersons' back stairway. They surmised that because it was in such an old house, because the back stairway served as a utility access for the mansion, the stairs where Mrs. Peterson was found were probably very steep.

News reports mentioned that police investigators wouldn't really understand certain factors such as the "orientation gradient," where people can become disoriented by subtle factors. There was much speculation about things such as the curves in the stairwell, the tread edges, and the handrails. News reporters speculated about the unusual size of the steps, noting that any fall, even a fall down three or four steps, could be very unforgiving. News reports reminded the public of the many factors that might make a person lose their view or vision, especially if the stairwell was dimly lit.

However, the children suspected, even though they hadn't made any public statements, that Kathleen and Michael had been drinking quite heavily on the night of her death. . . .

On December 12, 2001, the obituary of Kathleen Hunt Peterson appeared in Durham's *Herald-Sun* newspaper. Born in Greensboro, North Carolina, Kathleen had relocated with her family, and had spent her grade-school years in Lancaster, Pennsylvania, near the Amish

Country. She'd been voted "Girl of the Year" in high school, and she was quite the star. Not only was she the valedictorian of her class and the president of the debating club, Kathleen was the editor of the school magazine as well. After her graduation in 1971, Kathleen had chosen to attend Duke University, where she had been accepted as the first female student into Duke's School of Engineering. She had been a young woman of great initiative.

In her professional career, Kathleen Peterson had landed executive positions at Pritchard, Merck, and, ultimately, at Nortel Networks. For her achievements at Nortel, Kathleen had received countless awards. As a top executive at Nortel, she had traveled throughout the world, to Russia, China, Europe, and even to Vietnam. Beyond that, Kathleen Peterson was the only person—in the entire Research Triangle—to have received the honor of having a conference room named after her.

Kathleen was survived by her mother, two sisters, her brother, her five children, and her successful novelist husband, Michael. Knowing that Kathleen had so many admirers and supporters, and knowing that Michael held such a place of prominence in the community, the family made sure to mention that they didn't want any money to be spent on flowers. They requested that any donations be made to the Durham Arts Council in Kathleen Peterson's name.

But behind the scenes, with the police still present outside the mansion, with reporters still snooping for tidbits, things had gotten strange around the Peterson house. Michael had announced that he wasn't going to attend the public viewing at the funeral home. He had called his siblings, Bill, Jack, Ann, and Christensen, and had asked them not to attend Kathleen's wake.

Michael felt that the wake was a place for strangers. He didn't want the family subjected to all the public hoopla. He asked his sister, Ann, to contact the three girls in person. He wanted Ann to knock on their hotel room door, to advise them that the family would hold their own memorial in the privacy of their home.

When Caitlin was told about Michael's request, she called her stepdad immediately. She felt strongly about attending her mother's viewing, about honoring her mother's memory. She told Michael that she wanted to be reminded of all the people who loved her mom. Caitlin knew there were a lot of people who were planning to be there, and she couldn't really understand Michael's thinking.

"I want you to be at the house," Michael insisted. "I'm not going to the viewing. I don't want to intrude on you, but I would prefer for you to come home to be with me and your brothers and sisters."

"But I want to go," Caitlin told him. "I want to see my mother's friends. You know, my dad will be there, and my aunts and everyone."

"Well, I don't plan to be there. I'm not going because it's not something I believe in. If anything, I might go for the last five minutes," Michael said, "but it's not something your mother would want."

Michael asked to talk to Margaret or Martha, and Caitlin watched as Margaret picked up the receiver. Margaret listened to her dad, and didn't say much at all. Martha took the phone next. Neither of them said a word to protest their father's wishes.

But Margaret was visibly upset by Michael's demands. Caitlin could see that Margaret felt awkward, that her older sister wanted to attend the wake. Even though she wasn't saying much, Caitlin could tell that Margaret wasn't happy with Michael's request. Caitlin thought that

Michael, as usual, was being too over-protective. But in this case, his reasoning didn't make sense.

"Margaret, you should do what you want to do," Caitlin urged. "If you want to go to the viewing, these are Mom's friends."

"But Dad says we should all be at the house, as a family," Margaret told her. "He wants all of us to be together."

"This is our Mom," Caitlin said. "You should do what you want to do."

But there was no room for further discussion. Caitlin watched her sisters with a sense of confusion and disbelief. Margaret and Martha, whom her mom had raised as true daughters, were planning to honor their dad's decision.

Ten

Caitlin spent a lot of time crying at the wake. She had been accompanied by her grandmother Veronica and her aunts Candace and Lori. There was much sadness, and that was compounded by the number of people at the funeral home. There was a long line of people waiting to pay their respects, folks who had known Kathleen for years and years.

As the hours melted away, Caitlin felt she couldn't look at her mom. She had been aware of the dress her mom was wearing, she had chosen the particular coat and pearls to match, but she just couldn't get near the coffin. It wasn't that her mom looked horrifying. In fact, her makeup was wonderful. The day before, her brother Todd had even seen to the final touches.

But finally, as the procession of people began to dwindle, as people started to leave the viewing room, Caitlin began to inch her way over toward her mother. When she actually got close, standing beside her mom, she felt the need to look at all the flowers and photos that had been placed around her. Being close to her mom for the last time, Caitlin suddenly felt comforted by her mother's presence. Caitlin couldn't help but remain there. She absolutely didn't want to leave her mother's side.

With everything else fading into the background, Caitlin stayed frozen, just communing with her mother.

Her mom looked at peace. She looked pretty. Instead of feeling afraid, Caitlin loved being there beside her.

Then, the next thing she knew, Caitlin was informed that the funeral home would be closing. As much as it hurt her, Caitlin had to say her good-byes. It was so hard for her to walk away, but Caitlin knew she had to.

As she approached the funeral directors downstairs, ready to make her way out of there, Caitlin was told that Michael had placed a last-minute call. Michael and the rest of the family were on their way down to the wake. The funeral home had agreed to stay open for an extra few minutes. Caitlin was kind of upset about it.

Caitlin had already been through the trauma once. She had been through all the tears with her grandmother, her aunts and uncles, and cousins. But now, for Michael's sake, she would have to relive all of it again. She really didn't want to stay for Michael's arrival, but she had to. It wasn't just for Michael. It was for her brothers and sisters that Caitlin would endure.

Michael and his children arrived, all of them escorted by his brother Bill, and Caitlin joined along, being led upstairs again. By that time, the funeral directors had already taken Kathleen's jewelry off her, those things would be left to Caitlin, and they had already closed off most of the hallway lights.

It felt odd, the way the family had this moment of utter silence at the side of Kathleen's coffin. With the room as cold as ice, Margaret and Martha began to cry. Todd and Clayton looked shaken.

But it was Michael who was unquestionably the most physically upset at the sight of Kathleen. He was just so overcome with grief. He was shaking; then he began sobbing, holding on to the casket, where he knelt near his dear wife. Caitlin felt how much Michael was connected to her mom. She could see his pain. As she reached over to Michael to comfort him, Michael called her the "vision of her mother." Caitlin began to cry, and the other children stepped back.

Finally it was Caitlin alone at the coffin with her step-dad. Neither one of them had the strength to pull away. It seemed like forever, but Caitlin realized that Michael needed his private time to say good-bye to his wife, that he had to be the last one to see her , so she joined her brothers and sisters, who were already downstairs, waiting outside by the car.

The next day, for the funeral, Caitlin wore a dress that her mom had insisted she buy for her. Caitlin thought it was weird, the way that had worked out. She recalled going shopping over at the mall in Raleigh with her mom, the summer prior. There were two black dresses on sale, stunning dresses really, but Caitlin had liked one, and her mom had liked the other. In the end, Kathleen opted to buy both, even though Caitlin really never expected to wear the more conservative choice.

Yet, suddenly here she was, just months later, wearing that very dress that her mom so dearly loved. It wasn't black, actually, more midnight blue, and Caitlin was glad it was something her mom liked. She was glad that she wasn't wearing the same black sheaths that the rest of the family donned.

But the funeral became surreal, especially for Caitlin. Just as soon as she stepped out of the limo, it didn't matter what anyone wore, or what words were said. It was all just too unbelievable. There was no way for Caitlin to reconcile with the facts. It just didn't seem possible that her mom was never coming back.

For all of them, without doubt, Kathleen's service was painful. Nothing any preacher could say would lessen anyone's shock, would make their hurt go away. All the talk of Heaven, of all the angels in the universe, was of no consolation to the Petersons.

Kathleen's burial at the Maplewood Cemetery, right in

the heart of Durham, was even more difficult. Michael hadn't wanted a burial; he had wanted cremation. So it was only the immediate family in attendance, and with no headstone yet to mark the grave, there was this sense of overwhelming disbelief.

Immediately after the burial, the family went over to Manno's, a local home-style restaurant, where they ate a quiet meal. It was an uncomfortable time, really, especially because everyone knew that the police had come back to the Peterson house. The police had been there on the very night of Kathleen's wake; they had served a third search warrant. The Durham police seemed to be so uncaring about the family—they were indecent, really, as far as the Petersons were concerned. The way the police mishandled things, having the audacity to interfere with Kathleen's wake and funeral, it was as though they had no heart.

Most of the family had been made aware that the police had gone to test Kathleen's body prior to her wake. The police had actually served a fourth search warrant at the funeral home. It was unthinkable to them, but the police apparently had reason to administer a sexual assault kit on Kathleen. No one wanted to discuss it. There was an intruder theory that had become a part of the local media reports. It was just unreal to all of them that Kathleen's death would be so full of public speculation and rumor.

Kathleen's sisters, Candace and Lori, were anxious to leave the restaurant as soon as the meal was finished. They were exhausted, still in shock, and wanted no further part of the public attention their sister's death had brought them. Candace and Lori had already checked out of their hotel rooms. They wanted to get back to their lives in Virginia, to feel the safety of their homes, of their own beds. And as much as anything, they were concerned about their poor mom. Veronica, a woman in her eighties, who was going to take turns being hosted by her two remaining daughters.

As the day began winding down, it was Michael and Caitlin who slowly walked Candace, Lori, and the others out to the parking lot. Caitlin was saying very little, but Michael wanted to talk to Veronica, just once more. He wanted to share a private moment with her, to console her about the loss of her daughter, before she left the Durham area.

"I know how much you miss Kathleen. No one knows that as much as I do," Michael told her, his voice quivering.

"Yes, I miss her. I miss my daughter," Veronica said, breaking down into tears.

With that, Veronica leaned on Michael's shoulder. As Michael began to cry, Veronica's sobbing became tenfold. Michael was very emotional, trying to tear himself away, not wanting to say good-bye. Michael was feeling increasingly sorry for the whole family, but he was particularly sorry for Kathleen's mom, who never should have had to bury her own beautiful child. Michael promised to call Veronica in a week or two.

As he hugged Veronica one last time, Michael wanted her to know that she was always welcome back to his home. He wanted her to come back to visit him and the kids whenever she felt up to it.

"You know, I've always called you Ronnie," Michael said. "But now, if it's okay, I'd like to call you Mom."

The comment made Veronica cry all over again. She was already haunted by the idea that her daughter had died in that great big house. The thought of returning to that home—once filled with such life, such love—was too much for her.

Caitlin couldn't stop crying as she waved good-bye to her grandmother and aunts. Trying to break the sorrow, Candace asked her niece if she'd be up to Virginia to visit sometime soon. Caitlin thought she might drive through Virginia on her way back home from Cornell, so the family would have some kind of get-together.

Caitlin didn't really want to think about it, but Christmas was only two weeks away.

Eleven

It was not that Michael Peterson was being charged with any crime. It was just an investigation the Durham police were conducting, trying to conclude what, exactly, had happened to his wife.

As it was, the police had entered the Peterson mansion on the night of Kathleen's wake. They hadn't expected anyone to be home. They hadn't wished to confront Michael Peterson, his two sons, two of his daughters, or his brother Bill. The police had been blamed by the family for interfering with their going to Kathleen's viewing, but police had not requested that the family stay at the house that evening.

Kerry Sutton, Peterson's attorney and friend, had blasted the actions of police in the press, stating she was stunned by their behavior, by their insensitivity. But actually, it was Sutton who had advised Michael Peterson to stay in the house during the search.

The Durham police had a job to do. They were still investigating Kathleen's fall. And that job would continue, even while Kathleen's family mourned at her wake, even while they mourned at the Duke Chapel during her funeral service.

Most of Kathleen's family had found a way to put the police business on a back burner. Most of her family had found the strength to stand up and speak on Kathleen's behalf, especially on the day of her funeral. There was Caitlin, who said her mother's impeccable character was enough to give each of her children the strength to fulfill their dreams. There was Maureen Berry, who spoke of Kathleen's nonjudgmental nature, who said Kathleen was a uniquely upbeat individual, particularly with her husband by her side. There was Reverend Joseph Harvard, who told the congregation to keep the image of Kathleen dancing in their minds. The Reverend wanted people to remember Kathleen as she was, on the Friday night before her death. On that night, Kathleen had danced, until the early hours of the morning, in the arms of her beloved husband, Michael.

There were many testimonials about the love Kathleen shared with Michael. There were many people who felt the couple had been soul mates and they grieved for her widowed husband. As for Michael, he was so distraught about having lost his best friend, he was unable to get up and speak.

But regardless of the family's loss, regardless of the media coverage, the fact remained that it didn't matter how cold or calloused people believed the Durham police to be. The lead investigator, Art Holland, had observed a few curious things on the night of Kathleen's death, and the detective had reason to pull a number of search warrants.

In fact, a number of the responding officers and paramedics had some misgivings about the death scene. For one thing, there was blood on the sidewalk leading to the Peterson home, which didn't make sense. Mr. Peterson hadn't spoken to police at all that evening; he had been too distraught. But having blood outside the door, and having blood outside on a can of diet Coke as well, that didn't quite add up with Michael Peterson's claims in his 9-1-1 calls.

Beyond the blood in strange places, there were other

discrepancies. When Peterson placed the first emergency call, he reported that his wife was still breathing. But the paramedics at the scene noted that most of the blood around Kathleen was dry. According to the paramedics, Mrs. Peterson had been dead for some period of time . . . long before they arrived.

And there were other things that seemed out of place: a series of odd e-mails in Michael Peterson's desk, a broken crystal wineglass, Michael's athletic shoes and socks, which were all bloody, next to Kathleen's body, and an unwrapped condom that was filled with fluid that didn't appear to be semen.

After the initial police inventory was logged, the next search, which had been conducted the night of Kathleen's wake, turned up items in Mr. Peterson's home that were even more out of the ordinary. There were wild pornographic materials found in Peterson's office. There were unusual pornographic Web sites listed on his main computer. And hidden among Peterson's bookcases were strange things such as the *O.J. Simpson Notebook* and packs of unused condoms.

Not that Detective Holland was ready to charge Mr. Peterson with anything, but the detective was in a "conversation" with Jim Hardin, the Durham district attorney. And while Michael Peterson was asserting that Art Holland and Jim Hardin were treating him unfairly—showing people the newspaper columns he had written, columns in which Peterson had attacked DA Hardin and police officials for the gang violence and drug problems in Durham—the fact was, Jim Hardin was being very methodical about his job, as was Detective Holland. They were under an ethical obligation to determine what had happened in the Peterson home in the early morning of December 9, 2001. And they were in no rush to judgment.

Barry Winston, Peterson's attorney, told local news reporters that the investigation would clear his client.

Winston was advising Peterson not to speak with police because of what he called their "heavy-handed tactics." Kerry Sutton told the media that she hoped the police weren't going to persist in asking Mr. Peterson to "prove a negative." It wasn't her client's job to prove that he wasn't guilty. It was up to the police to show culpability . . . whether it be Mr. Peterson, someone else, or no one at all.

DA Jim Hardin had not yet submitted the investigation's results to a grand jury. The investigation was still open. The Durham police had asked his office to assist, and the district attorney was doing that, even though his office had not made any decisions.

As the investigation progressed, the police began looking at records of phone calls from the Peterson house and from the Petersons' cell phones. However, after a week of searching, no unusual phone patterns had turned up. The police could only characterize Mrs. Petersons' death as suspicious. Attorney Barry Winston would repeatedly insist to the media that his client Michael Peterson was innocent. Winston reminded people that the phone records proved one thing: Michael had done what anyone would do in his situation, which was to call 9-1-1.

To all of his supporters, the situation seemed obvious; Mr. Peterson's local political commentary had gotten him into a snarl. That was the opinion of all of his friends and family. People were concerned that Michael was slowly being framed. After being advised to search for a more powerful attorney, Michael agreed to make some calls. If the local officials were intent on blaming him, Michael needed to arm himself. Michael had plenty of net worth. And just to be safe, he decided he would make a round of phone calls.

Looking for the best lawyer that money could buy, Peterson fired Barry Winston in favor of David Rudolf, another Chapel Hill attorney, who had a reputation for being one of the best defense lawyers in the South.

David Rudolf was not only high-powered, he had just reached national attention for his victory in a case that involved an NFL player, Rae Carruth, the Carolina Panthers wide receiver. Carruth had been facing the death penalty on a charge that he had killed his pregnant girlfriend, but with Rudolf defending him, the NFL player was convicted of the lesser charge of conspiracy.

Although Peterson no longer wrote columns for the *Herald-Sun* newspaper, Peterson still kept his political views in front of the public by having his own web site, www.Hizzoner.com. However, in light of all the controversy, Mr. Peterson decided to pull down all of his political barbs. It was a sad commentary on civil rights in America, but Peterson felt he had lost his right to free speech. In light of the serious accusations being hurled at him following his wife's death, Peterson could no longer continue his free-wheeling attacks on the police and local officials. Peterson needed to focus on his innocence. Peterson needed to remind the community about how much he loved his wife.

In place of Peterson's political commentary about the dismal state of Durham affairs, Hizzoner.com would begin to show only one thing. It was a beautiful photo of Kathleen in a brightly colored dress. She was smiling, with sparkles in her eyes, standing on the spiral stairway in their mansion. Under Kathleen's photo, there was this loving caption, written by Michael's friend Guy Seaberg:

"All of us at Hizzoner.com mourn the death of Kathleen Peterson, a dynamic, wonderful and remarkable lady—a loving wife, mother and friend. Her passing is Durham's immense loss. Our love and sympathies to Mike, their children, and their entire family."

Twelve

In the South, David Rudolf's reputation as a criminal attorney was legendary. A close friend of former O.J. Simpson defense lawyer Barry Scheck, he had been described by Scheck and other colleagues as a legal perfectionist. Rudolf and Scheck met when they were both public defenders in the South Bronx. The two maintained a close friendship and a high regard for each other. Over the years, Scheck called Rudolf for opinions on all of his major criminal cases.

But it wasn't only Barry Scheck who thought the world of David Rudolf. Anyone who looked at his track record would agree that Rudolf deserved his high-powered reputation. Rudolf was not only brilliant, he was the type of attorney who would put an exceptional amount of energy into a case. Rudolf was a fighter, a believer in the justice system, and he enjoyed a challenge.

Above all, Rudolf had a tremendous amount of experience. He handled state and federal cases involving everything from drug conspiracies to sales of firearms. As far back as the 1970s, Rudolf was involved in sticky cases. In *United States v. Busic*, Rudolf acted exclusively as the counsel for a defendant in a federal trial involving a group of Croatian nationalists who were charged with an airplane hijacking and the murder of a New York City police officer.

Over the years, there were many examples of his victories, particularly in jury trials. There were prominent cases in North Carolina where David Rudolf successfully represented men who had been charged with murdering their wives. Rudolf excelled in that area.

There was one prominent physician whom Rudolf defended, Edward Friedland, who had spent four years as a murder suspect in his wife's death. The woman had been found slashed in the couple's home, and her doctor husband would have faced the death penalty, if convicted of the first-degree murder charges. But with David Rudolf at the helm, not only was the criminal case dropped, a civil case was filed to clear Friedland's name. In the civil matter, David Rudolf was able to win a jury verdict of $8.6 million.

Another accused husband whom David Rudolf defended was Charlotte businessman John Hayes. After hearing Rudolf's compelling argument, a panel of North Carolina jurors spared John Hayes from the death penalty, convicting the businessman of the lesser charge of second-degree murder in the slaying of his wife. David Rudolf had won the victory by mounting the first "battered-husband" defense ever heard in North Carolina.

David Rudolf was good; he was really one of the best.

But it was the case he handled on behalf of former NFL player "Rae-Rae" Carruth that won Rudolf his most public acclaim. Rae Carruth, a player for the Carolina Panthers, hung out in the fast circles of professional athletes. Along the way, Carruth had met a beautiful young woman at a party, Cherica Adams, who became his girlfriend, and later, the mother of his child. Adams, a twenty-four-year-old dancer who reportedly socialized with basketball stars such as Shaquille O'Neal, had been in love with Carruth. However, their romance allegedly soured when she told Carruth of the unexpected pregnancy. A few months after she shared the news, the expectant mother became the victim of a drive-by shooting.

The murder involved alleged associates of NFL player Carruth. One of those associates, a career criminal by the name of Van Brett Watkins, would later cut a deal with North Carolina prosecutors for which Watkins stated that Rae Carruth had hired him as a hit man.

Throughout the trial, David Rudolf was successful in launching an attack against hit man Watkins, maintaining that Watkins was psychotic. But another codefendant in the case, Michael Kennedy, testified that he had witnessed the drive-by shooting, that he had been in the passenger seat of Watkin's car on November 16, 1999, the day that four bullets ripped through Cherica Adams's body. Kennedy testified that Adams was driving down a dark road behind Carruth's SUV. According to his testimony, the codefendant, Rae Carruth, deliberately slammed on his breaks, blocking Adams's path, pinning Adams's car at the end of a dark alley.

On her deathbed, Cherica Adams managed to write a note that corroborated the other eyewitness accounts. In it, Adams stated that Rae Carruth had used his SUV to block her off on the road. Adams died a month after the shooting. Luckily, her son with Carruth, a healthy boy she named Chancellor, was born before her death, and the boy survived.

But regardless of the fate of the child's mother, by the end of the highly publicized case, David Rudolf had been able to create enough reasonable doubt. He began poking holes in the state's case by bringing up inconsistencies in the evidence, by questioning the credibility of career-criminal witnesses. To fortify his theory that Carruth was innocent, David Rudolf called upon the famed forensic expert, Dr. Henry Lee, whose testimony had helped O.J. Simpson get acquitted.

During Rae Carruth's trial, Dr. Henry Lee would take

the stand to say that the angles of the bullets at Adams's murder scene suggested that Carruth's SUV was not blocking Adams's vehicle. The famous Dr. Lee would testify that the first three bullets that entered Adams's car were at a ninety-degree angle, indicating that Adams's and Carruth's cars were parallel. David Rudolf was using Dr. Lee's testimony to support Rae Carruth's claim that he was innocent.

However, the state of North Carolina painted a portrait of NFL player Rae Carruth as a man plagued by bad financial decisions. To compound his financial worries, Carruth had suffered numerous injuries over the years, and then Carruth sprained his ankle again, just a month before his pregnant girlfriend's murder.

Ironically, after bail for $3 million was posted for Rae Carruth, the former NFL player decided to pick up and drive out of the state, driving in a white Ford Expedition. After a car chase, Carruth said he was headed for Tennessee because he "needed time to think."

Of course, the North Carolina jury hadn't completely bought into the notion that Carruth was innocent. Regardless of Rudolf's contentions, regardless of Dr. Lee's expert testimony, a jury of twelve convicted Rae Carruth of conspiracy to commit murder. For that, "Rae-Rae" Carruth was sentenced to serve at least eighteen years in prison.

For certain people following the NFL Panther's case, there seemed to be eerie similarities between Rae Carruth and O.J. Simpson. There were so many claims that each of these men had made—claims that didn't seem to add up. There was the expensive dream team each man had hired; there was all that reasonable doubt.

Then there were the alleged killers, who had no blood on their hands. And there was that odd phenomenon of the professional athlete, who, regardless of having been accused of murder, seemed to feel a sense of entitlement to freedom. It was as though these star players deemed themselves above the law.

But no matter what parallels people might have drawn, no matter what people might have thought of O.J. Simpson being found innocent, of Rae Carruth being found innocent of a first-degree murder charge, the truth was, their defense teams had fought the good fight. And in Carruth's case, it was David Rudolf who was able to combat the prosecutor's theory that the NFL player had masterminded the fatal shooting of his pregnant girlfriend. To all of his legal colleagues across the country, once again, David Rudolf had seen victory. The former NFL wide receiver, Rae Carruth, had been spared the death sentence.

And now, with the trouble facing Michael Peterson, David Rudolf would have his chance to prove his skills all over again. Because of his local celebrity, Peterson was under the scrutiny of yet another North Carolina prosecutor. And David Rudolf decided to defend the prominent Durham author, even before any indictment or formal charge had come down.

Peterson hadn't done anything wrong. His lawyer believed that. His family believed that. Together, they would beat the legal system. Michael Peterson knew it would cost him, but for a lump-sum retainer fee, Mr. Peterson could rest assured that David Rudolf would cover all the bases. If necessary, Peterson was told, the esteemed Dr. Henry Lee could be called upon to examine Kathleen's blood in the stairway. As he had done for Rae Carruth, Dr. Henry Lee would be willing to fly to North Carolina to see if he could determine what might or might not have happened to Mrs. Peterson in that mansion.

Thirteen

A special session of the grand jury was called to convene in Durham on Thursday, December 20, 2001, just eleven days after Kathleen Peterson's death. The grand jurors would hear evidence presented by District Attorney Jim Hardin, who had called the jurors back from their Christmas holiday. If the grand jurors so decided, the homicide investigation could be dropped. But it was also possible that they could issue an indictment, probably that same day, so Peterson and his team were gearing up.

Michael Peterson's friends would continue to talk about how loving and caring Michael was with his wife. From their impressions, he and Kathleen were so close, so very supportive of each other, there was no question that Michael would be cleared of any suspicions. The two of them respected each other. He called her sweetheart. In all the years they were married, he and Kathleen had never ever had a fight.

But on the day the grand jury listened to evidence and testimony from the state's key witnesses, Michael Peterson, the fifty-eight-year-old novelist who had written war stories, the decorated U.S. Marine who had served his country in Vietnam, was charged with first-degree murder in the death of his wife, Kathleen.

After the indictment was publicly announced, DA Jim Hardin was bombarded by calls from the media. The press wondered how serious the case against Michael Peterson really was. They wanted to know if Peterson would be facing the death penalty, but no one could get any answers. Hardin would make no comment about what penalty his office might seek.

Peterson's attorney, David Rudolf, would tell media that his client was not guilty of any criminal offense. Rudolf made comments about the one-sided nature of grand jury proceedings, making remarks to deflate the magnitude of the murder indictment. Rudolf wanted the public to realize that grand juries were held to the "lowest standard possible," and only needed to find a reasonable cause to believe a crime *might* have been committed. Rudolf felt confident that once Peterson's side of the story was known, his client would be fully exonerated.

But it didn't matter what Rudolf said. The murder indictment was there, and the public was stunned. The vast Research Triangle region was abuzz—everyone in Raleigh, Durham, and Chapel Hill—had their own opinion. Most of the people who lived there were well educated; they were involved in research, industry, and technology. They wondered how the Durham DA, with no witnesses and no murder weapon, would mount a successful case against Peterson.

It would be an entirely circumstantial case, people realized. There didn't seem to be anything that might point to premeditated murder. It was going to be a rough ride for the prosecution, especially with all of Kathleen and Michael's family working so hard, with David Rudolf and his team also fighting, to prove that Kathleen and Michael had the perfect marriage.

For the man who had been indicted, the day turned into a media event. Supporters wrote the local papers, applauding Peterson for hiring a prominent defense attorney. People believed it was a conspiracy, and they wanted Peterson saved from a possible death sentence. As for Peterson, he had always maintained that the American justice system was slanted. Peterson would assure his friends that he wasn't about to be railroaded by police. He felt certain that the DA hadn't done his homework. Peterson wasn't too concerned. If anything, he seemed annoyed about the charge filed against him.

Although grand jury sessions are closed to the public, Michael Peterson's first-degree murder indictment did name the three witnesses who testified.

They were: Art Holland, the lead Durham Police Department investigator in the case; Dr. Deborah Radisch, a state medical examiner out of Chapel Hill; and Duane Deaver, a North Carolina State Bureau of Investigation blood spatter analyst.

So the grand jury had seen the photos of the crime scene. They had reviewed the autopsy and toxicology reports. And they had been given an expert's evaluation about what the various blood patterns in the stairwell meant.

After learning of the indictment, on the afternoon of December 20, 2001, Mr. Peterson left his house on Cedar Street to head for the Durham County Jail. Driving his tan Jaguar, Peterson lead a caravan of four other vehicles. All the cars moved slowly, driving through the tree-lined streets that gave way to the downtown area of Durham. They passed the historic district, the remnants of former tobacco production, and wound up in an unpaved lot, where they parked across from the jail. It was there, on Mangum Street, that Peterson and his entourage were greeted by members of the press.

Dressed in a sport jacket and looking very dapper, Peterson was flanked by four of his children. His brother Bill and other family friends were there to support

Michael as well. Peterson was prepared to make his first public statement since Kathleen's death, and he told the group of reporters that he was an innocent man.

"I whispered her name in my heart a thousand times," Michael said. "She is there, but I can't stop crying. I would never have done anything to hurt her."

Not many people realized that Peterson was quoting a portion of an Emily Dickinson poem that had been read aloud at Kathleen's funeral. It was odd, especially to some family insiders who watched Michael on the news, to see him talking about his sorrow, about "whispering her name a thousand times," stealing the line from a great American poet.

As Michael Peterson ended his short speech, he spoke with a vehemence about the upcoming trial. It was clear now that Peterson was truly ready to fight the legal battle. And he was looking forward to his day of victory.

After a big good-bye to his family, Peterson walked, with his head held high, into the Durham County Jail. A somewhat-short but well-built man, Peterson sat himself down calmly, with his legs crossed. Looking like a man being persecuted, he waited very patiently; he had brought along a Bible and a pair of athletic shoes. For the esteemed novelist, the whole thing was a charade, a great insult. But Peterson did what he was told. He changed out of his expensive jacket and Italian loafers, and put on a regulation orange jumpsuit.

Because of the high-profile nature of the case, Peterson was housed in a single-man cell, in a section typically reserved for people with medical problems. The Durham detention officers said they were trying to keep Mr. Peterson's best interests in mind, but Peterson felt he was being singled out, being further degraded by having been placed in solitary confinement. While there, he began to write a journal, just to keep his mind busy. He wanted to keep a record of all of his thoughts, especially the thoughts of Kathleen. He wanted to remember her when she was still alive, when she was happy and content, and by his side.

Thomas Maher, a partner of David Rudolf who was now part of the team representing Peterson, told reporters that Peterson's family had never seen any problems in the marriage. Maher made statements about the strength of the Petersons' marriage, saying they were "a couple who made each other bloom." Maher characterized the Petersons as a couple who "finished each other's sentences."

Bill Peterson told reporters that the family had little chance to grieve "because of the unfair charges by police." With tears in his eyes, Bill assured the public that his brother had nothing to do with Kathleen's terrible accident. Nick Galifianakis, another supporter of Peterson, and a former U.S. congressman and prominent Durham attorney, told media that he was baffled by the murder charge. Like David Rudolf, Galifianakis was confident that the judicial system would establish his friend's innocence.

The day following Peterson's indictment, David Rudolf went to court to request that his client be released on bond. Rudolf mentioned the "roots" Michael Peterson had put down in the Durham community. He was asserting that a man of such character should not be held in a county jail, that Peterson could be trusted to await trial.

"Others in similar circumstances have been granted release on bond," Rudolf told the court, believing that Michael Peterson deserved the same treatment. Michael Peterson should be released, David Rudolf insisted, "not because of who he is, but because of how he has lived his life to this point."

But it was only partially true that Michael Peterson had been regarded as a pillar of the community. Indeed, he did live in one of the largest houses in the city. And he had owned property in Durham for many years, almost from the time he graduated from Duke in 1965. But if Peterson was a man with a following, he was also a man whom people disliked. He was a rebel. He caused trouble. He made people feel uncomfortable at times. He liked to brag about his military service; he liked to mention that he'd earned a Silver Star and a Bronze Star of Valor. Certain people were enamored with him, especially women. But others felt put off by Peterson's superior attitude.

Still, whatever people thought of him, good or bad, there were certain things that no one could deny. Michael Peterson had been successful as a novelist. He had written about Vietnam in three acclaimed novels, including the *New York Times* bestseller *A Time of War.* Beyond that, he had written a biweekly political column for the *Herald-Sun* newspaper that had gained so much attention, it almost led to a populist uprising. And there was the political history Peterson had in Durham. He had run for mayor in 1999, and had been supported most greatly by his wife, Kathleen.

Though Peterson lost in the mayoral primary, he still remained a familiar face in local politics. Because he was a public figure, and because his wife had so much belief in him, Peterson truly had a number of supporters out there. In 2001, Peterson had tried his hand at politics again, running for city council. But the political race became riddled with mudslinging, and in the end, Peterson lost to a longtime incumbent. His defeat was disappointing for Michael and Kathleen, but Peterson wasn't deterred. He would still play a role in politics, his family had rallied around him, and Kathleen, in particular, was ready to do anything to support her husband's ambitions.

Kathleen had known Michael before he ever wrote a best-selling book, before he ever dabbled in politics.

Though she hadn't met him until after his return from Vietnam and Germany, Kathleen was convinced that her husband was a man of principle and valor. She didn't need to see his bronze or silver medals to know that he had the courage to take a stand for people. She had watched him for over a decade, and he was a man of conviction, usually rooting for the underdog.

Even from an early age, when Michael had been a law student at the University of North Carolina, he had worked on behalf of a defendant in a famous homosexual sodomy case. The case stirred so much controversy, Michael left UNC law school and became an analyst for a defense consulting firm in Washington DC. And Kathleen admired that about Michael. He had always been a standout. Her husband had always taken the road less traveled. He was a leader, a man to be proud of.

When Peterson's DC firm sent him to Vietnam to conduct studies about how mechanized divisions could win the war, his vision of the war changed. Peterson suddenly developed an attachment to the soldiers fighting the war, and also a cynicism about war correspondents, whom he deemed hypocritical. After witnessing the reports of so many men being killed in action, reports that conflicted with the favorable media stories being played back in the States, Michael Peterson decided to leave his job and join in the combat. He enlisted himself in the marines.

In 1971, Peterson received an honorable discharge with a permanent medical disability. He retired with the rank of captain, and for the next fifteen years, he and his first wife, Patricia, would move with their two sons between Durham, North Carolina, and a small town just outside Frankfurt, Germany. Living near a U.S. Air Force Base outside Frankfurt, Patricia supported the family by working as a Department of Defense teacher, and during that time, Peterson struggled to write his first novel. At first, living among military personnel was good for

Michael and Patricia. They had their own established community of Americans, people to whom they were very close. For Patricia and the boys, that was a great support network. For Michael, however, as his writing began to take over his life, the friends around them didn't matter as much. He ultimately didn't care where he chose to write. Living in his fictional world, Peterson had become a loner.

Released in 1983, Peterson's first book, *The Immortal Dragon*, was a novel set in colonial nineteenth-century Vietnam. Though the book was no real success in America, many of his friends from the American Air Force Base admired it. The fact that the military community seemed to admire his writing skills was a perk for him. Michael was complimented on the veracity of his writing style and the vitality he captured in his first war novel. Michael was very happy to hear that. For him, being in print was a dream come true, and it had somehow put him on the map.

While many of the American military personnel in Michael's inner circle enjoyed reading the book, some of his friends, especially his close-knit group in Germany, had concerns about how racy the novel seemed to be. Some people didn't understand the need for so much gratuitous sex and violence in the novel, and they questioned Michael about it. Certain people were even offended by the obscenity in the book. Of course Peterson was cavalier about that. Sex and murder were what people expected. They were the only things that would sell.

It would be seven years before Peterson would put out his second book. But with the novel *A Time of War*, he had hit the big time, earning enough of an advance to buy the Durham mansion. By that time, he was already living with Kathleen, he had received his divorce from Patricia, and he was ecstatic about his good fortune. Life with Kathleen was better than he ever could have imag-

ined. Their lifestyles meshed; their personalities com-
plemented each other. They were finally able to live the
life they'd both yearned for, and they were making plans
to marry.

Being financially secure allowed Michael the freedom
to work at his own pace, which was important for a man
like Peterson, who took painstaking efforts to study the
origins of war, the governments and politics of Southeast
Asia. His novels were historically based, very intense
tales, and Peterson made sure that all his facts and fig-
ures were to the letter. Reportedly, Peterson had
received over $600,000 for *A Time of War*, a book that
centered on a fictional diplomat, Bradley Marshall. The
figure could never be confirmed, but there was proof
that the book had sold well, and had also been optioned
by a network for a miniseries.

But after that one *New York Times* bestseller, unfortunately, Michael Peterson saw no other real success. His
sequel to that novel, *A Bitter Peace*, was not received well
by the public. The book chronicled the evolved circumstances of Bradley Marshall, who made efforts to help
end the conflict in Vietnam in the early 1970s. The narrative presented Marshall as a man on a mission, as a
man of honor who tried to achieve peace in Vietnam.
Peterson had based one of female characters on Kathleen, and she was entirely flattered by that. His wife held
book-launching parties for him, and their friends all
agreed that it was a captivating work. Everyone was certain it would go bestseller. It would be a book that
readers wouldn't be able to put down.

With his first book out of print, with his *New York Times*
bestseller never having been transformed into a miniseries, Peterson needed *A Bitter Peace* to be a national hit.
But Michael and Kathleen's hopes for *A Bitter Peace* were
never realized. A reviewer from *Publishers Weekly* said Peterson's narrative was impeded by storytelling that fell

flat. The fact that his third novel was largely ignored by readers was a real blow to him, both financially and personally.

That was one of the reasons why Peterson's fourth book was all the more important for him. Aside from being a story he believed in, the book was a departure from war novels. For Peterson, who had never written a nonfiction work before, *Charlie Two Shoes and the Marines of Love Company* became a labor of love. The book told the real-life story of a young orphaned Chinese boy who was befriended by a company of marines during World War II. A tale that embodied what was still the American dream: "Charlie" was eventually saved from starvation in his war-torn region of China. The marines helped their friend Charlie make the odyssey to freedom in America. It was a years-long effort, but Charlie ultimately settled in the serenity and beauty of Chapel Hill.

In order to write *Charlie Two Shoes*, Michael Peterson worked with a coauthor, the North Carolina journalist David Perlmutt. Critically, the book was well received, and was even praised by Norman Vincent Peale in a 1993 quote, which was placed on its jacket. Michael Peterson had hopes that it would become the next *Saving Private Ryan*. As it happened, it was Michael's good friend Nick Galifianakis who had pushed the project along. Nick was hopeful about the potential movie deal, and knew that a film option had already been signed. There was much talk among the Peterson clan that the true-life story would be made into a film; and in the meantime, the book had a tremendous regional following, which was a blessing in and of itself.

Everyone knew it was a noble story, one of bravery and courage in the face of impossible odds. Everyone felt it was exactly the kind of project that Hollywood producers were looking for, particularly after the 9/11 terrorist attacks, when patriotism and brave soldiers were all front-page news. The timing was right, and Michael Peterson, as well as his many supporters, felt he had earned it.

In fact, Michael and Kathleen had been celebrating the movie option for *Charlie Two Shoes* on the night of her death.

But no one ever knew if an actual movie was going to be made. If real money was going to be paid, actors would have had to sign on, a director would have had to been attached, and none of these things had happened yet. There was no green light from a studio; there was nothing concrete. When the media asked Galifianakis to confirm the details about the film project, he said he couldn't discuss it.

The court motion filed by David Rudolf on December 21, 2001, asked that Michael Peterson be released from jail on a $1 million property bond. Rudolf argued that Peterson was not a likely flight risk. Peterson would use his mansion as collateral, and of course he would not skip town. Rudolf insisted that Mr. Peterson was a most worthy citizen.

But certain things had turned up about Michael Peterson, as a public figure, that made people wonder just how worthy he was.

There was his claim that he had earned two Purple Hearts for service in Vietnam. But in 1999, when Peterson ran for mayor, reporters uncovered a lie: the Purple Hearts were found to be a total fabrication. At the time, Peterson held a press conference to explain that his war injuries had been caused by a car accident in Japan. He told reporters that he hadn't ever explained the circumstances surrounding his Purple Hearts because the memories were too painful for him. Peterson insisted that he did receive the Purple Hearts, even though there were no military records of them, even though he couldn't produce the medals. Then there was a 1993 driving while intoxicated (DWI) charge against Peterson later reduced to wreckless driving, which had been discovered and reported by the media as well.

But even more curious to the general public was a 1994 incident involving his son Clayton Peterson, who was convicted for placing a pipe bomb in the main administration building at Duke University. Clayton Peterson, a onetime engineering student at Duke, claimed the bomb and the accompanying threatening letter were just a hoax. And even though Michael Peterson had tried to pass off the incident as a childish prank, his nineteen-year-old son would spend four years in prison.

Now, with Mr. Peterson facing a first-degree murder charge, each of his past failings would come back to haunt him. David Rudolf would do everything he could to distract the public from gossiping about Peterson's failed political career, about Peterson's "Duke Bomber" son, about Peterson's bogus Purple Hearts. And, in fact, none of that past history really mattered. The truth was, the man was being charged with murder, and all the gossip, all the spin, didn't make him a guilty man.

In direct response to the indictment, Rudolf reminded the public that the case was entirely circumstantial, and insisted to reporters that the crime scene police were relying upon was "hopelessly contaminated and mishandled from the beginning."

In one of Rudolf's defense motions, he criticized the police investigation. Among his concerns: friends and family members were allowed into the Peterson house before police began gathering evidence; items listed as being seized in police search warrants were never removed from the home; Michael Peterson and others had been allowed into the stairwell, destroying the integrity of the scene.

In an overwhelming attack on the prosecutor and the

Durham police, David Rudolf's motion suggested that the officials had rushed to judgment. In his view, even if it were possible that Kathleen Peterson's injuries hadn't been caused by a fall, the police and the DA were ignoring the idea that someone other than Michael Peterson could have been responsible for Kathleen's death.

Rudolf would begin to talk about a possible "intruder theory."

Rudolf told the court that Peterson's home was rarely locked. The defense attorney would note that in June 2001, an unknown intruder had entered the residence after midnight and had stolen a computer and a cellular phone. Allegedly, the Peterson house had been broken into on at least two other occasions, and the cars in their driveway had been broken into at least six times.

Rudolf asserted that if, by chance, someone had struck Mrs. Peterson, it was far more likely to have been an intruder. It was Rudolf's view that there was no evidence, no motive, to show that Michael Peterson was in any way responsible for the death of his wife. Michael and Kathleen Peterson were dutiful partners. There was never any trouble in their marriage. There was never any hint of physical or verbal abuse between them.

David Rudolf argued that in order to believe that Michael Peterson killed his wife, Peterson had to have gone from being a loving and respectful husband to a premeditated murderer overnight. And that concept, Rudolf claimed, was something that "strained credulity to the breaking point."

Fourteen

Without listening to any testimony or arguments, a superior court judge ruled that Michael Peterson would be held without bond. Awaiting a new hearing, which had been scheduled for January 22, 2002, Mr. Peterson, having dressed in street clothes, fully expected to be released on bond for the Christmas holidays. He slumped down in his chair and hung his head as Judge Ron Stephens announced his decision.

His attorneys, David Rudolf and Thomas Maher, were astounded. They had not only offered to arrange a $1 million property bond, but had also offered to have Nick Galifianakis, a former U.S. Congressman, monitor Mr. Peterson's whereabouts. To them, the decision had come from out of the blue. They had no explanation to give any member of Michael's family. The whole Peterson clan had come to Durham to support Michael—filling the courtroom in a standing-room-only crowd. But none of them could believe their ears as they heard the judge deny bond. They felt the court was treating the family harshly.

"This is absolutely unbelievable all around," Caitlin Atwater told members of the press, insisting that her mother and Michael had the "most amazing, loving relationship ever" and were "ideal parents." Caitlin and her four siblings were tearful and shaking their heads as they watched Michael being quietly led away by deputies to spend his second night in jail. As they struggled to subdue themselves, their tears quickly turned to indignation.

To the media, Caitlin became vocal and outraged about her stepdad being treated so unfairly. She told reporters that her mother would be "absolutely appalled" by the idea of Michael spending the holidays in jail, reiterating that neither Michael nor Kathleen would ever, in any way, harm each other. Her stepbrother Todd felt the judge's ruling was beyond unfair. In shock and disbelief, he said that having his father in jail would create "the most unbelievably heartbreaking Christmas" anyone could imagine.

David Rudolf promised the family that he would not give up easily. He was willing to do research to see if Judge Stephens's ruling could be contested in the state court of appeals. He told media that if police believed that Kathleen Peterson hadn't died from a fall, they needed to be "looking for an intruder" and not focusing on Michael Peterson.

Rudolf wasn't convinced that an aggravating factor existed. The attorney felt that Kathleen's death was more consistent with a fall, mentioning to reporters that the forty-eight-year-old Kathleen Peterson had been drinking on the night of her death. Rudolf also said that Mrs. Peterson had suffered "a couple of recent blackout periods." Though Rudolf didn't have any medical reports available, he was having independent experts examine the autopsy reports and other evidence.

Peterson's attorney felt it was improper to deny bond before the prosecution made at least some showing of an aggravating factor. But it was Jim Hardin's position that his office was merely complying with the law, which deemed they need only state that an aggravating factor did exist. The DA did not have to specify what that aggravating factor was.

* * *

In Michael Peterson's journal entry from his jail cell, entitled "Christmas Eve," the novelist said he was writing a journal in order to keep his sanity. Consumed with thoughts of his wife and children, he was writing, also, to keep his "horror at bay." No longer locked in solitary confinement, he was spending the night before Christmas with twenty-three other jail mates in the C-pod of the county jail. He felt sorry for all the men housed there. The place was so dank; the place seemed inhuman.

In one of Peterson's journal entries, he wrote sympathetically about the men he shared his sorrows with, categorizing sixteen blacks, six whites, and two Hispanics. These were a group of men who were once little boys, little boys waiting for Santa, perhaps with sugarplums dancing in their heads. Peterson wrote about the gestures of a "toothless Santa," an inmate in an orange suit, who handed out packages of Honey Buns bought for a few dollars in the jail's commissary.

Inside the cold, stark county jail, Peterson's life seemed upside down. His Christmas holidays, typically filled with eggnog and designer gifts, had become a time of unbearable grief. Not only was he unjustly housed in a jail cell, he was unable to see any of his family, not even his children. He had been allowed no local visitors for Christmas because of what the rules dictated.

Even though the jail had made a special meal for the inmates, feeding them the traditional mashed potatoes with gravy, cranberry salad with oven-baked chicken, the food was assembly-line caliber. And when the detention officers handed out little gift bags to the inmates, gifts provided by the Salvation Army, the bags held nothing but soap, deodorant, and toothpaste.

As Mr. Peterson sat in jail, helpless to do anything but write, the Web site he had created, Hizzoner.com, was providing the general public with information about a possible link between Kathleen Peterson's death and a man who had been charged with several break-ins near the Peterson home. The unnamed man had allegedly broken into homes on three streets within half a mile of Peterson's Cedar Street mansion.

The information about the burglar had been posted by Peterson's friend and Web site editor, Guy Seaberg. And Seaberg wanted the public to be aware that if, indeed, Kathleen's injuries showed an aggravating factor, if her injuries showed that her death was not an accident, then authorities had an obligation. Durham police needed to question the man already being held in jail for a rash of burglaries in Forest Hills.

Fifteen

"Michael wrote this thing about the police being out to get him," Caitlin recalled. "He was convinced that they had pulled a grand jury indictment just so he would have to spend Christmas in jail. He told all of us that the police were saying things about him that were not true."

As she sat alone in her room on Christmas Eve, Caitlin wanted to think about the happy times. She kept remembering one of the final conversations she'd had with her mom, when they had spoken during the early part of the Christmas shopping season. Back then, she and her mom were talking almost every day. Kathleen was checking in regularly with Caitlin about the gifts she was buying for Margaret and Martha, about the gifts she was buying for the boys. Kathleen had a knack for finding just the right jean skirt from the Gap, for finding just the right ski gear, and all those kind of things, but she liked to call Caitlin to be sure that she wasn't buying stuff that her kids already had.

As she continued to focus on happy times, Caitlin recalled that her mom had phoned all excited one day. It was a conversation she suddenly remembered quite vividly. Her mom was happy about the possibility of Michael's newest success—there was a film deal in the works—and her mom could hardly contain her glee.

"I have good news, honey. Really good news," Kathleen

said. "The producer of Tom Clancy's movies is reading one of Michael's books."

"Really? Does that mean we're going to be famous?" Caitlin asked, half teasing.

"Well, I've heard that this man is in the middle of making a movie with Ben Affleck. And they say that Ben Affleck is reading Mike's book right now. He might be interested in playing one of the characters."

"Is this for real?" Caitlin wondered. "Do you think Ben Affleck is really going to make the movie?"

"Well, it's up to his producer. This is the man who made *The Hunt for Red October*. So who knows? But if it happens, it might happen very quickly, which would really be a good break for Michael," her mom told her.

"Can you imagine if Ben Affleck decided to do it?" Caitlin asked. "Maybe I could be his date, and I could wind up going with him to the Academy Awards."

As Caitlin ran through the conversation in her mind, she recalled how happy her mom was in those final days of 2001. She and her mom just gushed, thrilled at the thought of a sex symbol being interested in Michael's work. In all their excitement, the two of them had gotten off on a tangent about the fancy parties in Hollywood. They talked about shopping for gowns, they had really gotten ahead of themselves, dizzy with the thought of Ben Affleck, the most eligible unmarried movie star they could think of. Not only was he gorgeous, but at the time he'd just starred in the epic film *Pearl Harbor*. The guy was a fantastic choice to play the lead in one of Michael's war novels. If Ben Affleck's producer signed a deal, they both agreed, there would be no stopping Michael's career after that.

But then, as Caitlin sat alone on Christmas Eve, as she continued to think about the details of their chat, she realized that her mom had offered no other information about the movie deal. Her mom said that Michael might have had some papers being drawn up, but she wasn't certain. Her mom really didn't know anything for sure.

The more Caitlin thought about it, the more it became obvious that she and her mom had gotten themselves all worked up over something that probably wasn't real. Caitlin had been down that road before. She'd heard that Michael had signed film options for a few of his books. Over the years, she'd heard a lot of talk and promises from Hollywood, but none of these things had ever materialized. Of course, when the deals would first happen, when the producers and agents would be calling, the whole family would stay excited for a while, dreaming and making plans about film stars. But now, with her mom gone, those dreams had died as well. As Caitlin began to cry herself to sleep, she had to come to the realization that Michael's career wasn't even worth thinking about anymore.

As she woke up to a lonely Christmas with her siblings still asleep, she faced the deserted house on Cedar Street in a quiet fog. Without the Christmas music playing, without the smell of French toast, Caitlin sat in the living room by herself with a cup of coffee. She stared over at the few gifts Kathleen and Michael had placed under the tree, and got a sick feeling in her stomach.

But when her brothers and sisters arose, they wanted to make an attempt to celebrate. Martha had wrapped everything, she had tried to make the Christmas tree look nice, and Margaret and Todd and Clayton were each making a strained attempt to look happy. They were all hoping that somehow things could return to normal for them, all except Caitlin, who couldn't even bring herself to eat. She didn't want breakfast; she didn't care about presents.

But for that day, at least, her brothers and sisters had decided to live their lives in a bubble. Caitlin had wanted to join a family of her Jewish friends, who had invited her out for a big Chinese dinner, but her siblings wouldn't hear of it. They insisted that they start a fire in the kitchen, and they began to prepare a big Christmas brunch.

Their house, now with one of the staircases boarded up, was one of the few places they could grieve their mother's loss in peace. They tried to find comfort in the decorations their mom had put up around the house for Christmas. Caitlin tried to find little things to laugh about, but she couldn't stand being in the house at all. She finally broke away from her siblings, insisting on visiting with her friends, whom she wound up joining at the Chinese buffet. For a few hours, Caitlin had tried to move on, to not think about death and sorrow, but once she returned back to Cedar Street, after the hours of daylight had passed and the night encroached, she, like her brothers and sisters, became filled with tears and rage.

The police were not letting up on their dad, which was just another horrible thing they had to deal with. They felt the world was conspiring against them, and they weren't talking to the police. By the end of Christmas night, each one of them retreated to their own bedroom, tearful and unhappy. It was hard to be in such a large empty home, to be there among the ruins of what was once Michael and Kathleen's place, a home with fires going, a home filled with music and laughter, abounding with such love and warmth.

The next morning, Bill Peterson came to the house to have a chat with Caitlin. He needed to talk to his niece about a few things, and the two of them sat alone together on the couch in her bedroom. Bill explained that Kathleen had died intestate, which meant she didn't have a will. He said that normally Michael would have been the administrator of her estate, but with all the legal accusations, there was no way Michael could fill that role.

"Todd said he would do it," her uncle Bill explained. "But it makes sense that you would do it, because you're her lone surviving child."

"Well, I'll do whatever I can," Caitlin said. "But I don't really know that much about it."

"Well, logistically speaking, we might have to sell the house," Bill told her. "We don't know what's going to happen, but we all have to pull together to get through this."

Caitlin listened as her uncle attempted to explain certain aspects of North Carolina law. She tried to understand what her responsibilities would be as the administrator of her mother's estate. After a while, Caitlin said she wanted to talk to her dad about the details. She felt she needed the common sense of her biological father, Fred, to help her understand all the legal jargon. And then, just as their conversation was wrapping up, her uncle Bill told her he had one other important thing to say.

"Caitlin, I've talked to Margaret and Martha about this last night," he began, "and this is something that I've known since I was fourteen years old, and since Michael was eighteen."

"Okay."

"You know, in life, everyone has skeletons in their closet, and no one wants them to come out," Bill said. "And Michael wants you to understand with all the stuff that's coming out in the press, there might be certain things coming out about his life that he wanted to keep a secret."

"What are you saying? Is it about my mom?" Caitlin asked.

"No. This is something that I've known about. It's something that's a part of Michael. And Michael wanted you to know. He wanted you to become comfortable with this because the media might try to make a big deal over it."

"What is it?"

"Caitlin, Michael is bisexual."

"Well, I don't really care," she said flatly. "I mean, what does that have to do with Mom?"

"It's not that," Bill assured her. "It's the media. You know how they can be. Look, I want you to talk with Margaret and Martha. I want you to all get comfortable with the idea before the media starts blowing it up, out of proportion."

Caitlin listened to her uncle's words, but they hadn't really fazed her. She was more concerned about the loss of her mom. She was more worried about Michael being in prison and how she would handle all the work around the Cedar Street house without either one of them being there to support her.

"I felt, like, the way Bill said it to me, that Michael maybe had an experience or two," Caitlin later confided. "I knew he had been in the marines, and I walked away thinking that maybe Michael had an experience at an early age. I thought maybe he still watched gay porno every once in a while. That was because of the tone and the way Bill said it. There was no explanation. Bill made me feel like it was just a casual thing that people might start talking about. And he didn't want me to think of Michael as a different person."

When Caitlin did go to Margaret and Martha to discuss it, each of the girls reacted the same way. They didn't really want to think about it. In part, they thought it was funny. They each snickered for a few minutes as they recalled a thick book Michael had in his library entitled *Short Gay Fiction*. When they were younger, each of them would take turns stealing it off Michael's bookshelves, hiding it in each other's rooms so they could accuse each other of being gay.

Back then, it was just silly teen stuff.

But now, with this news from their uncle Bill, the girls started to piece together a few other things. Michael had always been an eccentric person. That was part of his artistic side. But they realized that in his office, he had some weird artwork. There were certain items that glorified the male body . . . and then there was a pink flamingo displayed prominently by his fireplace.

Sixteen

David Rudolf, unsatisfied with the court's ruling that Peterson be held without bail, filed a motion asking for Peterson's bond hearing to be held at an earlier date. He began to compile a file of letters regarding Michael's character, letters that would be mailed to superior court judge Henry Hight, who would be taking over the bond hearing.

Among the supporters were Mary Clayton, a friend and neighbor of the Petersons for twelve years, who said she had many occasions to witness Michael, Kathleen, and their children in loving circumstances, at birthday parties, at dinner parties, on walks in the neighborhood. Mary Clayton hoped that the judge would allow Mr. Peterson to return home before his trial. She said he was a wonderful father and an ideal husband to Kathleen. She mentioned that just a few weeks before her death, while having lunch with Kathleen, the two of them had a conversation in which they both agreed that their husbands were perfect for each of them.

Another neighbor who wrote in was Bob Cappelletti. He said that he and his wife of twenty-four years had been entertained by the Petersons on many occasions. Mr. Cappelletti and his wife considered Michael and Kathleen to be dear friends. In his view, it was impossible to think that Mr. Peterson would commit the crime for which he was charged. In fact, after having witnessed the way Michael and Kathleen interacted, each being the perfect foil for one another, it would be hard to imagine how Michael could go on living without Kathleen.

This list went on, and many people planned to testify at the bond hearing, preferring to speak for themselves in person. What struck most of these people was how happy Michael and Kathleen were as a couple. One of her employees at Nortel had noticed that Michael and Kathleen would always stand very close to each other in social situations. Another friend would remember the parties the Petersons held for the North Carolina School of the Arts, parties they were happy to host at their spectacular home.

One person who distinctly stood out from the list of supporters was Patricia Peterson. Patricia was aware of Kathleen's sudden death. She had been contacted in Germany almost immediately, and had grown extremely concerned about the ramifications of Kathleen's horrible accident. Worried about the emotional state of her sons and her ex-husband, even from such a distance, Patricia had become a fervent supporter. Over the phone, Patricia Peterson had been interviewed by police, and David Rudolf had incorporated her statement into a motion seeking a new bond date for Michael Peterson.

According to Rudolf's motion, Patricia Peterson told police officers that Mike Peterson had never been violent toward her, that she never knew him to be violent toward anyone. Patricia asserted that Michael was never physically or psychologically abusive, and in her opinion, he was not capable of doing any harm to Kathleen, regardless of his frame of mind. Patricia Peterson characterized Michael and Kathleen Peterson as "intertwined." According to Patricia, they were a couple who "needed each other."

In the first week of January 2002, as her ex-husband sat in jail, Patricia Peterson took it upon herself to write

an editorial to the *Herald-Sun* newspaper to remark
about the breadth of Michael's character. In a very brief
note, Patricia attested to her strong marriage with
Michael, which had lasted thirty years. She commended
Michael's dedication to the welfare of their children.
She offered her sympathy for the death of Kathleen, stating that she, along with Michael and the rest of the
family, deeply mourned Kathleen's loss. Above all, Patricia stated her belief in the absolute innocence of
Michael Peterson.

On Friday, January 11, 2002, on a freezing night in
downtown Durham, a group of forty people gathered
outside the county jail to show support and seek
Michael's release on bond. Members of the group included Todd and Clayton Peterson, their sister Martha
Ratliff, a number of friends, and, of course, Bill Peterson, who spoke to the press on behalf of the family. An
attorney from Reno, Nevada, Bill was questioning a
process in which a DA was able to claim he would seek
the death penalty, hold a man in jail for weeks, then suddenly declare that the case against Michael Peterson
would not involve capital punishment.

Bill Peterson had been informed that the DA had decided not to seek the death penalty in the case. Without
knowing any further details, Bill was among the outraged members of Peterson's support group, who were
equipped with picket signs and candles. One unusual
character after another seemed to fill out the crowd.
There were local political activists, people who had supported Peterson's campaigns, and then there were those
who were there strictly out of loyalty and love for
Michael Peterson.

Mr. Peterson's former housepainter, Francisco Garcia,
was at the vigil to light a candle for the man who had

been such an unbelievably fair person. According to Garcia, Peterson had been a gracious employer, a man who offered nothing but kindness. Garcia stood outside in the ice cold of winter, happy to do whatever he could to support Peterson, because he truly believed in Michael as a good and honest man.

Members of the group held a variety of hand-painted signs:

PETERSON WON'T FLEE

A MAN WITH A FAMILY CAN ONLY RUN HOME

FREE OUR FATHER

As Todd Peterson expressed his father's gratitude, reading a dictated letter Michael had given him the night prior, he wished to thank everyone there who had shown their support. Todd said that his father was "utterly overwhelmed" when he found out about the vigil.

Earlier that same day, samples of head and pubic hair, along with samples of blood and saliva, were taken from Michael Peterson after a search warrant was executed at the county jail. Peterson's attorney David Rudolf could not be reached for comment. However, Kerry Sutton, acting as a friend of the family, told reporters that taking such samples was nothing unusual. Police were just doing basic crime-scene processing. . . .

Seventeen

Michael Peterson smiled and waved to a crowd of supporters at the bond hearing held on Monday, January 14, 2002. He sat silently as his two attorneys spoke on his behalf, and expected the proceeding to go very smoothly. But in a surprise move, DA Jim Hardin asked Todd Peterson to take the stand. Hardin produced a document in which Peterson had given power of attorney to his sons, Todd and Clayton, just one day after Kathleen was found dead.

Concerned that Peterson might have issued the power of attorney so his property could be sold, so he could liquidate and flee the country, Hardin was reluctant to let Peterson walk free on bond. Todd Peterson, furious at Hardin's suggestion, initially refused to answer any of the prosecutor's questions, describing them as "baseless and irrelevant."

When the angry twenty-five-year-old was instructed by Judge Hight to be responsive, Todd Peterson testified that the power of attorney had been signed over to ensure the financial welfare of the Peterson children and stepchildren, that there had been no talk of selling any property. Asked about when Todd last saw Kathleen alive, Todd testified that he'd seen her at their Cedar Street home at 9:45 P.M., December 9, 2001. At the time, Todd noticed that one or two wine bottles were open, and also that his dad had a bottle of champagne in hand, which they were drinking from two crystal glasses. Todd further testified that he went to a party that night, and returned home in the early hours of Sunday morning to find his stepmother already dead. Todd said his father was "utterly incoherent" when he arrived on the scene.

"He could not speak," Todd told the court, recalling his father's grief. "He simply cried, curled up on the floor, and cried and weeped and weeped. It was the most awful night of our lives."

Under cross-examination, Todd complained that police had threatened to arrest him five times on the night of Kathleen's death. Apparently, police didn't want Todd to speak to his father, and Todd resented their behavior, telling the court that the police conduct was "the most malice I have ever seen."

Following the proceeding, novelist Michael Peterson was ordered to surrender his passport. After promising not to leave the state of North Carolina, and posting an $850,000 secured bond, Peterson was granted a release from jail. He had put up his Forest Hills mansion as collateral. The house, which had been appraised at $1.2 million, held $870,000 in equity for Peterson. So the bulk of his Cedar Street home, his pride and joy, was virtually swallowed up by the court.

In order to cover the price of his defense, Peterson was going to have to come up with other resources. But most of those resources were yet to be liquidated. They were still tied to Kathleen Peterson's estate.

After being granted bond, Michael Peterson emerged from the county jail, flanked by David Rudolf and his family of supporters. Peterson gave a brief statement to reporters, telling them that all he really wanted to do was go home. He wanted an opportunity to spend time with his kids. He needed to spend quality time with them, and he needed to be at home, alone, where he could grieve for his wife.

That night was an emotional time for Michael and his

kids. They stayed up late, until almost 1:30 A.M., just hugging each other and treasuring their every moment. Even though they knew they couldn't make up for the lost Christmas, the children had left up the Christmas tree. They insisted that their dad open the presents under the tree left for Michael, marked "From Santa Claus."

They ate a big dinner, which had been brought in by Clayton and his girlfriend, Becky, who had gone to a nice restaurant and had ordered all of Michael's favorite dishes. All through dinner, the phone was ringing off the hook. People were calling to wish the family well. Those familiar with Peterson's columns, with Peterson's regular attacks on local officials, felt Michael had been jailed because of some retribution. Many who followed Peterson's political career felt that the DA and the police had taken glee in placing Peterson unfairly behind bars.

Close family and friends all knew that Michael was completely innocent. They were certain that Peterson had been held under false charges, and they were disgusted by the enthusiasm of the press, which had been covering the story with vigor. In many people's minds, the media had added unfair stress for Michael Peterson's kids, who were devastated by the loss of their mom, who felt humiliated and degraded by the trumped-up allegations against their dad.

Even though having their father back home was a huge relief, even though they knew he was an innocent man, the children realized that Michael would still have to stand trial for murder. There would be all kinds of publicity. All kinds of accusations. In between their tears of grief, they tried to understand what the sketchy and confusing details of the murder investigation really added up to. Nothing seemed clear. There was no murder weapon. There was no motive. The charge against their dad was just illogical.

For his part, Michael Peterson would go on local TV broadcasts almost immediately following his release, commenting about his difficulties in grieving for the loss of his wife. Peterson was making sure the public knew that he didn't plan to hide; being an innocent man, he would somehow carry on with life.

Since he was independent-minded, Mr. Peterson had no problem talking with the press about his feelings. He was candid about his sorrow for Kathleen's other family members, and he felt certain that the truth would have a way of winning in the end. It was, after all, the United States, where innocent people were still innocent until proven guilty. Peterson was happy to tell the media that he looked forward to his trial, proving his innocence in a court of law.

Also following Peterson's release from jail, the Peterson children had given an interview to the Raleigh-based paper *News & Observer,* telling a reporter they could not imagine their Dad having done anything to tear apart their family. The children called Kathleen their mom, and explained how good she was at keeping the family together. Kathleen was the one who insisted on cooking a feast every Sunday; Kathleen was the one who made sure that all of the children interacted with each other's needs and interests. To the reporter, Todd would assert, "We're probably a more loving and cohesive family than anyone I've ever met."

Todd felt the foundation of their family was built at the dining-room table, where many great stories and conversations had taken place. He recalled with fondness all the chatter, the animated laughter, and Margaret agreed with Todd, saying that there was such a good spirit among them that at times, the Peterson household felt "just like a big old Italian family."

Martha told the reporter that her ties to Michael Peterson went far beyond the laughter at the dinner table, citing her dad as the support system she could always count on in moments of crisis. According to her, Michael was "the most honest, sincere, kindhearted person anybody could ever know." Martha said that Michael had taught each of them "the right family values." Through Michael, she learned to trust her family, believing that her family "would be the only thing that would remain standing," should all else fail.

As the brothers and sisters chatted with the Raleigh reporter, relaxing in their living-room, where the tall Christmas tree with tiny white lights still twinkled, their dad remained out of sight. Todd believed that the criminal case against his father was an absolute sham. He felt, like so many others, that the local authorities were trying to quiet one of their biggest critics. Todd also felt, now with his father safe at home, that the state's case was beginning to unravel. He was convinced that the DA was stretching, going for a conviction with no basis whatsoever. And the other Peterson kids agreed. In their hearts, they remained confident that their dad would be acquitted.

However, Caitlin Atwater wasn't present during the interview to speak for herself. Todd was speaking for her, explaining that Caitlin was too distraught to be talking to the press. Apparently, Caitlin had gone back up to Cornell. Kathleen's daughter had chosen to isolate herself, unwilling to talk to the media about her grief.

As for the rest of them, they were sure that the worst was behind them. Michael had gone back to writing; Margaret, Martha, and Clayton were going back to their respective lives. None of them had complete faith in the justice system, especially after what they'd been through for so many weeks following Kathleen's death. But Clayton, who was busy rebuilding his life with a new round of college studies, felt that the worst of the nightmare was finally over. "It didn't seem real, it happened so quickly and was so outrageous," he told the reporter. "But, I mean, I don't think Dad is going back to jail."

Two weeks after Peterson had come home, his famed attorney had a run-in with the law himself. David Rudolf found himself in a courtroom in Chapel Hill—he was on trial for careless and reckless driving. Apparently, a rookie officer had stopped Rudolf in May 2001 as Rudolf was driving himself to the Durham Regional Hospital. The incident happened at 5:45 A.M., and Rudolf, who was in pain and heading into the hospital to have back surgery, allegedly swerved off the road, causing a tractor-trailer to slam on its brakes. According to the rookie officer's testimony, after Rudolf was pulled over, the attorney became irate and started cursing.

At the Chapel Hill District Court, one officer testified that Rudolf said something to the effect of "Do you know who I am?" Then he mentioned that he'd represented Rae Carruth. Rudolf denied making that statement, explaining that if he had mentioned Rae Carruth, it was only after the officer said something about recognizing him from television.

Whatever the truth was about Rudolf's bragging, no one could be sure, but five witnesses testified that David Rudolf used foul language to police, telling one officer, in an obscene way, that the officer was going to lose in court. Allegedly, while Rudolf argued with officers, he made a cellular call to a spokeswoman for the Chapel Hill Police Department at 6:00 A.M. Rudolf was looking for the Chapel Hill DA's telephone number, and the police spokesman later testified that she, too, could hear him arguing with police.

After other officers arrived on the scene, Rudolf was given a citation. The attorney then pulled away, spinning his tires, flinging mud and gravel on the officers and their cars. The officers claimed Rudolf was fishtailing, and pulled him over a second time, citing him for reckless driving again. District court judge Pat DeVine found Rudolf guilty of the second incident and ordered him to pay a $100 fine and court costs. Rudolf admitted that he lost his temper inappropriately, but he later would file an appeal to fight the ruling against him.

In the meantime, Michael Peterson was feeling bewildered and overwhelmed without having Kathleen in his life. His lawyer's recent squabble with the law was the last thing he cared about. Peterson was confident that his lawyer would be utterly prepared, that David Rudolf would be able to face whatever outrageous contentions the prosecution might put forth in his upcoming murder trial.

But no attorney on earth could have prepared him for the loneliness he was feeling, sitting in that big house, day after day, with nothing left but reminders of Kathleen. When his kids were still around, in the first week after his release, Michael had started writing. Hopeful that he could recover from the tragic accident, he continued writing day after day. Peterson was working on a book about politics and corruption in a small Southern town, but he discovered that his writing couldn't keep his mind off things, especially once his kids had all gone back to college.

With the love of his life missing, his writing didn't come as easily. The writing seemed empty. His spirits couldn't be bolstered, not even by his son Todd. Since Todd was attending a local college, he had decided to live at the Cedar Street home for a while, just to keep a watchful eye on Michael. There were times when Michael seemed so depressed, no one was sure what he might do.

There were many days when Michael broke down and wept. He would go and stare at Kathleen's grave, carrying a little bouquet of flowers, and he would just stand there frozen. Michael still wanted to be near her. Whenever he was by her grave, he felt Kathleen would want him to stay in Durham. But then, there were so many terrible memories for him at Cedar Street, and there was the malicious intent of the local officials. For Michael, living in Durham had become a real dilemma. Once his murder trial ended, he was seriously considering leaving North Carolina and moving far away—perhaps California, perhaps Japan.

But as he looked around their home—at all the objects he and Kathleen had collected from around the world, at the gifts they had received as wedding presents—Michael felt he couldn't bring himself to leave the place he and Kathleen had made their home. To uproot himself and lose every last inch of her, that was too much for him. At least, by having her things around him, he could feel he was still with Kathleen. More than anything, he wished he could have her back, and he had dreams of curling up with her on the couch, just watching TV, chatting and laughing. He would sit at home with the family dogs and watch episodes of *Law & Order*, dreaming of the days when he and his wife would stay home together, all snuggled up, all warm and happy.

Friends and family were still offering support, but that wasn't much comfort anymore. Peterson was having trouble regaining his balance. Without Kathleen, he couldn't seem to get back on his feet again. People still wondered why a special grand jury had been called. They wanted to know why there had been a presumption of guilt at the onset of Kathleen's tragic accident. Michael Peterson had no answers, really, to offer anyone. The roughest times for him were late at night, sitting in the darkness, wondering what the future would hold.

As it was, the autopsy report still had not been completed. DA Jim Hardin tried to explain that the case against Peterson was going to bring on a lot of scrutiny. Hardin claimed that he was working to protect the rights of Kathleen Peterson.

But people wanted to know about Michael's rights. Here was a man, sick with a broken heart, being accused of killing the only woman he had truly loved.

Eighteen

Just after Christmas Day, weeks after her mom died, Caitlin had gone to see her dad, Fred, in the eastern part of North Carolina. He lived near Beaufort, where things were peaceful, where the town seemed frozen in time. Caitlin always had a good visit with him and her stepmom, Carol, but this trip was different. Caitlin was restless. She couldn't be comforted. She decided to go up to Virginia, just outside of DC, to visit her aunt Candace, because her grandmother was up there, and her aunt Lori lived nearby. Caitlin hoped that seeing her mom's sisters, that seeing her grandmother, would somehow make things better.

But on her drive up there, she couldn't get the conversation she had with her father out of her head. Her father had sat her down the day after Christmas to have a "talk." He explained that Detective Art Holland was trying to get in touch with her, that he'd been calling the number at Cedar Street and was leaving messages. Caitlin hadn't known anything about it. She wasn't in charge of the phone machine, and most people called her on her cell phone. Fred didn't want to scare his daughter, but there were some real issues to be sorted out, the police had questions, and none of the other Peterson kids were willing to talk about anything. Fred was of the opinion that Caitlin should meet with the Durham police.

For a sophomore in college, who was not quite yet

twenty, Caitlin had a lot weighing on her already, just grappling with her own emotions, her schoolwork, and her immediate future. Even being mature for her age—the twists and turns of adulthood had come upon her too abruptly. Not only did she feel her whole family breaking down, not only did she have the responsibility of her mom's estate, but now she had investigators calling. With this new thought—about her mother possibly having been murdered—her life had become difficult, beyond anything she could have imagined.

In many respects, Caitlin felt torn. Her siblings seemed content to keep their heads in the sand, listening strictly to whatever Michael had to say. When Caitlin ran through the chat she had with her father, she recalled that he mentioned something odd. He said that David Rudolf had called, that Rudolf had advised that the whole family stick together because the police were going to try to drive a wedge between them.

"What do you mean, 'a wedge'?" Caitlin wanted to know.

"Well, I asked Mr. Rudolf," Fred said, "and he was just concerned that the police might want to start a problem between you and your brothers and sisters."

"But why would they do that?"

"Well, that's just it. It doesn't make sense. I asked Rudolf if he was advising us, acting as your attorney, or if he was acting as Michael's attorney," Fred told her. "And Rudolf said he was only representing Michael."

"Well, then, why should I be listening to him?" she wondered.

"Well, I don't think you should," her dad said. "Rudolf doesn't have your interests in mind. His interest is in Michael. You can do whatever you want. But I think it would be wise for you to listen to the Durham police."

"But why do I have to be the only one?"

"Your mother's estate is in your hands. There might be

a question about her life insurance policy. Why don't we drive down there together to see what they have to say?"

But Caitlin needed time. She asked her father to call Art Holland and stall. Fred Atwater delivered a message that Caitlin was thinking about returning to Durham, that he was hoping she'd be willing to listen to the facts. As soon as Caitlin felt open to it, Fred would call Detective Holland again to make an appointment.

On the ride to Virginia, Caitlin kept pondering the question. Deep inside, Caitlin felt nervous about it. She didn't want to face the police at all, especially when she was still convinced that this whole charge was about a grudge. There were so many police who hated her stepdad. And Michael had kept warning her to stay away. Her brothers and sisters were convinced of a conspiracy. As she looked to the sky, Caitlin kept asking her mother for guidance, but she wasn't getting any signs. For the first time in her life, it seemed she was truly on her own.

When she arrived at her Aunt Candace's place, Caitlin could sense that Candace, Lori, and her grandmother were all uneasy. After their initial hellos, after everyone had their feet up with sandwiches and coffee, there was a tone in the air, a thickness that could be cut with a knife. At first, no one was saying anything outright. Everyone was talking around the situation . . . but as each of them started to open up—Veronica, Candace, and Lori—it became clear that the circumstance surrounding Kathleen's death was more serious than any of them ever thought.

Her aunts and grandmother were trying to prod Caitlin, to find out exactly what she might know. They believed she might be aware of some foul play in the marriage. Having been the only one out of all of them who lived in that house with Michael and Kathleen, they were hopeful that Caitlin would have some answers, or at least some clues about the Petersons' relationship.

"They sit me down, and they just say they've heard all

this stuff about the bisexuality that they didn't know about," Caitlin recalled. "And one of the things that really freaked me out was when they asked me why I thought Michael was at the YMCA all those long hours every night, and all this stuff. And then, I was, like, the bisexuality thing was taking on a whole different level for me. And I didn't really want to think about it."

As her aunts filled her head, and her grandmother listened, Caitlin wasn't laughing about Michael's bisexuality anymore. When it had been just a book on a shelf, when it had been a joke that she and her sisters played as kids, that was one thing. But now, having to consider the idea that Michael could have been having affairs with men on a daily basis—Caitlin wanted it to be a fluke.

No one was pushing her. Her aunts were gently asking, just to see if Caitlin knew of any evidence that things were not happy in Michael and Kathleen's marriage. They were hoping Caitlin would have some story to tell. They were hoping that the reason Caitlin hadn't talked to the police was that she was hiding something, that she was frightened because she knew too much.

But Caitlin had nothing significant to relate about Michael's sex life. She considered her mom's relationship with Michael to be quite normal, quite loving, but it was also none of her business. In Caitlin's view, there was never any hint that Michael and her mom had problems in the bedroom. But then, Kathleen wasn't the type to discuss things such as that. Ever.

As for anything else unusual, there was a time when Michael hit her mother once. It was no big deal, but it was something her mom had mentioned. Caitlin said that was the only incident she could recall in the thirteen years her mom and Michael had been together. It wasn't anything they ever talked about. It was just something Kathleen had mentioned once, a few years back. Caitlin hadn't ever thought anymore about it.

"Well, honey, the thing is, there's a lot of blood in that stairwell. I've seen it," Candace said, "and we've all become concerned."

"We're going to go talk to Art Holland ourselves," Lori told her niece, "and it's not that we want to cause trouble, but frankly we think we need to do this. And we think you should be going back down with us to Durham to see what the police have to say."

"Well, I don't really want to look at the blood in the stairwell," Caitlin argued. "I mean, it's not something I really want to see."

"We understand that, Caitlin," Candace said. "We're not asking you to do that. But we've been talking to the police, and there's some questions that we have. . . . "

But Caitlin couldn't be convinced. She told her aunts that she might go, but she wouldn't give them anything more than a "maybe." Caitlin wanted to get down to Atlanta. She was meeting one of her best friends, Jen, in Virginia, and together they were driving to be with Becka and other buddies, close friends of Caitlin's who were her biggest support system. They were all going to be together for New Year's.

Caitlin didn't want to jump to conclusions. She was thinking very factually. She was questioning everything, everything Michael said, everything Todd said.

She was trying to determine what facts she knew, and what facts she didn't know.

"It was weird, because it felt like none of this had to do with my mom. It was already like a mystery, like a true crime novel," Caitlin confided. "It wasn't emotional to me at the time, because I was finding out facts, learning new information, and it was just like reading a book. My feelings were very separated. I was just working in the mode of, like, let's just get to the bottom of this. Even when I read the autopsy report, it was just words. It wasn't like it was my actual mom."

Nineteen

Caitlin had become influenced by her family's reaction. She was feeling pressured, and everything was scaring her. By the time she arrived in Atlanta, she was totally spooked. On New Year's Eve, she got a series of calls from both Todd and Martha. They were leaving messages on her cell phone, saying it was urgent that she call them back.

Todd and Martha wanted Caitlin to return to Durham for a TV interview. They were making her feel guilty about not sticking with the family. At that time, Michael was still in jail, and the kids were being hounded by the local media. They had arranged to tape a TV segment for the local news, and they wanted Caitlin to be present so that all five children could stand up for Michael.

Caitlin returned their calls and said she was stuck in a snowstorm in Atlanta. The roads were dangerous, she wasn't sure about doing TV interviews, and besides, this was about her and her mom. This was not about Michael. When she told Todd that she felt she should be able to do whatever she wanted to do, Todd began acting suspicious. He knew Caitlin had been to see her aunts near DC, and he was worried that Caitlin was jumping to the conclusion that Michael was guilty.

But Caitlin hadn't made any decision about that. She was angry that Todd was giving her an attitude. Both he and Martha were making her out to be some kind of bad person, accusing her of turning against the family. She tried to reason with Martha, she even tried to placate Todd by saying she'd try to find a way back to Durham, but really, all she wanted was some time to herself.

"There was no evidence that he was guilty of murdering my mom," Caitlin recalled, "but people were coming out with all these rumors about Michael being gay, and I didn't want to be unsupportive of him. But I also wasn't going to do a TV interview to say he was wonderful, because in my mind there was evidence that he probably cheated on my mom, and that wasn't okay."

The more Caitlin thought about Michael, the more she heard rumors that he'd approached gay male friends of the family—the more uneasy she felt about his leading a double life. Even if it was hearsay, too many people were coming up with details about Michael being sexually active with men. As Caitlin thought more about Michael's past, she realized he'd been courting some strange friends over the years. Back then, she hadn't ever thought about it. Back then, she was a kid with her own set of problems, and Michael's "friends" were of no concern to her.

"Michael would kind of adopt people at the gym," Caitlin confided. "There was this one guy, Roy, who was a wrestling guy and he'd stop by our house. This was when I was in junior high school. And thinking back, the guy was so blatantly gay. I started wondering, like, what was that guy doing at our house?"

As Caitlin tried not to think about it, as she sat in Atlanta with her friends, dodging phone calls from Todd and Martha, her friends convinced her to call Todd and give him another excuse. Todd and the others had already agreed to the first TV interview, and now the local papers were calling as well. Todd wanted a statement from Caitlin; he felt it was the very least she could do.

Todd felt Caitlin should support Michael. Todd was concerned about public opinion. He needed to show Peterson solidarity, and he wasn't going to let up.

"I didn't want to be there, and I didn't agree to be interviewed as a family," Caitlin confided. "They wanted my theory on how innocent I thought Michael was, and at first I said fine, I would talk about it. I said I'd call them later. But then, they kept calling and calling, and I couldn't get over how greedy they all were. They were insisting on getting my written statement. And I finally did tell them that I couldn't do any interview. That I was not going to talk about the questions."

As it happened, when the Peterson kids taped the first TV interview, Clayton had his girlfriend, Becky, with him. To the outside public the TV interview made it seem like there were five kids supporting Michael Peterson. Even though Becky hadn't been asked any questions, she had just been a presence for the cameras, any outsider looking at the television would have mistaken Clayton's girlfriend as one of the Peterson kids.

When Caitlin heard about that, she was furious. She felt Todd was being manipulative. It suddenly occurred to her that Michael was probably behind the PR campaign. When another story about the Peterson kids ran in the *News & Observer,* Caitlin was horrified to see that Todd had acted as her spokesperson. Todd had done a good job of making it appear that Caitlin was just distraught, that she wasn't participating in the interview because she was too emotional. But by that time, Caitlin had already called her father and had agreed to attend a meeting in Durham. Unbeknownst to Todd, she already had sat down with Detective Art Holland and Durham district attorney Jim Hardin.

Based on that first meeting, Caitlin and Fred Atwater had come to think about Michael Peterson in a whole new light. The officials had hard evidence pointing to

Kathleen having been murdered. The autopsy revealed seven scalp lacerations to Kathleen's head. Caitlin didn't want to look at the crime scene photos, but Fred had seen them. Like Candace and Lori, he, too, was disturbed by the overwhelming amount of blood. From the looks of the photos and the crime scene video, there was no way Kathleen could have died by having fallen down the stairs.

To make matters even more disturbing, the DA had presented some revealing information about Michael Peterson's past. Hardin could not offer proof, he could not yet give the full details, but there were suspicious circumstances that lead authorities to believe that Peterson might have been connected to another death during his days in Germany. . . .

Twenty

In early February 2002, David Rudolf confirmed to media that he had hired famed forensic scientist Dr. Henry Lee, who had testified for the defense in the O.J. Simpson murder case. It was in part due to Dr. Lee's testimony that the Los Angeles jury had found O.J. Simpson innocent of any crime. During that trial, Dr. Lee stated that he found three "imprints" on the terracotta walkway on Bundy, the famous crime scene that Lee himself photographed. Lee further testified that these imprints did not match the size-twelve bloody shoe prints, made by Bruno Magli shoes, that prosecutors said belonged to O.J. Simpson.

In Dr. Lee's O.J. Simpson testimony, his findings revealed a "parallel-line imprint," as well as another "imprint," which did not match O.J. Simpson's shoes. This inferred the possibility of a second assailant being at the crime scene. Dr. Lee's testimony, therefore, challenged the prosecution's theory that O.J. Simpson was a lone assailant. In essence, Dr. Henry Lee managed to challenge the core of the prosecution's case against the former NFL star.

In response, one of the FBI's senior experts on shoe prints, William Bodziak, testified that Dr. Lee's findings were faulty, that one of the "imprints" Dr. Lee had photographed from the walkway on Bundy was actually an

indentation in the cement, a trowel mark made by
workers in the laying of the cement years earlier. But
it was Dr. Lee's testimony that stayed in the minds of
the jury. His theory that shoe prints at the scene might
have come from a second assailant was enough to place
a reasonable doubt in the jurors' minds.

Even though Dr. Lee was struck down by comments
refuting his findings, even though testimony by FBI shoe
print expert Bodziak debunked Dr. Lee's "parallel-line
imprint" theory on virtually every level, the jury in the
O.J. Simpson case remained impressed by Dr. Lee. They
didn't seem to care about the disputed facts. They saw
Dr. Lee as a highly intelligent, world-renowned gentleman. His discredited testimony, therefore, hadn't had
any sway with the jury whatsoever.

In the trial of the century, it was Dr. Henry Lee who
had the greatest impact. He was a man who came off as
worldly and sophisticated. He was seen as a sincere expert, a man who worked more often for the prosecution
than the defense. By the vast majority, Dr. Lee was considered to be the best in his profession. And, after the
O.J. Simpson verdict, media from all over the country
hailed him as America's top forensic expert.

In most everyone's view, Dr. Henry Lee was the best
witness money could buy. So when local media in North
Carolina discovered that the nationally known forensic
scientist, the coauthor of twenty books, was on his way
down to Durham—headed there from his home base at
the University of New Haven in Connecticut—they were
anxious to report the story, printing glowing portraits of
the "forensic sleuth."

David Rudolf had asked Dr. Lee to make a special trip
down, to take a look at the stairwell in the Peterson mansion, and Lee arrived on Valentine's Day, 2002, entering
the gorgeous abode on Cedar Street, where he was
greeted by a very humble Michael Peterson.

Of course Michael Peterson was ecstatic, as was David Rudolf. They knew Dr. Henry Lee wouldn't be there if he hadn't believed in Peterson's innocence. Dr. Lee would be looking for anything exculpatory. In particular, he would look at the bloodstain patterns to determine exactly how Kathleen Peterson might have taken such a terrible fall. Both Peterson and Rudolf believed that Dr. Lee was the right man to determine what, if anything, could be gleaned by the blood patterns and other forensic evidence left behind on the staircase. Certainly, having a man such as Dr. Henry Lee on their side would bode well for Michael Peterson.

There was much local fanfare regarding the presence of Dr. Henry Lee. Not only had both top newspapers written stories about him, ABC's *20/20* had flown in a news crew to film Dr. Lee in the Peterson stairwell. Himself a media star, having testified not only for the defense of O.J. Simpson, for the defense of William Kennedy Smith, and in the famous unsolved case of JonBenet Ramsey, Dr. Henry Lee had caused quite a stir in the Triangle region of North Carolina.

Once the hubbub settled, after Dr. Lee had jetted off on a plane, David Rudolf reminded local media that the case against Michael Peterson was circumstantial, again accusing police of mishandling the crime scene. The attorney told the media that he viewed the blood evidence on Peterson's stairs as one of the most important factors in the case. The interpretation of the cast-off spatter, Rudolf asserted, would be something that people would interpret differently, and David Rudolf looked forward to the Michael Peterson case becoming a battle of the experts.

Up until that point, the autopsy results and photographs had remained sealed. The public remained in limbo about the culpability of Mr. Peterson, and his attorney was asking that the gruesome photos of Mrs.

Peterson be kept under seal, partially as a courtesy to the family, who had been through so much agony over Kathleen's unfortunate death.

Within days after Lee's whirlwind tour through Durham, Kathleen Peterson's sister Candace Hunt Zamperini felt compelled to contact a columnist at the *Herald-Sun* newspaper. Acting as a spokesperson for the Kathleen Hunt Peterson's family, Candace wrote a statement regarding David Rudolf and his public presumption that he was representing the entire Peterson family in their desire to keep Kathleen's autopsy results and photographs away from the public eye.

Candace stated that, even though the release of the devastating autopsy photos would fill her family's heart with sadness, Kathleen's family had agreed that the documents and photographs needed to be made public in order that the truth about Kathleen's death be discovered. Candace also wrote a comment about David Rudolf, whom she insisted did *not* represent Kathleen's family. She noted the "confusion" that had "arisen from misrepresenting the relationships of people in Kathleen's life," asserting that Mr. Rudolf had never spoken with her or any member of Kathleen's family.

Candace said that she and the rest of Kathleen's family took "great umbrage with Mr. Rudolf taking the liberty to speak for any of us" concerning the case against Michael Peterson. Candace made it clear that, while Michael had been Kathleen's husband, he stood accused of murder, thus he no longer held the position of "family," as far as she or any of Kathleen's immediate relatives were concerned. Candace pointed out that Kathleen's family was comprised of her mother, two sisters, one brother, and one daughter, all of whom were united in the common mission of discovering the truth about Kathleen's death.

Two days after Candace's scathing comments hit the

local paper in Durham, David Rudolf sent a letter to Kathleen's sister at her home in Virginia. Rudolf had read that Candace and other members of Kathleen's family were upset because he was claiming to speak for her family. He said that, to his knowledge, he had never done such a thing, but if in some way he had "created that impression," he was truly sorry. Rudolf said that he hadn't meant to cause Candace or any of Kathleen's family any additional pain. He explained that he was only trying to "effectuate the wishes of Michael and his children" by asking that Kathleen's autopsy photos not be available to anyone.

Rudolf emphasized to Candace that the request to seal the autopsy results and photos had nothing to do with determining the truth about what happened to Kathleen. Rudolf said he fully respected Candace's beliefs, but he wanted her to know that Michael was just as interested in determining the truth about what had happened to Kathleen as she was.

Rudolf maintained that the autopsy photos would be available to all lawyers, experts, and jury members. He explained that the public release of such material would in no way contribute to the real search for the truth. The truth, Rudolf explained, would come from qualified experts who had reviewed all the evidence, who would testify in a court of law. The real truth of Kathleen's death, Rudolf wrote, would not come "from armchair analysis by pseudo experts" who would be contacted by the media "to pump up their ratings for sweeps month, which happens to be February."

David Rudolf hoped that Candace and the rest of Kathleen's family would keep open minds about the facts in the case, that they would wait until the trial to make their judgments.

But already, the state's experts had expressed opinions about the cause of Kathleen's death, deeming it a homicide. Candace and Caitlin, as well as other members of Kathleen's family, had been made fully aware of the details. While Rudolf insisted that other qualified experts might disagree with the state's findings, he could never convince Candace Zamperini of that. Candace had been to Durham. At first skeptical and defensive of Michael Peterson, once Candace had seen the photos of the crime scene, once she read the autopsy reports, there were questions that couldn't be answered so easily. The photos and reports detailed the seven severe lacerations to Kathleen's head. And there appeared to be defensive wounds to Kathleen's hands and wrists, indicating that she had been fending off an attack.

As the attorney closed his letter to Candace, Rudolf spelled out the two questions that he considered to be key in the case regarding Michael Peterson. The first was, what actually happened? Rudolf said he needed to discover if there was an accident or a homicide. That was a question for his experts to determine, once they had the chance to review the reports of the medical examiners and other state's witnesses. The second question was, assuming the state's conclusion that Kathleen Peterson had been beaten to death was actually correct, "who did this?"

In Rudolf's opinion, that was a question he could address. In his letter, the attorney assured Candace that Michael was innocent of the charges against him, stating that if Kathleen was beaten, "it was certainly not by Michael," who was still expressing his love for Kathleen.

Twenty-one

The first autopsy examination issued from the Office of the Chief Medical Examiner at Chapel Hill was signed by Dr. Kenneth Snell. The decedent, Kathleen Hunt Peterson, had been viewed at the Cedar Street house at 7:40 A.M. on December 9, 2001, when it had been determined that the probable cause of death was a closed head injury, blunt-force injury to the head, due to a fall down the stairs.

The narrative summary Dr. Snell wrote stated that Mrs. Peterson was found at the bottom of the stairs by her husband or her son—and that friends and family members were notified before EMS was notified. When the EMS did arrive at 2:40 A.M., the husband admitted to having put towels under Mrs. Peterson's head. Dr. Snell noted some blood had partially been wiped up on the stairs with paper towels. Dr. Kenneth Snell also made a notation that there had been alcohol consumption on the evening before her death.

Dr. Snell recorded blood still present in the stairwell, and wrote that it appeared Mrs. Peterson hit her head on the top step above the corner, hit the floor in the corner of the stairs, and then landed at the base of the stairs on her back. The medical examiner further noted that the blood spatter appeared to support the scenario of a fall. His findings suggested Mrs. Peterson's death was an accident.

However, once Kathleen Peterson's body was transported to Chapel Hill, a full autopsy examination was to be performed by Dr. Deborah Radisch. As a matter of record, the 120-pound body of Mrs. Peterson, an adult female clad in a brown fleece sweatshirt and white sweatpants, was determined to be in "good general condition." There was evidence of medical intervention noted on the skin of her right lower abdomen, but otherwise, Mrs. Peterson's body, with its brown hair and green eyes, was basically intact, prior to the event of December 9, 2001.

Dr. Deborah Radisch, a seasoned pathologist with a stellar track record, would carefully write both an internal and external description of the body of Kathleen Hunt Atwater Peterson. Her pathological diagnosis included a long list of injuries:

Multiple lacerations to the posterior scalp.
Multiple contusions to the posterior scalp.
Subarachnoid hemorrhage with cerebral convexities.
Early acute ischemic neuronal necrosis.
Fracture, with hemorrhage, of the left thyroid cartilage.
Contusions of the back, posterior arms, wrists, and hands.
Multiple small abrasions and contusions to the face.

Dr. Radisch noted that hair was grasped in Mrs. Peterson's right and left hands, which was collected and submitted as evidence. There was no visible tissue seen under her fingernails, but it was noted that Mrs. Peterson did have crusted blood beneath her nails. There was a small chip discovered on one tooth. There was also dried blood on the bottoms of her feet, and dried blood on her face.

Mrs. Peterson had three contusions over her right eyelid, a contusion on her right ear, and a linear vertical abrasion on the right side of her neck. Beyond that, she had three linear horizontal abrasions over her left eyebrow. Also, there was a horizontal abrasion over the bridge of her nose, two small linear horizontal abrasions over her left eye, and a small abrasion over her lip.

Dr. Radisch counted at least seven distinct lacerations on the posterior scalp of Mrs. Peterson. Several of those lacerations were complex: one was a tri-pronged linear laceration measuring 3 inches vertically. Located 2½ inches away, there was a second tri-pronged laceration measuring over four inches vertically. Continuing along Mrs. Peterson's scalp, the lacerations were measured out in vertical and horizontal intersections, one of which had a deeply undermined edge. In addition, there was a 1-inch flap of skin removed from the left side of her scalp.

There were no skull fractures found, and Mrs. Peterson's brain was not swollen. Her system contained a blood alcohol concentration of .07 percent, just one point below the legal driving limit. There were trace amounts of chlorpheniramine, Cyclobenzaprine, and nicotine detected in her blood specimen, and Valium was present in a small concentration as well.

While the initial examination by Dr. Kenneth Snell indicated the death was due to a fall down the stairs, Dr. Deborah Radisch listed the cause of death as being due to severe concussive injury of the brain, caused by multiple blunt-force impacts to the head.

Blood loss from Mrs. Peterson's deep scalp lacerations may also have played a role in her death, but Dr. Radisch's final report concluded that the severity and location of the lacerations to Mrs. Peterson's head were the primary cause of death. In her medical opinion, those lacerations were indicative of multiple impacts received as a result of a beating.

About the final autopsy results, one particular item stood out to neuropathologist Dr. Thomas Bouldin, who later examined the body of Kathleen Peterson: consistent with the acute ischemic neuronal necrosis present in her cerebrum, there existed *rare red neurons.* Those red neurons would only appear if Kathleen Peterson had experienced a decreased blood flow to her brain for perhaps two hours before her death.

Twenty-two

At the request of the Durham Police Department, a bloodstain pattern examination was conducted on certain items of clothing submitted to the North Carolina State Bureau of Investigation Crime Lab. Special Agent Duane Deaver had taken possession of ten paper bags of evidence and had examined them in the Molecular Genetics Section of the bureau, and Criminal Specialist Dennis Honeycutt was present during the examinations. Agent Deaver's report, filed just after Valentine's Day, on February 19, 2002, concluded the following:

Item#1. A pair of shorts, collected from Michael Peterson, Brooks Sport brand, size 36, 100% cotton. The front of the shorts were heavily bloodstained. The blood had soaked through to the inside fabric of the pockets, and bloodstain on the front of the shorts, which had also been diluted, had formed a "V" pattern. There were smears, contact stains, and blood spatters visible on the shorts. Of particular interest was the blood spatter on the *inside* of the right leg of the shorts.

Item#2. Four white athletic socks, collected at the bottom of the Peterson staircase, with soaking and smear stain in blood.

Item #3. A pair of Converse brand men's 8.5-size athletic shoes, low-cut, leather. The soles of each shoe were bloodstained. The right shoe had spatters, drips, smears, and contact stains in blood on it. The left shoe had the same. When the shoes were examined for a second time, by Special Agent Joyce Petzca, other points of interest came up. The toe of each shoe had blood spatter that came from a source of blood *directly above* the toes.

Item #4. A knit short-sleeved shirt collected from Michael Peterson. Navy in color, size large, the shirt had a heavy odor of perspiration about it. Dark bloodstains were visible on the left chest, and on both sleeves of the shirt. The dark color of the shirt, however, prevented a complete examination of the bloodstain characteristics.

Also in a sealed paper bag were items identified that had been collected from Todd Peterson. Of interest was a size-large shirt, gray in color, Structure brand, which had contact stains in blood over the top of the shoulders and the top of the sleeves. The front of the shirt had contact stains in blood from the collar down to the middle. The back of the shirt had contact stains in blood, along the left shoulder blade.

Of further note was a pair of jeans collected from Todd Peterson, Perry Ellis brand, size 34" x 32". On the front of the jeans, smears of blood could be seen above the right pocket. Contact stains of blood were found on the right side of the leg, in the crotch area. On the left side of the leg, contact stains could be seen along the inseam, just below the crotch. On the back of the jeans, a contact stain in blood was found near the hem of the right leg.

Also collected in the brown paper bags were the items of clothing worn by Kathleen Peterson on December 9, 2001. A dark-colored fleece top, size petite, was stained heavily with blood around the collar, and down the back. The tail of the shirt was soaked in blood.

There was also a pair of white sweatpants, size medium, L.L. Bean brand. Unlike the fleece top, which revealed very little, the pants collected from the body of Kathleen Peterson, had quite a few points of interest. The pants had a story to tell. On them were found:

A) Soaking stains of blood on the front of the pants, primarily around the waist area.

B) A diluted bloodstain visible along the crotch of the pants, down each side of the leg.

C) Contact, drips, and smears visible on the front of the pants.

D) Blood spatters visible on the front right and left legs of the pants.

E) Diluted bloodstains in the seat area of the pants.

F) Blood spatters visible on the back of the right leg of the pants.

G) A shoe track, transfer stain in blood, found on the *back of the right leg* of the pants.

The shoe track, it was later revealed, would match the size-8.5 Converse sneaker belonging to Mr. Michael Peterson.

Twenty-three

Also at the request of the Durham Police Department, a bloodstain pattern examination had been ordered for the stairwell, as well as in the kitchen area of the Peterson mansion. Conducted by Special Agent Duane Deaver, with Crime Scene Investigator Eric Campen and Crime Scene Investigator Angie Powell also present, the testing began at 5:07 P.M. on January 9, 2001.

Duane Deaver, an SBI agent since 1985, had been involved in over five hundred criminal cases, and was the State Bureau of Investigation's chief instructor for bloodstain pattern analysis. Briefed by Detective Art Holland, Deaver began an in-depth examination of the area. Being very cautious and conservative in his analysis, the testing of the crime scene took him almost six hours to complete.

For the purpose of the report, Deaver numbered the stairs from top to bottom, one to eighteen. In the hall outside the staircase, blood spatters were found on the wall, and on the header over the hall leading to the kitchen area. There were two drops on the header, 114 inches above the floor, as well as three drops of blood on an adjacent wall. Each of these drops showed a downward path, an *origin from above the drops*. Agent Deaver believed this cast-off blood was created by some object being swung in an upward motion.

In the front of the stairwell, there was a pair of foot-printlike transfers in blood. A photograph provided to Agent Deaver showed Kathleen Peterson's body seated in the same spot. The photo showed that the victim's feet were bare, and had bloodstains on the bottoms. To the expert, these stains indicated that Mrs. Peterson had stood up in her own pool of blood.

Transfer stains in blood could be seen on the trim molding, and finger and hairlike transfer stains were visible on the trim. There were drips in blood going from the floor to forty-six inches in height. A light switch to the left of the trim molding had a transfer stain in blood on it. One particular piece of trim, along the inside of the stairwell above step fifteen, had fingerlike transfer stains in blood. There were three individual stains at the end of the handrail, making it appear as though someone had been trying to pull herself up.

On the north wall at the bottom of the stairs, the area over steps sixteen, seventeen, and eighteen, a large smear of blood was noted. What was interesting about this was that this smear of blood had another blood spatter pattern *on top of it.* That meant there was fresh blood on top of dried blood.

The blood spatter patterns that covered the north wall, including the entire width of the stairwell, were found to rise to a height of seventy inches above the highest step on the stairwell. On the east wall, an unstained area was found in the middle of a bloodstain pattern. This so-called "void" area was approximately ten inches long and four inches wide, and a careful reconstruction of the blood spatter patterns on this wall revealed two points of origin for the patterns.

After measuring the two points of origin for the blood, Agent Deaver noted that a minimum of two blows were delivered to cause the source of blood in the corner of the wall above step seventeen. It was possible that these bloodstains resulted from Kathleen Peterson's head being struck as she was standing.

Blood spatters above steps sixteen and seventeen were also examined for points of origin. A line of blood spatter was noted in a pattern that ran above the steps, matching a place where a metal chairlift was located. The chairlift was an unused wheelchair-type device that had been installed by previous owners. The device had blood spatter on it and bloodstains behind it.

Drips, smears, and transfers in blood were noted on the surface of numerous steps, and were found on the *riser* between steps sixteen and seventeen. Oddly, above step fifteen, when a reconstruction of a blood spatter pattern was made, a point of origin was found to be twenty-seven inches up from that step.

Deaver concluded that a minimum of one blow had been delivered to cause the source of blood above step fifteen. In addition, a blood transfer on step fifteen was noted to have sharp edges and looked as if it had been created by a heavy object. Drips were also seen on a piece of floor molding in the stairwell, with a fingerprintlike transfer.

On the landing at the top of the stairs, a transfer stain in blood was made just above the riser, on the underside of the wood flooring. According to Deaver's measurements, that blood spatter came from a source *directly above* the stain.

After further study, the SBI agent also concluded that someone attempted to clean the stairway near where Kathleen Peterson's body was found. The wall next to her body showed certain runs in the pattern of blood, indicating that a liquid had been applied to that place. One particular step, toward the bottom of the stairwell, near where Mrs. Peterson's head was resting, showed that an effort had been made to clean the step entirely.

Based on the patterns of blood, the various locations of smears and cleanup, Agent Deaver had no doubt that someone had struck Kathleen Peterson repeatedly. After further analysis of the photographs taken of the victim's clothes and of the crime scene, the expert also surmised that the bloodstain patterns on Mrs. Peterson's pants showed that her body had been moved in positions *other than what* he observed at the scene.

In the kitchen, Agent Deaver found further evidence of foul play. There were transfers in blood on a cabinet that contained two shelves of drinking glasses. The transfer stains were fingerlike and were discovered on the knob of the cabinet. Directly below the cabinet, Deaver found a drop of blood on the kitchen countertop, with two drinking glasses and an open wine bottle sitting near the sink basin.

The sink looked messy, with a large pasta pot and a food strainer covering the drain in the sink. When Agent Deaver raised the pot, he could smell the odor of alcohol coming from the drain. The smell of alcohol was so strong, it was clear that someone had poured a good deal of wine down the drain, perhaps an entire bottle.

As he concluded his findings, there was no doubt in Agent Deaver's mind: someone attempted to stage the scene.

Twenty-four

Michael Peterson was born in Nashville, Tennessee, but his family moved to Virginia when he was young, where he graduated high school, moving on to earn a B.A. in Political Science from Duke University in 1965. When the intrigue of war drew the Duke graduate to Vietnam, Peterson felt it would be the perfect experience and setting for him. He expected to write "the great American war novel."

When Peterson arrived in Vietnam, he was quite anxious and considered to be gung ho. Commissioned as a lieutenant, he was assigned to a small outpost, called Oceanview, located in the northernmost region of South Vietnam. His battalion was small, comprised of no more than thirty men. And by the time he arrived there, in the middle of 1968, Lieutenant Peterson found himself and his men in a tough position.

The platoon he was with had the job of defending a region that the North Vietnamese Army wanted control over; the Oceanview outpost was just at the edge of the demilitarized zone that separated North and South Vietnam. According to marines in his battalion, by early 1969, Peterson and his men were having a growing problem with North Vietnamese soldiers who would sneak inside American bases with explosives.

Just months after Michael Peterson's arrival, the official log of the unit's activities recorded that on the night of February 22, 1969, numerous positions across South Vietnam were being attacked by the North Vietnamese Army. At Oceanview, the fighting would continue for six hours. As Michael Peterson, the highest ranking officer at Oceanview, recalled the events of that night, he said his outpost spotted enemy troops through night-vision telescopes. Peterson himself, from his command bunker, saw twenty-five enemy soldiers descending near Oceanview. It was a life-and-death situation and his outpost was in jeopardy.

In recalling the incident, Peterson would confide that he demanded his patrol not shoot at enemy troops until he gave the command. Even though Peterson would later claim that instead of listening to his order, his patrol panicked and opened fire, in an interview that was taped right after the battle in 1969, Peterson had said something different: he had admitted that his crew opened fire on his order.

Whatever the case, when the crew from Oceanview had opened fire that night, killing two and wounding others, it was Michael Peterson who was finally able to stop the firing, long enough, at least, to pull his marines back to the command post. In a dramatic moment following the return of his men, Peterson's nineteen-year-old radio operator, Corporal Jack Alfred Peterson, died in Michael's arms, saying, "I hurt, Lieutenant, I hurt."

Michael Peterson would later incorporate part of the Oceanview battle into his novel *A Time of War.* It was a novel that was so epic, Peterson's editors would liken it to the James Jones masterpiece *From Here to Eternity.* Calling Peterson's account a "classic story of Vietnam," the book jacket described *A Time of War* as "a richly textured novel" that captures "the essence of a time and place." Indeed. Peterson did recount the 1969 battle in one scene in particular, which detailed a lieutenant who sent two men to their death. In that same scene, Peterson described a marine who had to be restrained for being angry at the lieutenant for deliberately getting their men killed by sending them out on patrol.

Perhaps it was based on true life, certainly much of it was fictionalized, but in any case, *A Time of War* was Peterson's way of chronicling the brutal action he'd witnessed in the fields of his remote outpost. True to his own account of what happened that night, one of the marine warriors, who dies in the lieutenant's arms, repeated the same real-life line, "I hurt, Lieutenant, I hurt."

But the recollections of Michael Peterson, while dramatically fictionalized in his war novel, were never entirely confirmed by all of his former battalion marines. Apparently, Peterson's memory of the Oceanview battle, was not quite the same version that everyone else had recorded. One of the members of Peterson's company, Corporal Leo Hazelton, would later tell reporters that Michael Peterson panicked. Hazelton would confide that as the North Vietnamese soldiers began to descend on Oceanview that night, Michael Peterson had to be restrained because the lieutenant was "running around in circles."

In Hazelton's reported account of the 1969 battle, when Michael Peterson learned that no reinforcements were being sent to his outpost, Peterson acted as if "the world was coming to an end." Another marine who was at Oceanview that night, Dennis Coney, recollected that when things got really heated at the outpost, "somebody had to grab Michael Peterson and slap him," forcing the young lieutenant to face reality.

At the end of the battle, the North Vietnamese withdrew before dawn, never having injured any member of the Oceanview outpost. The men who died, it turned out, were killed by members of their own battalion. Of

course Lieutenant Peterson would continue to claim
that it was his *troop* who panicked and opened fire, un-
knowingly killing members of their own patrol. But Leo
Hazelton and others would assert that the Oceanview
troop lost American soldiers because they acted on
Michael Peterson's panicked command. "Peterson didn't
know it was our own people," Hazelton later told the
News & Observer.

Michael Peterson would deny being the cause of any
battle fire; he would maintain that his troop panicked because the enemy was chasing them. Of course one could
never know the actual truth about the 1969 battle. Some
of the enlisted men blamed Peterson for the "friendly
fire" deaths of their fellow soldiers. Others in the Oceanview troop would praise Lieutenant Peterson for his
valiant efforts, claiming Peterson behaved like a leader,
that Peterson was able to get them through the night.

After the battle was over, for his successful defense of
the Oceanview outpost, Michael Peterson received the
Silver Star of Valor. At the end of his tour of duty, Peterson also received the Bronze Star for leadership in
combat. For many years following that 1969 battle, Peterson would tell the story of how he was injured that
night in Vietnam, the night his radio operator was killed.
According to stories told by Michael Peterson, his radio
operator had stepped on a land mine when he was
killed, a land mine that sent shrapnel into Peterson's leg,
earning him a Purple Heart.

But there was never any documentation of a Purple
Heart in Michael Peterson's military record, nor was there
any record of a land mine exploding. When Peterson ran
for mayor of Durham in 1999, when he was forced to
admit that in actuality he was injured in a traffic accident
in Japan, Peterson would explain that the accident happened just after he left Vietnam, and would claim that

he spent months in a hospital with dying and wounded soldiers.

To members of his shocked family, who didn't understand why Michael would misrepresent something as significant as a Purple Heart, Peterson would claim that his memory of that time period was too painful for him to discuss in further detail.

Years later, when local reporters later speculated that Michael Peterson's Vietnam combat might have shaped Peterson's character, that the 1969 battle might have had some bearing on the man standing trial for murder, it would be Peterson's attorney David Rudolf, who would rush to Peterson's defense.

Disappointed over the *News & Observer* article that detailed the differing stories of the "Battle at Oceanview," Rudolf felt it was unfair for local reporters to bring up old stories about Vietnam. Rudolf would assert that, even if it were true that Michael Peterson panicked in the first few minutes of battle, all that mattered was that his client "pulled it back together and won a Silver Star."

Twenty-five

After his three-month recovery in Japan, Michael Peterson joined his wife, Patricia, in the Frankfurt region of Germany, where she was teaching elementary school at the Rhein-Main Air Base. It was the early 1970s, and Patricia Peterson was happy to have Michael back by her side. She had missed her husband dearly, and was anxious to start a family. By the mid-1970s, Patricia and Michael had become the parents of two beautiful boys, Clayton and Todd.

All of them enjoyed the expatriate life, spending their time with the American military families on the base. For Patricia, working for the Department of Defense was a way of fulfilling her dream. She loved being an educator, and raising her children away from American materialism was an extra bonus. Michael was happy to be a part of the air force's base as well. He spent his time writing, jogging, working out at the gym, and he socialized with a small group of Patricia's friends.

Patricia's best friend was Elizabeth McKee, a level-headed young woman who had expatriated herself from America in the late 1960s. Also a schoolteacher at the Rhein-Main Air Base, Elizabeth was happier living overseas. Liz was very fluent in German and French, she enjoyed traveling around Europe, and she was good at teaching. Children of military families on the base flocked to her.

Elizabeth had many friends, and as time passed, she became extremely close with both Michael and Patricia Peterson. In many ways, they had become like family. In fact, Michael and Patricia became such close companions, they even talked Liz into spending a summer with them in Durham one year. It was back in the late '70s, the end of the hippie era, that Liz agreed to stay with Patricia and Mike in the Durham home they still owned. The three of them became very close during that summer in North Carolina, especially after Liz had some kind of abrasion surgery done to her skin at the Duke University Medical Center. Liz needed special care, and the Petersons became a great source of love and support for her.

Back in Germany, in the early 1980s, Elizabeth met Captain George Ratliff at a party held at the Air Force Officers' Club. If ever there was love at first sight, the two of them experienced it. George and Liz fell head over heels. An air force navigator who was almost ten years her junior, George Ratliff had come from a small Texas town. George was already married and divorced from his Texas A&M sweetheart, and his air force friends recalled how elated George was when he first met Liz. Even though they came from different backgrounds—she was a New England girl with a love of classical music, he was a Texas cowboy who drank beer—the two of them became inseparable.

On their wedding day in early 1981, Liz and George glowed. They had chosen to have a small civil ceremony at the Gothic-gabled Roemer City Hall, a medieval building that suited their storybook romance. Elizabeth's matron of honor was Patricia Peterson. George's best man was fellow air force navigator Randy Durham. Elizabeth wore a simple white dress with a garland of roses in her hair; George wore his military whites. The pair looked stunning, and shared vows that people believed could never be broken.

Missing from the occasion was their friend, Michael Peterson. He was the only person who avoided the reception, which was held in a small town called Klein-Gerau. Everyone there was absolutely delighted on that occasion. One of Elizabeth's sisters had flown over from New England, as had some of George's family, and Elizabeth and George were the two happiest people on earth. After a romantic honeymoon spent in a castle hideaway, the couple moved into an exquisite cottage in Klein-Gerau. They enjoyed the peace of living in a country setting, not far from the air force base, and it came as a big surprise when Elizabeth got pregnant right away. Shortly before Christmas of that same year, she would give birth to their first daughter, Margaret, a healthy, happy girl. They nicknamed her Gigi.

When Margaret was born, Patricia Peterson was one of the friends who helped out at the hospital in Wiesbaden. People recalled that Elizabeth couldn't believe how blessed she was at the time. To Elizabeth, it was a miracle that she'd found such a brave young man who adored her, that she was actually starting a family at her age, in her late thirties. And George was equally ecstatic. A quiet and shy type, he had always dreamed of having a true love with someone, of sharing a lifetime together.

A navigator on C-130 airplanes, large aircrafts, the size of 737 commercial jets, George Ratliff was a highly regarded officer in the U.S. Air Force who frequently spent long stretches away from his home. His main duty was to deliver troops and supplies along the Berlin corridor, but he was also called upon for certain top secret missions. George never discussed his military service, not even with his wife, and Liz understood that. There were certain things that Liz didn't need to know about.

Her main concern was that her husband remained safe. She trusted that the officers in George's squadron were all top-notch, but she worried about his dangerous missions.

George and Liz Ratliff were living in the Cold War era, which meant George and his fellow air force officers were flying over Communist territory. His squadron supplied "special support" for the U.S. military, and often their missions were veiled in code, deemed "highly sensitive." For the most part, Liz was content to keep uninformed about the secret military aspects of her husband's life. She really only wanted to know George as a loving husband and devoted father. Liz appreciated her time together with George. The two shared a unique bond, a rare connection that many people never find. The two of them would communicate without talking, and whenever he was home, George and Liz enjoyed happy times. Still crazy in love with each other, the two would soon learn that Liz was pregnant again. The news came very quickly, and George and Liz were elated to add Martha into their lives, just a little over a year after Margaret was born.

In his four years of service in Germany, George had become close with Major Bruce Berner, a senior flight officer who often flew back and forth between Frankfurt and Berlin. Flying special missions together along the three Berlin corridors of East and West Germany, the two men became good friends.

"It was always a real pleasure to listen to George direct a mission," Major Berner would recall. "There was a sensitive navigational mission that he was dealing with all the time, which was serious business. He was actually standing up for most of the flight, navigating, directing the flight, directing every little turn that we made. And George would do it with a smile, so he was a really pleasant guy to be in that position, to essentially lead the crew."

At the same time that George and Bruce were getting to know each other, the two officers' wives, Elizabeth

Ratliff and Amybeth Berner, also began developing a tight friendship. Even though Liz was much older, Amybeth being in her twenties, both women had been raised in New England, and both women preferred European ways. As they shared their philosophies and perspectives, Liz and Amybeth found they had so much in common, Liz became like Amybeth's big sister. Liz was a role model for Amybeth, who felt hopeful that she too could be such a patient mom, such a loving spirit, if and when she might have her own child.

And Liz had her fun side. She liked to sip champagne with strawberries, she liked to shop in big cities, and she enjoyed a five-star restaurant now and then. It was through Liz that Amybeth would learn more about the finer things in life. From Wedgwood china to how to arrange place settings, from fine wines to Laura Ashley prints—Liz knew about these kind of things. And Amybeth loved learning about the beauty of a particular lace pattern or the simplicity of a certain wildflower arrangement.

A newlywed who was trying to start a family of her own, Amybeth enjoyed spending time at home with Liz and her girls, admiring all the special care Liz took with her daughters, Margaret and Martha. Liz was musically inclined, so she would sing to the girls, she would play the piano and the guitar. Liz went out of her way to make things special for the girls, and Amybeth felt that being around Liz was an enchanted experience. She and Bruce lived in Graefenhausen, a town a few miles away, where most of the other American military officers were. She and her husband were neighbors to Michael and Patricia Peterson, so the whole group became very chummy. Over the months, and then the years, the Berners, the Petersons, and the Ratliffs got to know each other well. They socialized together on occasions, and traveled in groups to cities throughout Europe.

"Officers' wives tend to live according to protocol," Amybeth confided, "but the women in our squadron were very kind. Nobody had a snooty attitude, not in our squadron. In our small group, people were very personable, very caring. Maybe it was because it was Special Missions. Maybe because our husbands were gone a lot, and we needed each other."

Twenty-six

As George and Liz Ratliff continued to become closer to Bruce and Amybeth Berner, they all agreed that life in Germany was more enjoyable than it was in America. It was easy to go on trips, it was easy to hang out and do things socially, and no one focused on American materialism. No one tried to outdo each other with designer labels, no one placed burdens on each other by having to keep up with the latest toys. People in Germany seemed to be above that nonsense. The Europeans seemed more cultured. They talked about art and music, they talked about interesting films. And their sensibility seemed much more pleasing, especially to Elizabeth Ratliff.

Elizabeth wanted to make sure that her daughters remained in Europe. She wanted them to be cultured, she wanted them to have a slower-paced and peaceful life. But she also wanted them to have more of a "world consciousness" than most Americans had. It was very important to Liz that her girls would grow up with a worldly sense of being. Liz herself had grown tired of America. It was Liz's upbringing in Rhode Island, perhaps, that felt too puritanical and too hypocritical for her.

Liz had been raised by nuns in a Catholic school, and the nuns had been so strict and unforgiving, they had scolded her for the smallest reasons. Things like wearing patent leather shoes were considered too sexual. The nuns implied that men could see up Liz's skirt in the shoes' reflection. Liz found these kind of teachings absurd, and by the time she turned twenty, Liz announced that she planned to leave New England for good. Instead of seeking fame and fortune, Liz wanted to travel the globe, and she spent time traveling throughout parts of Asia and Europe before landing her teaching job in Germany.

Feeling the same way Liz did, once he met his wife, George became intent on staying in Germany as well. He was quite happy being a part of the 7405th Operations Squadron, flying classified missions throughout Germany and in other undisclosed parts of the world. He planned to continue his work for the U.S. Air Force, operating out of Germany, for as long as possible. But just months after Martha was born, Captain George Ratliff left on a mission to Central America, and he died under mysterious circumstances.

George Ratliff was on a top secret mission outside Panama—he was there during the time when the United States was making preparations for an invasion of the island of Grenada.

George's friend Bruce Berner hadn't flown that particular mission, known as "Goat Rope," because his wife, Amybeth, had suffered a serious back injury and was hospitalized in Wiesbaden for a month. Bruce had to stay at home to care for Amybeth until she could get back on her feet again. On the day George Ratliff died, Bruce Berner happened to be at his unit's highly secured building on the base, working in the room where messages were transmitted. Often his squadron would receive directives from the Pentagon. But on that given day, when his commander took the call, Bruce Berner learned that George Ratliff, his thirty-four-year-old buddy, had mysteriously died in his sleep.

When Bruce's commander told the rest of the squadron

about the sudden death, there was a lot of silence that followed. No one else had died on the mission, and there was no reasonable explanation why George Ratliff had died so young. There would be an autopsy report to follow, but because of the secret nature of George Ratliff's work, that information would not be released for years.

When the word of George's death reached Liz, she couldn't accept it as true. Bruce was the person who helped break the news. Others surrounded her, trying to console Liz—but it was as if her own heart melted away when she heard that her husband had died. George's friend Randy Durham received a one-day clearance to Panama to retrieve Captain Ratliff's personal effects, and then to accompany his body back to Bay City, Texas.

In Germany, with no one else to turn to, Elizabeth leaned on Michael Peterson, who helped her make the necessary arrangements for handling all the military paperwork, and for flying back to the United States for the funeral. At a loss because the military would not reveal any details whatsoever about George Ratliff's death, Elizabeth's other friends felt grateful that Michael was able to pick up some of the slack for the widow. Being a former marine, Peterson was good at dealing with military red tape. Michael had always been close with Liz. They were mutual admirers of each other, and he took on her plight without question.

But Michael's shoulder was not strong enough. From the moment of George's death, everyone around her could see that Elizabeth had no real will to live. At the burial ceremony in Texas, on October 27, 1983, Randy Durham presented Elizabeth with the American flag that had been draped over George's coffin. The widow was accompanied by Michael Peterson. She had been greeted by members of the Ratliff family, people who, understandably, shared her shock and grief. But Liz could not be calmed. Her grief was overwhelming. Her tears wouldn't end.

Just before she left Texas to return to Germany, Liz confessed to her sister-in-law, Connie Ratliff, that she wished to join her husband in death. Liz confided that she had roamed the Ratliffs' expansive property, hoping and praying for the universe to take her to Heaven.

But Elizabeth had her girls.

She knew she had to return home to them.

Liz felt she couldn't bear to go back to her house, so she sent word through Michael and asked that her friends have all of her belongings moved out of the cottage in Klein-Gerau. A crew of people got together and packed everything up, knowing that Liz was unable to face that pretty cottage alone. As for her girls, they were too young to know what was happening. People were pitching in, doing whatever they could to make life more bearable for Liz and her daughters. But of course, the girls would never remember any of that.

Michael was helping with the money Liz had gotten from George's insurance policy and what was owed to Liz from the military. And Patricia was helpful with the girls, trying to get them settled in a row house, located just a few doors away from the Peterson place, in Graefenhausen. But for Elizabeth—her life, as she knew it, had ended. Her days of being a stay-at-home mom were over, she would return back to teaching, and she began hiding behind a wall. Amybeth, who had lost her dad at a young age, knew how devastated someone could feel. Amybeth would go over and talk to Liz every day, trying to see if there was anything she could say to raise her friend's spirits.

"I know that you feel really bad," Amybeth would tell Liz, "and death is a horrible thing. But I know that eventually you're going to feel better."

"No, you don't understand," Liz would insist, "he was the love of my life."

And so it was that Liz could not be consoled. She would somehow go on, for the sake of her girls, but Liz was only going through the motions of existence. She would set special breakfast tables, she would sing little songs, she would spend weekends stitching pretty quilts—but having to do all of that at the end of every workday just left Liz feeling even more drained and depleted. As the weeks passed, and the holiday season approached, Liz began to slide into a deep depression.

Her sadness became greater. And there seemed to be no end in sight.

Liz had asked that most of George's things be placed in a special room in the house. She also had his clothes placed in her bedroom. She had some of them put away in closets and drawers. She had a pair of George's eyeglasses and other little items of his strewn around the room, as if George were still living with her.

Michael Peterson thought Liz was crazy. He had trouble dealing with Liz's mood swings. Other people would talk to her about her moods at length, trying to get her encouraged about being a new mom, trying to make Liz realize how fortunate it was that she had two beautiful daughters. She needed to celebrate Christmas, to have parties for their birthdays; there was so much life ahead of her.

Her good friends Thomas and Cheryl Appel-Schumacher, who also were connected with the air force base, tried their best to support Liz emotionally. They wanted her to be strong for her girls, and because Liz was so tearful and sad, they had grown quite worried about Margaret and Martha. Being one of the most practical of Liz's friends, Cheryl didn't want to see Liz grieving all the time. She knew it was unhealthy for the girls to see their mom so tearful. Cheryl would insist that Liz not allow herself to go to that dark place. She would encourage Liz to concentrate on the future, helping Liz regain her sense of faith.

But Liz loved George so much, she was so lost without him. She retreated into negative thoughts about herself. She began telling people that she'd lost hope. Elizabeth didn't think that anything would get better. She blamed herself for not being a good enough person. She started to believe that she had never deserved a man as wonderful as George.

Twenty-seven

Just months before George Ratliff died, Michael Peterson had published his first novel. The folks at the military base were impressed, particularly since the book was published in America by Signet, and was released as a mass-market paperback. It seemed that Peterson was on his way to a promising career, and to the people who counted on him, like Patricia and Elizabeth, that was a wonderful thing.

However, having a book on the stands about Vietnam didn't mean that Peterson was absolutely admired by the military personnel around him. Many thought of Peterson as a braggart. They would hear him go into details about the Central Intelligence Agency and would cut him off. Ranking officers in the military didn't need to hear any of that kind of bunk. In any context, trying to sound connected to the CIA was ludicrous, yet Peterson would sometimes assert just that. For certain people, Peterson was a complete turnoff. He might have had some success as a writer, but he was largely considered a misfit. For one thing, Peterson was a night owl, he kept strange hours. For another, he often seemed to disappear on weekends, he was somewhat shady. To most straight military people, Michael Peterson was a wanna-be. He joked a lot and was fun to be around, but he wasn't the type of guy anyone would want to get close to.

"I saw him as the husband of a schoolteacher who was trying to make a living at writing," Bruce Berner confided. "I wasn't interested in reading any of his books, or any of his stories, because I saw him as an oddball. It wasn't that I had anything against Michael at the time. It's just that I wouldn't have felt comfortable talking to him intimately."

As it turned out, even though they were next-door neighbors, Bruce and Amybeth Berner didn't really see Peterson all that much. Michael Peterson would usually sleep in the day and work in the evening. Bruce and Amybeth would notice that Michael would spend hours away from home, either at the air force gym or away on some mysterious business.

No one in their group recalled seeing Michael Peterson on any regular schedule. He often let his wife and kids do things on their own, only occasionally accompanying his family, even on their trips to other parts of Europe. In fact, it was Bruce and Amybeth Berner who took Patricia, Clayton, and Todd on one of their very first visits to Paris. The boys were young, and Bruce had his two girls from his first marriage staying with him, so the two families made the trip together, doing all the usual tourist things, seeing the Eiffel Tower, eating at fine French restaurants.

"The fact that Michael wasn't available to go to Paris, I probably didn't think too much about it," Bruce recalled. "I had already decided that the guy was going to do pretty much whatever he wanted to do, and it wasn't going to make any sense to me. He would get up late in the day. He would decide he'd go out and exercise in the gym late at night. Maybe he'd go out and run at two in the morning. I mean, this is the way he was."

Everyone around the Petersons pretty much accepted that Patricia was the breadwinner, and Michael was the free spirit. That was the nature of their relationship.

They didn't seem to act in unison, especially when it came to sharing the responsibility of raising the boys. In terms of communication, one-on-one, Michael was good with his boys. But Patricia doted on the boys, and babied Todd and Clayton even up to the time that they were ages eight and ten.

As for the day-to-day drudgery of household chores, most of that fell on Patricia. Michael had become pre-occupied, even more so after George's death, when he took on all the responsibility of caring for Elizabeth and the girls, and the Ratliff estate. Michael had become intensely involved with the military, fighting to get Liz paid, fighting to get George's autopsy, fighting to discover the truth behind his death.

It would be years later that people would learn that George Ratliff was found to have had traces of cyanide in his system, that George had died of a sudden heart attack, that he had been taking special medication for a heart condition, prescribed to him by doctors in Germany. People later wondered if George's medication had been tampered with before he left on his mission.

Because Michael was put off about doing any household chores, friends felt sorry for Patricia. Friends got the impression that Patricia was pleasant, that she had her hands full with her kids, but she wasn't entirely happy. When weekend events would come up, if Michael was not around, Patricia would make up excuses for him. She would never really say what her husband was busy doing, but neighbors would know that Michael Peterson's silver Mercedes was gone, that he was off on a romp somewhere.

Some people thought it was sad, the way Patricia would be alone so much, the way she had to take on most of the housework and the breadwinning of the Peterson household. They saw her as a very nice lady, but also as a passive person, easily controlled by Michael. It was strange that Patricia, as close as she felt to George Ratliff, had opted not to go to the funeral in Texas. It was weird that she never questioned Michael's time spent with Elizabeth, which grew more and more frequent as the months after George's death passed.

Patricia, in a sense, had become Michael's shadow. Amybeth saw her as a odd woman, someone who rarely changed her outfits, someone who wasn't very good at taking care of herself. Amybeth couldn't really picture Michael with Patricia, especially since he was so buff, such a good-looking man with a well-kept physique. Patricia dressed in prairie-style clothes, and was the opposite of Michael in every way. Amybeth and other people sometimes wondered if Michael had become romantically interested in Liz.

Not that Liz would consider it. Not for a second.

But folks were talking, through the grapevine, and finding out little things that led them to believe that Michael might have developed a secret crush on Liz. There was the knowledge that even though Patricia was Elizabeth's matron of honor, Michael deliberately chose not to attend George and Elizabeth's wedding. Later after the wedding reception, Patricia made up excuses about Michael being busy at the gym.

"It was almost like Patricia wore blinders," Amybeth recalled. "She wouldn't see anything bad, she would only see good. It was like she refused to look at things that were bad or difficult. She only wanted to be sweet."

But if people suspected anything about Michael, they didn't talk about it very much. They knew better than to suspect that Liz would be interested in her best friend's husband, and watching the interaction, they would notice that Liz, like Patricia, was usually quiet and passive around Michael. If anything, Liz was pursuing Patricia's friendship more than she was Michael's. But since Michael had a "take-charge" personality, it was easy to see how he could control the communication and intrude among the three of them. As for Liz's girls, Margaret and Martha, obviously it was Michael, with his take-charge attitude, more than Patricia, who would be the one to look over their well-being.

As days and months went by, Elizabeth was shifting her perspective somewhat, trying to participate in the lives of her daughters, even bringing them to social gatherings at friends' homes in Graefenhausen. Whenever Michael was present, he would become the center of attention, the entertainer at any given dinner or birthday party. People liked to sit around and let Michael tell stories. He was that type of guy, filled with tales of exotic travel, and he had a bellowing voice that took over any room.

People noticed that Michael never really gave them any personal details about his life. His stories were always focused on political events, or on details about a certain place in time. There was nothing ever said about his childhood, about his schooling, or even about his Vietnam experiences. But then, no one ever paid it much thought. Michael was a tremendous storyteller; he was witty, bawdy, intense, and very insightful.

Finding herself always tired and overwhelmed, Elizabeth decided to try out a nanny, Barbara O'Hara, a beautiful young woman who was unhappy working for a family who lived just down the street. Barbara loved the two little girls and was very good with children, and Barbara and Elizabeth hit it off right away. Within a week, Elizabeth decided that it would be best for Barbara to move in with her full-time. The girls needed constant attention and Liz couldn't keep burdening her neighbors while she was busy teaching.

The arrangement with Barbara O'Hara turned out to work very well for Liz. Her girls loved Barbara, they were learning new things with her every day, and Barbara fit

right in with the group of Elizabeth's friends as well—
the Berners, the Appel-Schumachers, and the Petersons.

With Barbara around, there was music played in the
house, there was some semblance of normalcy again,
and everyone was happy to see that. Michael took a fond
liking to Barbara, and even though she was much
younger, the two became buddies. Michael and Barbara
would sometimes go out together on weekends. There
was nothing sexual about their relationship, but the
two shared their own bond. Whenever Barbara wasn't
baby-sitting, it seemed, she'd find time to run off to
Darmstadt or somewhere, often tooling around with
Michael.

Amybeth would recall thinking it was strange—seeing
the two of them together. Amybeth and Barbara had also
become friendly, and she would sometimes question Barbara, wondering why the young woman was spending
so much time with Michael.

Peterson seemed to act like a kid around Elizabeth's
nanny. He would hang around with her alot . . . but Amybeth could never get a straight answer about what the
two of them did together.

Twenty-eight

As a nanny, Barbara O'Hara grew close to Margaret and Martha, but as she continued to work for Elizabeth Ratliff, eventually their opposite lifestyles began to clash. Barbara was younger and full of life. She was staying out late; she was still a party girl. Elizabeth, on the other hand, was a homebody. She still didn't like to hear loud music. She didn't like to hear noise. Still somewhat pensive and brooding, Liz wanted order in her life. After a number of months of uncertainty, Michael suggested that perhaps Barbara should find her own place. Actually, it was Michael who helped Barbara move out. He was the one who found her a perfect apartment close to Liz's place.

Things worked out better that way, for everybody. Liz could have her peaceful weekends, her quiet weeknights. And Barbara, after a weekend of fun, would appear chipper every Monday morning, ready for a week of full-time work. Even as small children, Margaret and Martha were happy with the arrangement. They loved Barbara, their nanny spoiled them. But there was nothing better than spending time with their mom, who made sure they were dressed up like little dolls, showing them off to all her friends who would stop by for visits.

By the time Barbara was happily living on her own, working for Elizabeth as a daytime nanny, almost two years had gone by since George's death. It was a time period when Elizabeth was finally having some breakthroughs. With her daughters getting older, walking and talking independently, and looking so much like George, Liz was beginning to come around to see the positive side of life. As a surprise, Liz decided she would throw a big anniversary party for her friends Tom and Cheryl Appel-Schumacher. It was just before Thanksgiving, the start of a new holiday season, and it would be the first joyful event Liz was hosting since she became a widow.

As Liz had always done in the past, she put all of her heart and soul into the party, going to great lengths to make it an event. Liz wasn't just throwing a wedding anniversary celebration for Cheryl and Tom, she was opening her home to all of their family and all of her dearest friends. Cheryl and Tom had just arrived back from the States, and Liz had the party completely under wraps. Liz had everything arranged so they would be totally surprised. It was something she was doing as a welcome-home gift for them.

Back to her old self, Liz went all out, as did her friends, each preparing mouthwatering appetizers and extraordinary desserts. Liz wanted everything she did to be homemade, created from scratch, and she filled her home with candles and chose selections of classical music as she prepared all day Saturday for the special occasion. Liz felt like she was coming back to life, and because she enjoyed things that were refined, she wanted nothing but the best for her friends. As she set her tables and placed her serving platters out, Liz decided on Beethoven to start. She would serve the best French champagne and accompany it with caviar.

But when it began snowing on that particular Saturday, Liz became a bit panicked that the party might not be pulled off. She was hoping the snow would stop. She didn't want any cancellations. And then, to complicate matters, Liz had a bit of car trouble when she went to pick up some last-minute groceries. Suddenly Liz was worried about her own personal safety as she realized that the road conditions were really bad. She decided she needed to make arrangements to take her BMW in for service right away.

The thought occurred to her that someone might have tampered with her car; she had no idea why it was acting strangely. Even with the party approaching, she could take no chances, and as soon as she made it home, she phoned Michael. Luckily, he was there when she called to ask if he'd follow her over to the dealership. Of course Michael agreed to help her out.

But at the time, Michael was busy, on his way out. He suggested that he follow her over to BMW on Sunday, deciding it would be best for Liz not to worry about the car that night. To make life easier, Patricia got on the phone to say it would be no problem for Liz to catch a ride to work with her on Monday morning.

For a few days prior to the surprise party, Elizabeth had been getting some hang-up calls that had been making her nervous. On that same wintery Saturday afternoon, just minutes after she spoke to Michael, Liz called Amybeth looking for Barbara. It temporarily had stopped snowing, but the roads were still dangerous, and Liz told Amybeth that she was hoping to catch Barbara or get a message to her, because she needed to ask Barbara to spend the night.

"Why do you want Barbara to stay there tonight? You'll have so many people in the house already," Amybeth wondered.

"I've been having stress headaches lately and sinus headaches," Liz told her.

"Well, I've been having those myself. It's the allergies from the farmers' fields. I can drop you by some tablets I take—"

"No. No, I would really like Barbara to stay with me tonight," Liz insisted. "I've been getting some hang-up calls this week, and I think someone might be watching the house."

"Hang-up calls? What do you mean?"

"It's just someone calling me a bunch of times this week. Three times a day, maybe," Liz told her. "I don't know what it means. But I've been feeling eerie around the house."

"Do you have any idea who it might be?"

"Absolutely none. It's the craziest thing. I pick up the phone and someone is there faintly breathing. But they're not saying anything."

"I'll call around to see if I can find Barbara, okay?" Amybeth said. "But if you need to, you and the girls can always come stay with us."

Of course Liz would never impose on people like that. She promised Amybeth that she would make sure all her doors were locked every night, and then Liz moved the conversation back to the subject of the party. As Elizabeth finished listing the various dishes friends were preparing for the surprise, Amybeth asked if there was anything else she could do, anything Liz could think of that might make her feel better.

But Liz really had nothing in mind. She was sorry she'd worried her friend, and said she was going back to finish her chores of the day, expecting to see Amybeth and a houseful of people by early evening.

Twenty-nine

People didn't remember Michael staying for very long at the party. Elizabeth didn't seem to mind, nor did anyone else seem to notice, because there were so many people who showed up. To everyone's glee, the surprise was pulled off. Cheryl and Tom couldn't get over all the trouble everyone had gone to, and they were thankful to see their friend Liz had gotten herself back into the swing of things. The party was a great success. There was the right mix of people, the right hue of lighting, and people laughed and drank well into the night.

But Liz had confided at one point that she was still feeling uncomfortable about being alone in her home. It was early on in the party that Liz had pulled Amybeth aside in the kitchen and the two had a brief chat. Liz was still very nervous that someone was hanging around the back alley. She felt certain that someone was watching her. There had been more hang-up calls on that day, and there was a question about why her car was acting up.

Amybeth wanted to know if Liz had been dating anyone secretly. She thought, perhaps, that Liz had a thwarted love interest on her hands. Liz confessed that there was a man she had been interested in, but nothing had come of it yet. Liz wouldn't name the man, and Amybeth didn't feel it was the time to press the issue.

With the party going on, their conversation shifted rapidly, and Amybeth didn't discover much more.

Worried about her friend, Amybeth wasn't sure what to think. She couldn't understand why her friend was acting so paranoid. Liz was giving her mixed signals, and Amybeth tried to decide if she should say anything to her husband, Bruce.

"Liz asked Barbara again, when she was at the party, if Barbara would stay over. She said she wasn't feeling right," Amybeth recalled. "Liz was feeling weird, like she wasn't feeling safe around the house."

But when Barbara said she wasn't available, apparently Liz didn't say much to try to persuade her. As Amybeth listened to their exchange, she decided not to say anything to Bruce. There was no need to worry her husband in the middle of a party, especially when it seemed like Liz might very well have been overreacting.

Amybeth took note that Liz had spoken to Barbara in a very casual way about staying over at the house. To Amybeth's surprise, Liz hadn't confided any feelings of being in danger. Elizabeth merely wanted to know if Barbara might consider spending the night, just to help her out a little.

Barbara had become more like family to Elizabeth, the two of them had a sincere relationship. They felt they could level with each other. They didn't need to stand on ceremonies, and spending the night was something that Barbara did whenever she felt like it. Even though Barbara had her own apartment, Liz still kept Barbara's room intact, and Barbara was always welcome to stay.

But Barbara didn't really have time for Elizabeth that particular evening. The nanny wasn't really all that close to Cheryl and Tom Apple-Schumacher, and with all of their family around, people who were strangers to her, Barbara didn't feel the need to be present for the wedding anniversary party.

Barbara told Liz she was already committed to go else-
where that night. People later discovered she might have
met up with Michael Peterson. Whatever Barbara's plans
were, Elizabeth realized her nanny had not come over to
celebrate with Cheryl and Tom. Her nanny was there, really, for Margaret and Martha's sake.

The girls were all dressed up in little lace dresses; it
was a big occasion for them to be hosting guests in their
home. Barbara had stopped by to spend a little time with
them, bringing them a platter of cookies. They were pre-
cious girls, their nanny loved them, and she wanted to
gush over their fancy outfits and their mom's beautifully
decorated party.

With their frilly ankle socks and patent leather shoes,
Margaret and Martha spent the evening downstairs with
the adults until they were finally too tired to stay awake.
For much of the night, Liz seemed joyful, happily serving and joking with her friends. When she had kissed
Barbara good-bye early on, Liz said she was glad that Barbara had a chance to see how beautiful the girls looked.

Elizabeth never knew where Barbara disappeared to.
She didn't have time to worry about it, especially after
most of her guests had gone, leaving her alone with Tom
and Cheryl to handle the cleanup.

The next day, Elizabeth took her girls sledding in the
fresh clean snow. It was an enjoyable afternoon, followed
by a visit to the Petersons' home for dinner. After having
a quick bite to eat with Michael and Patricia, it was time
for Liz to get home with her girls. It was early Sunday
evening, and Michael would follow Elizabeth to the
BMW dealership, where she would drop off her car.

Thirty

Barbara O'Hara arrived at Elizabeth Ratliff's house early on Monday morning, November 25, 1985. She had taken a taxi to get there, and she asked the driver to wait for a minute because something seemed strange. There were lights on in the hallway and the living room, which had never been Liz's habit, and after remembering the conversation with Liz on Saturday night, the nanny was concerned about things looking out of place.

As she rushed to the front door, she realized it wasn't locked.

And then, at her feet, at the foot of the stairs, there was a body lying there. In a panic, Barbara began shouting for Liz to come downstairs. She kept shouting Liz's name, and then she ran upstairs to see where Liz was. There was blood all up and down the stairway. Barbara was horrified to see that the two girls were asleep in their beds, all alone.

Barbara grabbed the upstairs telephone to dial the Petersons, but the phone line was dead. Running back down the stairs, with the taxi driver still waiting outside, Barbara suddenly realized that she was looking at Elizabeth, practically unrecognizable, at the bottom of the staircase. Elizabeth was lying in a pool of her own blood, and Barbara felt Elizabeth's body, searching for a sign of life.

Barbara noticed that Elizabeth still had her snow

boots on, which struck her as unusual, since Liz never wore shoes inside her house. Running back outside to the taxi driver, Barbara signaled for help. The nanny felt sick to her stomach, like she was about to throw up, and she didn't know what to do first. She wanted to get the girls out of there, away from all the blood before they woke up. She wanted to get medical people there, hoping and praying that Elizabeth was still alive. But with no access to a phone, she only had the taxi driver to assist her. Barbara realized she'd have to ask the kind stranger to watch over the house while she ran down the street, over to the Petersons' place.

Michael got up out of his bed to find Barbara frantically crying at his door. Patricia hadn't left for work yet, and the two of them listened to Barbara's hysterical pleas. Michael followed her over to Elizabeth's immediately, where they both looked in horror at Elizabeth Ratliff, who was lying facedown, bleeding, at the bottom of the stairs. As Barbara sobbed, leaning against her friend's neck, feeling the warmth in Elizabeth's body, Michael Peterson leaned down to feel for a pulse.

"I think she still might be alive," Barbara told him. "See if she's breathing."

"She's dead, Barbara," Michael said. "I believe she's dead."

"No, she's not. Her skin is still warm," she insisted.

"There's no heartbeat," Michael said.

Rushing back up the stairs, Barbara O'Hara ran to wake up Margaret and Martha, dressed the two girls, and then wrapped them in blankets. The nanny left with the two of them in her arms, taking the girls out the back, down the back alleyway. Barbara had never used the fire escape before, but she could not risk letting the girls see their mother and all that blood. Even though they were quite young, even though they might never remember the scene, Barbara thought they could wind up being traumatized.

When Michael Peterson ran back to his home, he found that Patricia had already dialed for emergency help. Within minutes, Barbara had arrived at the Petersons' place with the girls, whom the taxi driver had helped her deliver. Still in a panic, Barbara left the girls with Patricia, running next door to get Bruce and Amybeth Berner. Having no time to wait for the Berners to dress, Barbara asked that they go and try to help Liz at her home.

Barbara was shaking, but she had to contain her fright for the sake of the children. Margaret and Martha knew that something was amiss, but they had been seated in the kitchen of the Peterson home. With all her strength, Barbara tried to put on a happy face. She decided to act as rationally as possible, hoping to divert the girls by feeding them breakfast.

Michael had already gone back to tend to Elizabeth, and now that Barbara was watching the girls, Patricia went running over to her friend's house as well, just horrified to see what had happened to Liz. Patricia was in tears, but always allowing Michael to be in control, she listened to his advice and got out of the way. There was nothing any of them could do to save Liz. They had gotten there too late.

As Bruce and Amybeth arrived, they were both shocked at the amount of blood at the foot of the stairs. Elizabeth was covered by a blanket, her head was barely visible. But her feet and snow boots were standing out, and Amybeth recognized the shoes. Michael Peterson was pacing, waiting for the emergency crews to get there.

Bruce ran up the stairs to check things out, to examine all the doors and windows, looking for signs of an intruder. Amybeth, unwilling to step near Liz at first, went back to the kitchen, where she found Patricia Peterson sitting by herself, just in a complete state of shock.

To Amybeth, Patricia looked like some kind of wax figure. As Amybeth joined Patricia at the kitchen table, Mrs. Peterson was sitting in a daze, having nothing at all to say.

"When I first got there, there was no real interaction. Just nothing. Patty was like a vegetable, sitting there in front of the window," Amybeth recalled. "She was sitting at the kitchen table, not moving. Then she put her hands on her head, shaking her head. And then I remember her talking about coffee. Patty wanted to make coffee."

Amybeth realized that Patricia Peterson was not going to be of any help. In fact, Michael's wife seemed to be in la-la land for most of the day, unable to say or do much. When Cheryl and Tom Appel-Schumacher got there, just minutes after Bruce and Amybeth arrived, they, too, were struck by the amount of blood. With all the commotion, neighbors were waking up, American neighbors who wanted to see what was the matter, but Cheryl and Tom kept anyone else from entering the house. It was a dramatic scene, quite horrifying, and there was no need for others to be involved.

The authorities had not yet arrived, but Michael mumbled something to Tom and Cheryl about what he thought might have happened. There was the possibility that Elizabeth might have had some kind of stroke or something, that she'd fallen down the stairs and had bled all night long.

"The whole scene was bizarre," Amybeth confided. "Patty was basically in the kitchen and didn't move out of the kitchen. She's talking about coffee. She keeps making more coffee. And Michael is basically standing right at the front door, by the stairs, waiting for whoever it was that was supposed to come. But he's not talking that much. He's not saying anything much, which is not like him."

While Bruce Berner was up at the top of the landing, he looked around to see if anyone had been hiding behind some of the boxes that Liz had stacked. But there was no indication of any intruder. From all the blood along the stairway, Bruce had trouble believing that Elizabeth had died from a fall. But Michael Peterson had surmised that a fall had occurred, he'd told Bruce about Elizabeth's rare blood disorder. Elizabeth apparently had some kind of rare disease, similar to hemophilia.

Michael seemed to know a lot about Elizabeth's medical history, and said he'd been concerned about her because she was complaining of headaches. Michael thought Elizabeth could have fallen, perhaps from a dizzy spell.

Bruce would later call his squadron to ask to be excused from flying that day, but before he left the scene, the air force pilot had some questions of his own he tried to answer. Bruce hadn't seen very many dead people, and he had no experience with people falling, but there was something about the stairway that didn't seem right.

"The main thing I remember is, I did walk up the stairs, and there was a splattering of blood," Bruce confided. "It was right above my left shoulder, toward the top of the staircase. And I remember thinking, someone would have a really hard time banging their head against that part of the wall and making that splatter there."

As Bruce mused at the top of the stairs, looking at the tiny spots of blood, he tried to put himself into Elizabeth's position. He wondered whether small splatters would show up so high on the wall if he himself got dizzy and landed against the stairwell. Bruce thought it might be possible, but not likely. Bruce examined the texture of the wall, and once he realized that it had a rough surface, he wondered why there were no scrape marks on the stairwell. Wouldn't someone have scraped themselves as they fell?

There should have been scrapes or smears of blood. But there weren't any smears. Only tiny droplets.

Amybeth finally summoned the courage to join Bruce up on the top of the stairs. Devastated by the amount of blood, she looked in disbelief at the unusual blood spatter. The blood reached way above Amybeth's head, it was all the way up toward the top of the staircase, and suddenly she had a chilling thought.

"Bruce, this is a crime scene," she whispered.

And her husband very much agreed. But just then, the German police had arrived downstairs and the Berners could hear them speaking to Michael.

Peterson was telling them they were in the home of an American military family, asserting that the military police were on their way.

"Americanish," Peterson kept saying to the German police.

Bruce and Amybeth could hear the German police asking questions. Before they went downstairs, they took a last quick look around Liz's bedroom to see if anything was out of place. They were hoping to see signs of a struggle, but they found everything in perfect order.

The only thing that seemed unusual was something that Amybeth had noticed when she first arrived. She noticed it the minute she sat down with Patricia at Liz's kitchen table. Amybeth found it odd that Elizabeth's table was blank, bare of the girls' porcelain cereal bowls and drinking cups. She didn't mention anything about it to Patricia at the time, but Amybeth knew it was not like Liz to forget about the breakfast table for her girls.

The special breakfast setup that Liz always carefully placed out for Margaret and Martha before she went to bed every night was distinctly missing.

Thirty-one

"There's been an accident." Michael called Elizabeth's family to report. "Liz fell down the stairs and died."

Michael was on the phone with Margaret Blair, Elizabeth's sister, making arrangements to meet her in Bay City, Texas, where Elizabeth Ratliff would be buried next to her husband, George. The news came as a total shock to Margaret, who could not understand how such a thing happened to her responsible and loving sister.

Margaret was aware that Liz suffered from an odd hereditary ailment called von Willenbrand's Disease. Margaret also knew that Liz had hospital workups done in Germany regarding the disease, having been told that her bleeding disorder would be impossible to cure. Elizabeth's normal blood-clotting agents were deficient. Any cut or injury could cause a serious internal hemorrhage. Von Willenbrand's was like hemophilia. There was not much the doctors could do. They advised her to stay away from blood-thinning agents such as aspirin.

When Margaret asked if Liz's fall had caused much blood, Michael supposedly lied about it. He didn't want to alarm Margaret; she was so upset already. So Michael reportedly told Margaret that her sister only had "a little bit of blood behind her ear." He said he had been at Elizabeth's house, that he and Patricia were looking after the girls, who were doing fine, and said they were waiting for the authorities to come back with an autopsy report.

Michael explained that because of the military protocol, Elizabeth's autopsy results would probably take time. Having suffered with Liz about the secrecy behind George's death, Margaret Blair already knew the drill. Elizabeth was a Department of Defense teacher. There would be all that red tape again. Michael told Liz's sister how sorry he was about the accident, and mentioned that the investigation by the German police had indicated that Elizabeth's cause of death was a cerebral hemorrhage. He thought Elizabeth might have suffered a stroke.

Earlier that day, when the German police had arrived on the scene, Michael Peterson had given them an explanation of what might have happened. The German authorities hadn't seen anything suspicious, so when the Germans heard Michael Peterson's account of Liz Ratliff's medical history—learning of her bleeding disorder, learning that Liz Ratliff had been complaining of severe headaches two weeks prior to her death—it seemed obvious that her demise was due to the fall. They hadn't determined anything technically, but the German authorities were handling the matter.

Because Elizabeth's death did not occur on a military base, the German authorities had jurisdiction. Even though the American authorities would respond to the scene also, sending an army criminal investigator, Major Steve Lyons, to take notes on the death, it was the German authorities who were calling the shots. When Major Lyons appeared, asking what he could do to help, he was informed that the death was probably an accident, that the investigation was already under way.

There was a German emergency doctor on the scene who had found bloody spinal fluid in Elizabeth's spinal column. The German doctor's findings were consistent with cranial bleeding *sustained by a fall down the stairs.* The German doctor noted that Elizabeth Ratliff had scalp lacerations, but these lacerations were considered to be secondary to her terminal fall.

Once the German police had arrived asking questions, once the American authorities had arrived to follow up, Amybeth and Bruce Berner were convinced that the teams of police were doing a thorough job. They had waited around in the living room, expecting to be questioned, but to their amazement, they had been politely introduced to the police by Michael Peterson, and were never spoken to again.

Major Lyons had seen Elizabeth Ratliff lying on the floor in a pool of blood, but the Berners noticed that Lyons didn't walk up the entire staircase to look for other evidence. The Berners weren't told that Major Lyons's presence was strictly cursory. None of the civilians at the scene were sure about what kind of backup the American military was providing to the German police.

On the day Elizabeth had been found dead, Bruce and Amybeth Berner, Tom and Cheryl Appel-Schumacher, had all witnessed the police doing their jobs. They had witnessed a German doctor using a syringe to take spinal fluid out of Liz's body. But Tom and Cheryl were too upset by the gruesome scene. They wanted to stay clear of Elizabeth's body, and became involved with calming down Barbara, and making sure that other neighbors stayed away.

As for Bruce and Amybeth, however, they really had suspicions. They believed that further testing and autopsy results would come back to prove something other than a natural death. Neither one of them could be sure who might be held responsible, but they believed there had been an intruder.

The Berners had checked all the windows and doors,

but, with the exception of the front entrance, they were all tightly locked. Bruce and Amybeth had also checked around the outside of the property, noticing that, aside from Barbara's prints on the fire escape, there were *no other footprints in the snow.* The Berners had looked outside everywhere, around the laundry area and the back patio—but all they could see was fresh, untouched powder.

While she was still at the scene, Amybeth found a moment to talk to Barbara on the side, and she asked Barbara about the strange location of Elizabeth's body. It seemed weird that Liz was positioned as if she were *resting* at the bottom of the stairs. It didn't look like the natural result of a fall. Amybeth continued to press Barbara about it, and Barbara finally alleged that Elizabeth's body had been moved. Barbara claimed that earlier that morning, when she had first arrived at the house, Elizabeth's body was in a different position. According to Barbara, Liz's body was facedown on the stairs, her head down, her feet up, practically in an upside-down vertical position, leaning against the staircase.

Amybeth couldn't figure out why someone would have moved Elizabeth off the staircase. It made absolutely no sense, so she kept harping on Barbara, insisting that the nanny provide more details. Barbara finally blurted out that she thought Michael had moved the body, but of course Amybeth wouldn't hear of it. Michael had become Elizabeth's dearest friend. He was her main support system. Amybeth couldn't believe it would be in Michael's character at all—he loved and respected Liz too much—to do such a thing.

Amybeth didn't want to think anymore about it. She knew Barbara was hysterically upset, and she thought the nanny could be imagining things. For most of that day, Barbara was blathering. Half of what she said had ended up in a stream of tears. At one point, when Amybeth asked Barbara about how strange it was that Liz's breakfast table setting wasn't there, Barbara had no answers. The cute little Peter Rabbit bowls, the girls' special place mats—none of that had been arranged. Barbara agreed that it was odd, knowing that Liz usually set those things out at 10:00 P.M.. But Barbara was focused on the fact that Elizabeth's body was still warm. Even though Liz's body had been covered fully by a blanket, the nanny remained in a state of denial, hoping that someone would come forward to say Liz's death wasn't real, that Liz could be saved.

When the German police had first arrived, as they were trying to determine whether Elizabeth Ratliff had already been dead before she hit the floor, Amybeth Berner decided to listen to their conversations. She could speak fluent German, and she overheard them discussing the spinal fluid. She also overheard Michael telling the Germans that they were not needed there, insisting that this was an American matter, that the American military police were on their way. Amybeth wasn't sure who was really in control of the scene. The German police hadn't been there long before the American authorities arrived, and the teams of men seemed to be working together.

Major Steve Lyons had remained at the scene long enough to recall that there was one man on hand, who seemingly wanted to dominate the situation. The man seemed to be in control of the flow of information to police, voicing his belief that Mrs. Ratliff may have *blacked out* at the top of the landing and then fallen down. But Lyons couldn't recall, when asked years later, if that man was Michael Peterson.

In all the confusion, no one was sure what had happened. Amybeth remembered that as she overheard the investigators talking, she had grown increasingly concerned and nervous, worried that the German police were listening to Peterson's information, and not processing the death as a crime scene. She recalled that the Germans *did not* seem to be studying the stairwell carefully.

She recalled that when the Americans got there, the military police seemed to be taking directions from the Germans. She recalled thinking that all the authorities on the scene had rushed through their business. They had breezed up and down the stairway without taking pictures or measurements. Amybeth wasn't sure whether anyone had focused on the tiny spots of blood spatter that she and her husband had noticed.

But Amybeth Berner really had no right to interfere in the official police investigation. The authorities were doing their jobs, and they didn't want any civilians in their way. Amybeth was disturbed that the teams of police had come and gone so quickly; it felt as though they had finished their reports within fifteen minutes. But Amybeth was assured by her husband that the police teams would come up with their own interpretations, in time. She and Bruce had discussed the situation, and they each felt that the authorities would eventually recognize that a crime had taken place.

When the German police completed their investigation, they told Major Steve Lyons that they believed the cause of death was natural. The German police had seen no signs of struggle. There were no personal effects removed from the home, and no evidence of an intruder. Major Lyons concurred, but in accordance with autopsy protocol, just to make it official, Elizabeth Ratliff's body would be sent to an American military hospital for further testing.

"I thought these guys were special investigators," Amybeth recalled. "The military police who were there were supposed to be one notch above everyone else. They were supposed to be brighter and quicker."

Elizabeth Ratliff, a forty-three-year-old mother of two,

had been examined by a doctor at the Armed Forces Institute 97th General Hospital, and her autopsy results had been stamped out by the Armed Forces Institute of Pathology in Washington, DC. Elizabeth Ratliff's autopsy protocol, her slides, blocks, and tissue, had been reviewed and coded—and the chief of the Division of Forensic Pathology had signed off on the report, in agreement with the findings of Major Larry Barnes from the 97th General Hospital in Frankfurt, Germany, who had performed the autopsy on November 27,1985.

Elizabeth Ratliff's autopsy report had come back with the following diagnosis: sudden death due to spontaneous intracranial hemorrhage, complicated by von Willenbrand's Disease; natural.

"We had some trained Germans come in there, we had a group of Americans who called themselves investigators, and we had a coroner," Bruce Berner reflected. "We were told that they were all doing a job separate from the others. We were told that they were all looking into it. And we figured we knew what the outcome was going to be. But that's not the outcome we got."

At the time of Elizabeth Ratliff's death, Amybeth Berner had recently discovered she was pregnant. Having a difficult pregnancy from the start, Amybeth had already suffered miscarriages, so even though she harbored suspicions, her husband insisted that Amybeth focus on her own health. The military protocol had cleared any ideas that the Berners might have had regarding foul play. Amybeth's suspicions—that some spy or unknown love interest might have killed Elizabeth— would lead to nothing more than idle gossip.

In the final analysis, the experts had deemed that Elizabeth Ratliff's death was the result of an accident. Their friend had taken a horrible fall, and because of her rare blood disorder, she bled quickly, before any adult could get her to a hospital.

There was much grief in the months that followed Elizabeth's funeral. Margaret and Martha Ratliff were old enough to realize that they had lost their mother, and the girls were extremely upset. All of Elizabeth's friends mourned for the children. But the guardianship of Margaret and Martha had been willed to Michael and Patricia Peterson, and people took comfort in knowing that the girls were in good hands.

Everyone agreed that the Peterson family would watch out for the Ratliff girls' best interests. They trusted Elizabeth's instincts, and her last will and testament, written just months after George's death, had expressed her desire to have Michael and Patricia Peterson become the guardians of her two little girls. Elizabeth was adamant about wanting Margaret and Martha to be raised in Europe. Before Elizabeth signed her will, the Petersons had promised that, should anything happen to Liz, they would honor that wish.

As for everyone's individual sorrow, there was nothing people could do or say to bring Liz back. They would have to come to terms with Elizabeth's death, and find peace in the memory of her beautiful spirit. Friends and family would now have to try their best to focus on sweet little Margaret and Martha Ratliff. It was such a tragedy—the girls, so young, had been left complete orphans.

Thirty-two

On December 12, 2001, sixteen years after Elizabeth's death, Detective Art Holland received a phone call from Margaret Blair. The Durham police paged Holland with an urgent message from a woman in Rhode Island. The call had something to do with Margaret and Martha Ratliff.

"That's when it all started. She told me who her sister was, and that she died in Germany in 1985, found at the foot of the steps, " Holland confided. "Now I've got two women dead at the foot of a flight of steps, and both women know the same man."

The call from Elizabeth's sister came just days after Kathleen Peterson's death, at a time when all of Michael Peterson's friends and neighbors were telling Holland about the good character of Michael Peterson, and what a perfect husband he had been to Kathleen.

The day after Kathleen's demise, Blair had spoken to both of her nieces to express her sympathy for the loss of their stepmom. The girls were in shock. Both of them knew the history of their mom, Elizabeth, who had died from a fall down the stairs. Margaret and Martha both thought it was just a horrible coincidence.

Even though she was their same blood, by the time of Kathleen Peterson's death, Margaret Blair had become a virtual stranger to her nieces. There was nothing she felt she could say to them. It was obvious that they both believed their dad, Michael, was completely innocent of any wrongdoing. Her nieces thought that Michael Peterson was being taunted by the local media and Durham police. The Ratliff girls had clearly fallen under Michael's spell. Over the years, there were problems that Michael Peterson had created between Margaret and her nieces. There were sticky situations, some fights over the girls, but Michael had won those battles. He had managed to make Margaret Blair feel unnecessary.

Back in 1985, when Margaret Blair had first learned that Michael Peterson was legally in control of Elizabeth's daughters, she was surprised that her sister had left the care of her children to someone outside their family. There had been a time in the early 1990s, when Margaret Blair had tried to adopt Margaret and Martha. It was a time when the girls were spending their summers with Blair at her home in Rhode Island, and Margaret and her husband had become very attached to Elizabeth's daughters. Even though her sister's will had specified that Michael and Patricia Peterson be their guardians, Margaret Blair hoped that the Petersons might relinquish their legal rights.

Margaret Blair fought to become their legal mom.

But those years had become a difficult period for everyone. As it happened, Margaret and Martha Ratliff felt torn between two households. Margaret Blair ran a very strict Christian home, and the Ratliff girls, very young and impressionable, were led to believe that because Michael Peterson and Kathleen Atwater were living together, because Michael was still technically married to Patricia, they would be better off living full-time in Rhode Island.

It wasn't merely the fact that Michael and Kathleen were living in sin, it was the reality that the Ratliff girls were being shifted around from place to place. They had

Michael Peterson, best-selling novelist, on trial for the murder of his wife, Kathleen. *(Courtesy of The News & Observer)*

Kathleen Peterson became the first woman to earn a master's degree in engineering from Duke University. *(Courtesy of Fred Atwater)*

Kathleen and her first
husband, Fred Atwater,
celebrate as newlyweds.
(Courtesy of Fred Atwater)

Kathleen in her younger days,
visiting Disney World.
(Courtesy of Fred Atwater)

Kathleen with her daughter
Caitlin, on a camping holiday.
(Courtesy of Fred Atwater)

Margaret and Martha Ratliff in Germany, dressed European style by their mom, Elizabeth. *(Courtesy of Amybeth Berner)*

Amybeth Berner and Michael Peterson's first wife, Patricia, enjoy a fine dining establishment with their children in Paris. *(Courtesy of Bruce Berner)*

Left to right: Amybeth Berner, George Ratliff, and Carol Durham,
at a get-together at the Berners' house in Germany.
(Courtesy of Bruce Berner)

Left to right: Former nanny Barbara O'Hara, Martha Ratliff,
Amybeth Berner, Margaret Ratliff, and Bruce Berner, as they
enjoy a meal at Elizabeth Ratliff's table. *(Courtesy of Bruce Berner)*

The entrance gate to the Peterson mansion on Cedar Street. *(Author's photo)*

The Peterson mansion swimming pool, where Michael Peterson claimed to have been sitting as his wife died inside their home. *(Author's photo)*

Caitlin Atwater, daughter of Kathleen Peterson, fought for justice for her mother. *(Yearbook photo)*

Michael Peterson on trial for first-degree murder in Durham. *(Courtesy of Robert Olason)*

Left to right: Todd Peterson, Margaret Ratliff, Martha Ratliff, and Michael Peterson. *(Courtesy of Robert Olason)*

Lead defense attorney David Rudolf. *(Courtesy of Robert Olason)*

Left to right: Bill Peterson, Michael Peterson, friend and supporter Doug Hinds, and attorney Kerry Sutton. *(Courtesy of Robert Olason)*

Left to right: DA Jim Hardin, ADA Freda Black, and defense attorney Thomas Maher, who would continue to represent Michael Peterson after his conviction. *(Courtesy of Robert Olason)*

Judge Orlando Hudson, Jr.
(Author's photo)

Lead Detective Art Holland of the Durham Police works with CSI outside the Peterson mansion. *(State's exhibit)*

Of the two crystal wineglasses from the night in question, neither contained Kathleen's finger-prints, but Michael Peterson's finger-prints were visible. *(State's exhibit)*

Investigators surmised that the wine had been poured down the sink, to make it appear that Kathleen Peterson was drinking heavily the night she died. *(State's exhibit)*

The back stairwell in the Peterson house remained boarded up and covered with blood for almost two years. *(State's exhibit)*

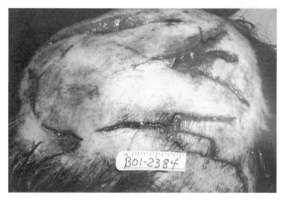

Kathleen Peterson's scalp reveals deep gashes and strange pitchfork-like patterns. *(State's exhibit)*

BO1-2384

Kathleen's blood-soaked body the night her husband "discovered" her at the bottom of the stairs. *(State's exhibit)*

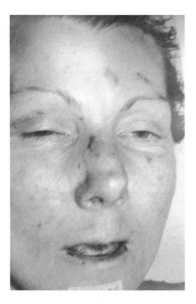

The lacerations on Kathleen's face were considered evidence of a struggle. *(State's exhibit)*

The shoe print from Michael Peterson's sneaker appeared on the back of Kathleen Peterson's sweatpants. *(State's exhibit)*

The blood spatter on Michael Peterson's athletic shoe appears to show drops of blood that fell vertically, perhaps dripping from an object. *(State's exhibit)*

A close-up of the bloodstains, with small drops of blood spatter, on the inside of Michael Peterson's shorts. *(State's exhibit)*

A Diet Coke can showed traces of blood and unidentifiable mixed saliva. *(State's exhibit)*

A model replica of the Peterson staircase used by bloodstain expert Duane Deaver. *(State's exhibit)*

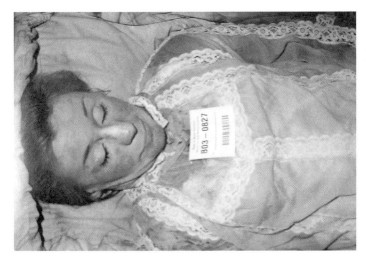

Elizabeth Ratliff as she appeared upon her exhumation in 2003,
18 years after her death. *(State's exhibit)*

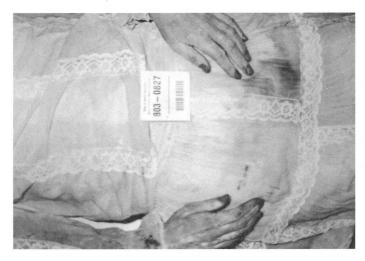

Medical examiners were shocked to see the condition of
Elizabeth's corpse, complete with flesh, fingernail polish,
and makeup. *(State's exhibit)*

The legs of Elizabeth Ratliff reveal the perfect condition of her wedding gown and stockings. *(State's exhibit)*

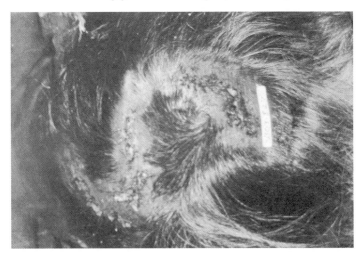

Elizabeth Ratliff's scalp shows lacerations similar to the ones suffered by Kathleen Peterson.
(State's exhibit)

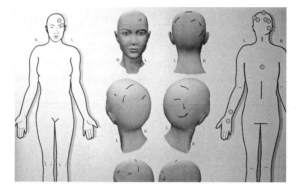

Diagrams of the scalp lacerations to Elizabeth Ratliff.
(State's exhibit)

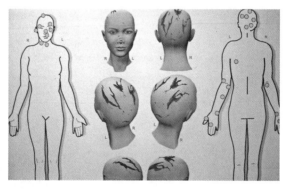

Diagrams of the scalp lacerations to Kathleen Peterson.
(State's exhibit)

Amybeth Berner testifies about her suspicions against Michael Peterson in Elizabeth Ratliff's death.
(Courtesy of Robert Olason)

Famed forensic expert Dr. Henry Lee concluded that Kathleen Peterson's death was "inconsistent with a beating." (Courtesy of Robert Olason)

Michael Peterson exchanged e-mails with former male escort "Brad" (center) in an attempt to arrange a paid homosexual encounter. Here, ADA Freda Black questions Brad's attorney, Thomas Loflin III. (Courtesy of Robert Olason)

Candace Zamperini, Kathleen's sister, holds a replica of the alleged murder weapon. (Courtesy of The News & Observer)

Caitlin Atwater being comforted by her aunt, Lori Campell, while waiting for the final arguments to close.
(Author's photo)

Local residents bought all of the contents of the Peterson mansion during an estate sale in November 2003.
(Author's photo)

General Summary Information			
DOC Number: T261129		Inmate Status: ACTIVE	
Name(s): PETERSON, MICHAEL			
Demographics			
Gender: MALE	Race:	WHITE	
Age: 59	Birth Date: 10/23/1943		

Michael Peterson's mug shot. He was sent to the Nash Correctional Institution to serve the rest of his life in prison.
(Courtesy of the North Carolina Department of Corrections)

lived with Michael and Patricia in Durham, they had lived with Michael and Patricia in Germany for a while, and then they wound up living with Michael and Kathleen and her daughter Caitlin in a kind of makeshift family.

Three-three

There was a letter Michael Peterson had written to Margaret Blair, dated July 18, 1990, which made his intentions quite clear. At the time, there had been a misunderstanding about the girls, and Michael was enraged about it. By then, Patricia and Michael were separated, they were fighting over the children, and Patricia had somehow led Margaret Blair to believe that the Ratliff girls could stay, permanently, in Rhode Island.

Michael's letter to Elizabeth's sister was lengthy, and it covered a number of points. He was very thankful that Margaret Blair had hosted the Ratliff girls for part of the summer, but he was angered by the heavy dose of religion that the girls had been subjected to. Michael mentioned that, being raised in an Italian Catholic home, he understood Blair's Irish Catholic background, but he felt that Margaret Blair's religious beliefs bordered on fundamentalist fanaticism. He didn't agree with Margaret's teachings. He didn't feel it was appropriate for her to be telling the Ratliff girls what to believe, and he wrote that her slight "fanaticism" was something that Liz had been utterly against.

Michael Peterson disagreed completely with the ideas Margaret Blair had, not only regarding religion, but also with her parenting style in general. He found nothing wrong with Margaret and Martha watching TV shows such as *The Simpsons,* or movies such as *Gremlins.* The prejudice against these innocent forms of entertainment was a good example of how religious righteousness could become controlling and unhealthy. Michael was specific about the fact that he didn't like the way Margaret and Martha had returned to Durham—suddenly filled with a "smug" belief in God. Michael didn't want his girls going around quizzing people on their religious beliefs.

It wasn't that he was trying to sever Margaret Blair's relationship with her nieces. That was not his intention. But Michael had thought long and hard about the Ratliff girls, and things were going to be different. After much soul-searching, Michael wrote, he had determined he would accompany his wife, Patty, back to Germany. Patricia Peterson had accepted her old job as a second-grade teacher for the Department of Defense, and Michael and Patty and the four children would be living together as a family. Michael explained that the matter of giving the Ratliff girls to Margaret Blair for adoption had become a moot point.

There were many reasons Michael had for deciding against any possible adoption. Of course he didn't really need to explain himself, because Elizabeth Ratliff's will, on file in Matagorda County in Bay City, Texas, was very clear. But still, Michael realized that Margaret Blair had grown so attached to the girls, she deserved some kind of reasoning behind his decision.

Peterson wrote that he had been the "sole male figure" in the girls' lives ever since the time their father, George Ratliff, had died. For seven years, Michael claimed, he had been their active father. He had taken care of Margaret and Martha from the time they were babies, from the time Martha was just an infant. And then after Elizabeth had died, Michael had become the "sole continuous link" in their lives.

Peterson talked about George Ratliff's will, which had also designated him to be the guardian of the two girls. Upon George's death, Elizabeth had changed the order of the guardians—it was something she had done after examining all the possibilities of the guardianship. It was Elizabeth's conscious choice, as verified in her will, that Michael and Patricia Peterson become the girls' guardians, excluding any family.

Michael wrote that he considered this guardianship a sacred trust. He outlined how, for five years since Liz's death, he had acted in Margaret and Martha's best interests, loving them, comforting them, nursing them, and counseling them. Not only had he taken them to doctors and dentists, he had been to their recitals and plays, he had sat on the school board and had attended the PTA.

Even though Michael never legally adopted the Ratliff girls, as their guardian, he considered them his children. He had been there to listen to their sorrows, to laugh at their jokes—he had overseen all the aspects of their lives. Michael thought it would be terribly harmful if the Ratliff girls were made to feel like a commodity, if they felt like they could be adopted by someone else, just passed on, losing all sense of continuity in their lives.

Peterson believed that all of the girls' aunts and uncles—George Ratliff's brothers and sister, as well as Elizabeth's sisters—were playing an important role in the girls' lives. He wanted those connections to remain in place. But none of those distant relatives, he felt, could provide that function of "anchor" as well as he had. No matter what special bond the girls had developed with Margaret Blair, or any other family member, Margaret and Martha needed the stability and love that only he had given to them. Michael had become an integral part of their lives, and he felt it was his duty and honor to continue to act as their dad.

Michael was happy that both sides of the girls' family—Elizabeth's and George's—had tried so hard to become a presence in Margaret and Martha's lives. He was appreciative of that, and grateful for their support. But Michael hoped that Margaret Blair and the rest of the relatives were appreciative of his efforts also. Michael had a special commitment to the girls. It was a commitment that nobody would ever be able to understand.

Deep in his heart, Michael believed he was the best choice to raise the Ratliff girls. He was the right person to guide them. And he loved them.

Thirty-four

Caitlin remembered the way Michael felt about the Ratliff girls. He was very attached to them, and they seemed to love him. Margaret and Martha had been Caitlin's favorite playmates, and the Ratliff girls seemed quite settled over at the Peterson house. They considered Michael and Patricia to be their parents. Way back when Caitlin first met them, Margaret and Martha couldn't remember any details about their real mother, they couldn't recall any exact details about Germany. All they knew was what they had been told.

But all was not well at the Peterson house.

It was Caitlin, even at a very young age, who noticed that Michael and Patricia didn't seem happy together. Caitlin was aware of the dynamic that had developed between Michael and her mom, and to her, it was obvious that Michael was becoming more fond of Kathleen every day. From her backyard, Caitlin would watch Michael and Kathleen slip away into her mom's bedroom. She was just an elementary-school kid, but she had an idea that they might be kissing—that something was going on. Margaret and Martha would eventually join Caitlin in her suspicions, especially when Michael began the process of trying "separations" from Patricia in those early years, in the late 1980s.

By 1990, the summer that Margaret Blair had tried to

adopt Margaret and Martha, Michael and Kathleen had become firmly entrenched in the lives of the three girls. That summer was a time that Caitlin would remember very well. When the Ratliff girls left for New England, Caitlin missed having Margaret and Martha around. In a way, they had become like sisters to her.

For his part, Michael was overly annoyed that Margaret Blair would even suggest adopting the girls—she had no legal right to do that. He decided that he and Kathleen should take a trip up to Rhode Island that summer, just to check on the girls' living circumstances. Of course Kathleen brought Caitlin along, who was thrilled to be able to visit with her best friends.

When Michael made the arrangements for their trip up north, he never said it, but he had reason to believe that Margaret Blair's home wasn't the best place for Margaret and Martha. He acted as if he were curious. For his own peace of mind, he wanted to know if Margaret and Martha were truly happy in New England. If that wasn't the case, he planned to bring them home to live in Kathleen's house, and Kathleen was in support of that.

For Caitlin, the idea of Margaret and Martha returning to Durham would be a dream come true. Being an only child, she loved having her best buddies around. Without the girls, Michael and Kathleen were no fun to be with, and Caitlin hadn't exactly adjusted to having her parents being split apart. She didn't mind having to spend time alone with her dad, Fred, but Fred couldn't really entertain her. Caitlin loved her father, but she didn't feel comfortable in his downtown Durham loft. It wasn't exactly a home to her, and she missed the neighborhood kids.

Before they took the trip to Rhode Island, Michael claimed he wasn't sure about the fate of Margaret and Martha Ratliff. All along, Michael was saying that he would abide by whatever the Ratliff girls' decision was. He wanted Margaret and Martha to know that it was their choice—that they alone could decide where they might be happier. Michael originally had planned to spend just a few days in New England, but after the first day of their arrival, Michael chose to extend their stay to a week.

Caitlin had packed some of her favorite Barbie dolls and other toys—and the girls seemed to be enjoying each other so much. As Caitlin recalled, throughout the visit to Rhode Island, Michael and Kathleen would spend much of the day at the Blair household, allowing the girls a chance to play for hours. Margaret was happily married with kids of her own, so her house was always busy and alive with laughter. Michael thought it was nice that the Ratliff girls had gotten to know their cousins, but he also noticed that Martha seemed extremely attached to her aunt Margaret. Being the baby, that seemed only natural, but Michael was disturbed to learn that Martha might prefer to remain in New England, to live with Margaret Blair and her family.

Michael explained that there were other priorities to consider. Michael said he wanted it to be Margaret and Martha's decision, but he kept reminding the Ratliff girls that if they decided to stay in Rhode Island, they would be going against their mother's dying wishes. He told them that Elizabeth's will had designated that they live with *him*. He mentioned that their birth mother had big plans for them, explaining that Elizabeth had left New England for a reason, that she hadn't wanted her children to be raised there.

The Ratliff girls had so much fun playing games with Caitlin, they finally admitted that they missed their former life in North Carolina. When Michael suggested that they all fly home together, Margaret and Martha agreed. Before they knew it, Margaret and Martha had joined them at the airport, where plane tickets were purchased for all of them to return to Durham. The girls' belongings had been packed up, and some of them were taken on the plane. The rest of their summer things were left with their aunt, to be shipped at a later date.

Being back with Michael was a difficult transition for the girls, especially in the beginning of his separation from Patricia. Michael had moved them to Germany and then back to Durham, and it took Margaret and Martha some time to think of him as a true dad. The girls hadn't felt at home in Germany—they were much happier living back in English-speaking America—but by the time Michael and Kathleen had gotten married and moved into the Cedar Street house, the Ratliff girls finally felt like they belonged.

They accepted Michael as their father and were comfortable with Kathleen, who had gone to great lengths to treat Margaret and Martha as daughters. Over the years, she'd done everything she could for the Ratliff girls, had given them birthday parties and special gifts. Every Sunday, Kathleen and Michael would make a point of doing things together as a family. There were vacations and excursions, and there were always big holiday gatherings that Kathleen would turn into magical occasions.

It would take years, but eventually Margaret and Martha called Kathleen their mom. And that was appropriate, because Kathleen was the person who put most of the effort in with them. She focused as much on Margaret and Martha as she did on Caitlin, and she would encourage each of the girls to communicate every night at the dinner table, asking them about their day, about their schoolwork, and about their views on the world.

"My mother was always wanting us to discuss things, and Michael always had a more outlandish view," Caitlin confided. "If you hit on a topic that he wanted to talk about, he always had the better story. You would end up listening to him because he was a very educated man, and he knew history, like from B.C. It was clear you couldn't compete with that. But it was Mom who genuinely tried to push for us to share. She wanted to hear what we had to say."

Kathleen would ask that each of the girls come to the table with three topics to discuss. There were always stories, there were jokes and anecdotes, and, as the years passed, the girls recognized the significance of their nightly family dinners. That was, until they became teenagers and were suddenly not as concerned with world events and homework reports. It all seemed tedious, the obligatory family dinner, complete with three full courses and dessert.

Caitlin recalled that as they got older, the dinner table at the Peterson house would sometimes feel like a scene out of *American Beauty*, where everyone was forced to speak, where there would be some awkward stretches of silence. At times, Kathleen would get caught up talking about what she was doing at work. Her job was high-powered. She was traveling to Canada and Asia for Nortel Networks—a company in the high-end electronics field.

By 1999, Nortel Networks, a Canadian company, formerly a manufacturer of telephones, had become a household name, competing with the American telecommunications giant Lucent. Nortel Networks was standing toe-to-toe with the high-tech networking company Cisco Systems, and Kathleen Peterson's job responsibilities, as well as her income, were skyrocketing.

At times, Kathleen, whose job entailed writing about Nortel equipment, would get too technical in her nightly dinner discussions about her fast-growing company. Her daughters couldn't keep up with all the information Kathleen would try to impart, and sometimes, neither could Michael. When Kathleen would bring up Nortel, the girls would stare across the dinner table, trying to understand what she was saying. But they couldn't comprehend it all. Often they would sit and listen silently, just to placate her.

If their mom would get too specific, the girls would sometimes stare off into space, or would explain that Kathleen was losing them, asking her to change the subject. Margaret and Martha and Caitlin didn't really care about Nortel announcing a half-billion-dollar deal with Sprint and MCI WorldCom to launch trials of Nortel equipment. They didn't understand what it meant for Nortel Networks to be able to transfer data at ten gigabytes per second.

They really didn't want to know about it. They were in their fun years, busy with high-school concerns. They had boyfriends, dances, and loads of friends to occupy their minds. They would try to be polite whenever their mom would give details about Nortel—it was all well and good that she changed jobs a lot and was climbing the corporate ladder—but the girls didn't really want to hear about phone systems being hooked up in Asia or third-world places.

They'd never heard of half the technical stuff their mom talked about, and they would defer to Michael to move the conversation back to politics or social issues, to more familiar ground. As far as the girls were concerned, the Internet and the wireless world were great for e-mailing, but all the high-tech gunk that fueled it sounded more foreign to them than Greek.

Thirty-five

In February 2002, not long after Caitlin and Fred At-water went to Durham to meet with Jim Hardin and Art Holland, Caitlin called her sisters to try to reason with them. Margaret and Martha were both back at college, and Caitlin was able to get hold of Margaret on the campus of Tulane.

Shocked by the details in the autopsy reports, Caitlin didn't want to flat-out tell Margaret that their mom had been beaten. It was a subject she preferred not to speak about on the phone. Caitlin just wanted her sisters to see the truth. Caitlin hadn't taken sides; she was still giving Michael the benefit of the doubt. But she felt that once Margaret and Martha read about the seven lacerations to Kathleen's head, without even looking at the photos of the wounds, they would realize that their mom had been killed by someone, perhaps an intruder.

"Margaret, this is about Mom," Caitlin pleaded. "You need to read the autopsy report. You need to understand that she didn't fall down the stairs."

"Dad says not to read it," Margaret said. "He says it would be too upsetting and that the things they've written in the reports are not true."

"You need to read it for yourself. You need to know what happened to Mom. She was beaten," Caitlin told her.

"I don't want to read it," Margaret insisted. "Dad already told me what's in there, and he says the reports are wrong."

"She was our mother. This is about Mom," Caitlin argued. "This is not about Dad."

But Margaret had made up her mind, and she told Caitlin not to bother calling Martha, who felt the same way. Neither of them had an interest in seeing bloody photos and autopsy reports filled with nasty accusations and things that would traumatize them all over again. Their dad had assured Margaret that he would be exonerated in court.

Michael Peterson had convinced the girls of his innocence by leaning on the opinions of experts. Among the experts in his corner that he bragged about was, of course, Dr. Henry Lee, who had already made a trip to the house, who had brought in a crew from *20/20*. Michael had given the Ratliff girls inside information, he had promised them that the top forensic expert didn't believe there had been a crime.

Michael had bragged about the appearance of Dr. Henry Lee to everyone on his side of the family. Kathleen's immediate family had no idea, but they would watch in horror when ABC aired the *20/20* story in April 2002. Kathleen's sister-in-law, Cynthia Woodward, happened to catch the program; it was a profile piece on Dr. Henry Lee. As the news team followed Henry Lee to the back staircase, Woodward recognized the entrance to the Peterson mansion. She recognized the furnishings, and was mortified to see Kathleen's dried blood everywhere, in close-up shots.

Dr. Lee took a pair of tweezers to show reporters that he was retrieving tissues and hair samples from the bloody wall. There was dried and smeared blood on the walls behind him, and beneath his feet, there was blood all along the steps. Though the Michael Peterson case was never mentioned during the *20/20* segment, Cynthia Woodward went numb, devastated to see the great amount of blood. When they learned about the broadcast of the Peterson stairwell, some of Kathleen's family members wrote editorials expressing their shock. They were beside themselves, and couldn't believe that the news team could be so insensitive.

Of course Michael Peterson was pleased that the *20/20* segment had aired. The segment was powerful. The image of Henry Lee finding "hidden tissue" made it seem like the expert was trumping the North Carolina authorities. The piece had punch. Attorney David Rudolf was shown in one of the shots, standing outside the Peterson house. He was in the background, having a friendly chat with Dr. Henry Lee.

It was further proof of his innocence, Michael would insist to his family.

And, according to Michael, it wasn't only Dr. Lee, the top national forensic expert, who believed in him. Peterson insisted that David Rudolf had a very strong case lined up. He insinuated that Rudolf would show proof that the Durham police had a vendetta against him.

Michael wanted his daughters to sit tight and wait for the trial. He swore that the day would come when numerous experts, who were in complete disagreement with the state's autopsy findings, would testify in court.

As for Margaret and Martha, they just wanted to go about their business, to work hard at getting good grades in college. They weren't willing to watch the news anymore, they were sick of all the drama, and they didn't even try to see the *20/20* piece when it aired.

Margaret and Martha felt sorry that Caitlin made the mistake of listening to the Durham police. They felt their sister was being misled, that Caitlin was believing in false charges. Like Clayton and Todd, the Ratliff girls had always been worried that Caitlin might fall prey to all the rumors circulating about their dad. They had hoped it wouldn't affect them, that Caitlin wouldn't begin taking sides, but after Caitlin's persistent conversation with Margaret, nothing would ever be the same.

"When I hung up the phone with Margaret, I was very upset. I didn't want to talk about it anymore," Caitlin confided. "At that point, I decided that she was my mother and not theirs. I couldn't believe that my mom could have these daughters for a total lifetime and they were not willing to find out what happened to her. But that was the pattern with them. They were so brainwashed by Michael, they were not willing to listen to anything."

Thirty-six

When she had returned to begin her next semester, Caitlin Atwater, the nineteen-year-old Ivy League student, was no longer the typical college coed at Cornell. She was happy to be back on campus, and was moving forward with her classes, but apart from a few distractions from her friends, there were certain weird things happening that were making life more difficult.

In early 2002, with the trial still a long way off, as Michael Peterson's defense team prepared for battle, Caitlin found herself confronted with a number of strange requests. She had received a number of e-mails regarding estate matters, and she had questions and concerns about what they meant.

There was one e-mail in particular, in which Bill Peterson, on behalf of his brother, was making an odd suggestion. Attorney Bill Peterson wanted Caitlin to understand that the $1.45 million life insurance policy for Kathleen Peterson would not be paid out until Michael's innocence was determined. Bill wanted to be clear that if, for some reason, Michael was found guilty as charged, the entire proceeds of the life insurance policy would pass to her. Caitlin would be the only heir, according to Bill Peterson's interpretation of her mother's insurance policy.

If, however, Michael was found to be not guilty, then all the insurance money would go to him. Through the e-mail, written by the estate attorney on Bill's behalf, Bill Peterson was suggesting that, since Michael was looking to raise money for his defense, Caitlin and the estate could agree that the insurance money could be paid out to the estate. Then the estate, with Caitlin's blessing, could "loan" half of the insurance money to Michael, and Michael would give her a mortgage on the Cedar Street home.

If Michael was found innocent, the estate would pay him the other half of the proceeds. If he was found guilty, the estate would then foreclose on the mortgage, paying the money back to Caitlin. Bill Peterson and the estate would make sure that Caitlin Atwater was protected. Caitlin would not be giving up her rights, the e-mail seemed to suggest.

When Caitlin forwarded the e-mail to Fred, he was flabbergasted.

It was a lose-lose proposal.

He told his daughter that under no circumstances should she agree to such a proposal. He reminded her that, even if Michael had the right to the insurance money, which was not a given, Michael Peterson had already mortgaged most of the value of the Cedar Street house to post his bond.

Though Caitlin wanted to believe in Michael's innocence, though she had spent thirteen years becoming a part of his "family," Caitlin was growing leery of the man she called stepdad. Michael had written to her, early on, after Kathleen's death, asking Caitlin to listen to her mother's voice. He wanted Kathleen's voice to be the "only voice" Caitlin would listen to. Michael wanted Caitlin to sort through all the chaos, to sort through the "cacophony of voices," and try to hear her mother speaking the truth to her.

There wasn't a moment that went by when Caitlin didn't think about her mom. There wasn't a moment that she didn't hope for an answer, that she didn't pray that an intruder had something to do with her mom's death. Caitlin couldn't bear the idea that her loving step-dad would have been responsible for killing anyone, and she grieved privately, trying to think of what her mother might say about the accusations and police reports. Caitlin was afraid she might never know what actually happened to her mother. She had no idea who might be held responsible, and no clue as to why anyone would want to kill her. The whole thing was a mess.

With all of her mother's encouraging words through the years, Caitlin would find strength in knowing that Kathleen always expected her to do great things. Caitlin remembered that her mom wanted her to be a success-ful woman in the workforce. There was no doubt that Kathleen felt that Caitlin was well above average in in-telligence. All of Caitlin's grades and high scores through the years proved that, and Kathleen had always made it known that she didn't want any of Caitlin's smarts to go to waste.

Caitlin had aspirations to become a lawyer, and after her mom died, she had no choice but to become legally savvy. In her own way, as legal documents and requests came to her, Caitlin began to piece together the puzzle behind her mother's death. Reading the reports and finding out her rights, Caitlin sometimes believed she was earning her law degree ahead of time. As the evidence came in—about specific bloodstains, about a possible murder weapon, about the Peterson family finances—Caitlin grew more concerned that the man she had shared a home with was someone she had never really known at all.

The reality started to plague her. More and more each day, Caitlin was coming face-to-face with the idea that Michael Peterson was a cold-blooded monster.

Thirty-seven

While officials in Durham County were waiting for a final inventory of Kathleen Peterson's estate, a preliminary accounting of her assets showed that she had a net worth of just above $250,000. Surprisingly, even though she was helping to make the mortgage payments, Kathleen Peterson did not own any part of the Cedar Street mansion. Mrs. Peterson's worth included a personal bank account with about $1,600, vehicles valued at $17,895, stocks and bonds worth $5,600, a half-interest in some rental properties, valued at $176,000, and an Individual Retirement Account worth $52,000. The value of her Nortel Networks retirement plan and her life insurance policy were listed as unknown.

Prosecutors thought it peculiar that Kathleen Peterson died with so little net worth. Her salary at Nortel Networks was in the six-figure range, and she was living so large, it seemed like she had millions. People surmised that there was more money somewhere, that Kathleen Peterson's net worth would prove to be greater. For one thing, Kathleen's joint checking accounts with Michael were valued at about $20,000, but that was money that reverted back to him at the time of his wife's death.

In mid-April 2002, Citibank filed a claim against the estate of Kathleen Peterson for more than $13,000. The credit card charges in her name had come from places such as California and Louisiana, states where Martha and Margaret attended college respectively, and there were also charges from New York, which were purchases made by Caitlin. The overall bill had been run up over a long period of time, and it included transactions made in Fort Lauderdale, where the Petersons had vacationed in November 2001, in addition to Christmas purchases made in Durham, just weeks before Kathleen died.

The Citibank claim against the Peterson estate made the front page of the local news sections, and folks in the Triangle region were shocked to learn that the Petersons had let so many charges pile up, not only with Citibank, but with Bank of America, Bank One, and other banks as well.

By that time, the prosecutors in Durham had already begun studying the Peterson financial situation, looking for a possible motive. Through the efforts of a North Carolina State Bureau of Investigation agent, the DA office would discover that, at the time of Kathleen's death, the Petersons were over $140,000 in debt, carrying credit lines spread across twenty active accounts.

Even though the Petersons owned some small pieces of property, apart from the Cedar Street house, records showed that no one in the Peterson family had much equity in those parcels. Prosecutors learned that while Michael Peterson was purporting to be a wealthy, successful novelist—buying late-model cars and filling his home with expensive antiques—Mr. Peterson, in fact, hadn't earned any substantial income in years. Aside from a modest military pension, Peterson had no money coming in that they could trace—not from royalties or from film options.

To prosecutors, it looked as though the Petersons were surviving solely on Kathleen Peterson's $145,000-a-year income—and were affording the additional luxuries that made up their high-end lifestyle by living on credit. When prosecutors had the Petersons' cash flow boiled down to gross numbers, there was evidence that for three years prior to Kathleen's death, the Petersons were spending $100,000 a year more than they were taking in.

When word of the impending Citibank lawsuit was printed in the *Herald-Sun* newspaper, providing all the details about Kathleen's estate finances being in disarray, Michael Peterson hit the roof. He felt publicly humiliated, and was furious that the newspaper reported specifics about their bills being unpaid from places such as Toys "R" Us and US Airways. The last thing Peterson needed was a public perception that he and his wife were in financial straits. He shot off an e-mail to Caitlin, insisting that she clear up the problem. As the administrator, Michael wrote, it was *her* responsibility to settle the credit card debt and any other outstanding bills.

Michael wasn't just angry, he was irate. He wrote that Kathleen would have been "out of her mind" if she had been alive to read about such shame being brought to the family. He wrote that he'd been very "polite" and had tried to keep silent about things, but now, he told Caitlin, "this estate matter better get unfucked immediately." And if Caitlin didn't take care of the problem, Michael threatened, he would go to the police to report the $100,000 worth of jewels and furs that were missing from his wife's belongings. In the e-mail, Peterson suggested that the $100,000 worth of missing merchandise could easily pay for all the estate debts.

The only problem was, when the "missing" estate items were accounted for, all that was taken from the Cedar Street house were a few Louis Vuitton and Gucci handbags, Kathleen's pearls, and some small pieces of matching jewelry. Caitlin had these items appraised, and, apart from the sentimental value, she had been informed that the jewelry was not worth much.

The pearls, which Michael had bought at an estate sale and were supposedly owned by Lana Turner, weren't authenticated. They were the pearls that her aunts had given to Caitlin after her mom's wake. It was at that time that Caitlin also received her mom's designer handbags. The items hardly added up to tens of thousands of dollars. And aside from that, Michael was wrong in thinking these possessions were his. It was Caitlin who had a right to keep the goods, by law. Caitlin Atwater was the administrator of the estate, and she had already placed her mother's pearls and jewelry into a safe-deposit box, waiting for the estate to be settled.

Caitlin Atwater hadn't done anything illegal. Caitlin hadn't caused trouble for the estate, nor had she stolen anything. Her aunts were the ones who suggested that Caitlin take a few of her mom's handbags, but Caitlin had left the Cedar Street house with very few mementos from her mom. Mostly, Caitlin packed her own personal belongings, her sentimental stuffed animals, her favorite summer and winter clothes. Caitlin had never tried to set foot in the house after the Christmas season was over. The place gave her the creeps. She never wanted to go back there.

But in his e-mail to Caitlin, Michael ranted and raved, trying to make her feel guilty, holding her responsible for the problems she and Kathleen's other family members were causing him in the media. Michael said that his silence was over. He seemed ready to strike back at Kathleen's family, and not only was he planning on "going public" about the "missing" goods, he was also threatening to report Caitlin's aunt Candace to the Internal Revenue Service.

It seems Candace Zamperini, in her rage over Henry Lee's appearance on *20/20*, wrote an editorial in which she called Dr. Lee "hired help." In retaliation, Michael was ready to file a report about Candace's South American housekeeper, Jean, whom he thought the IRS people would be interested to learn about. The thing was, Candace was paying her housekeeper on the books. She was filing tax returns and doing everything on the up-and-up.

But Michael Peterson didn't know that.

He just assumed his threat was valid.

In his lengthy e-mail, Michael berated Caitlin for refusing to watch *20/20*, telling her that she, more than anyone, should have been interested in what Dr. Lee had to say concerning her mother's death. Michael wondered if anyone honestly thought Dr. Lee would compromise his reputation for a few bucks involving a case in Durham, North Carolina. He told Caitlin that she should listen to Dr. Henry Lee, rather than "the idiots" who investigated the case.

Michael blamed the cops for destroying the family that Kathleen had spent so many years putting together. As Michael had predicted from the beginning, and as Todd had predicted, it was no surprise that Caitlin had turned on him. Michael felt Caitlin was being hypocritical. In his view, Caitlin's public comments and her behavior were mind-boggling. Michael wanted to be spared the "horseshit" about *20/20*. He claimed that Caitlin's mother would have been much more upset about her autopsy photos being released to the press than about her house being shown on *20/20*. Michael was certain that Kathleen wouldn't have cared one bit about Dr. Lee being on their staircase.

Michael wrote that he knew Caitlin was in agony. He was sorry that things had turned out to be so dreadful. He still wanted Caitlin to contact her sisters—he insisted that Kathleen would want that. And he claimed that, no matter what, he still loved Caitlin.

But for all the love he supposedly had for Caitlin and Kathleen, Michael was acting in ways that were completely contradictory. From the moment Kathleen died, it was one thing after another. For starters, Michael was refusing to pay for Kathleen's cemetery plot. The place Caitlin and Candace had chosen to bury Kathleen happened to be in the old part of the Maplewood Cemetery, and therefore required a family purchase of four plots. For some reason, Michael felt the estate should pick up the tab. Michael apparently didn't like the idea of dealing with headstones and grave plots, and he wrote a separate letter to Kathleen's estate. In this epistle, he explained that he was "philosophically opposed" to any kind of burial and he preferred cremation.

Caitlin was mortified when she received a copy of Michael's letter, reading in his own words that he was refusing to pay the funeral bills. He was leaving it on the estate to sort out the matter of all the funeral expenses: Kathleen's monument, burial plot, as well as the unpaid $800 flower bill, which Michael said had been placed under his name, without his permission. Michael had written to implore the estate to pay the bills, particularly the bills for Kathleen's coffin and flowers.

If the estate couldn't come up with the money, Michael Peterson claimed he was ready to contact the police, and possibly his insurance company. Michael didn't care about the Citibank claim, but he certainly did care that Kathleen's funeral matter be settled, even if he had to *loan* the estate some money himself.

Caitlin was horrified by the details in Michael's correspondence, both to her and to the estate. It was one of many times that Michael was using the memory of her mother to haunt her, to make her feel like a disrespectful and dishonest person. Caitlin wasn't really familiar with paying estate bills. She hadn't let things slip on purpose; she just had too much on her plate. Dealing with attorneys and all the legal mumbo jumbo, especially when it involved both civil and criminal aspects, was too much for her.

She was still a kid. And she was grieving and in shock.

Caitlin felt terrible that her mom's grave site had become cause for argument, that there seemed to be no peace for her mom's soul. With the constant news items, the brewing legal battle, and Michael's weird behavior and threats, her life was becoming a living hell.

The worst of it was, even though Caitlin had seen the circumstantial evidence, a part of her wanted to believe in Michael's innocence. There was a part of Caitlin that had a soft spot for Michael, and she found herself remembering all the good years, all the vacations, all the holidays, the fun times.

But Caitlin would continue to discover that Michael was not the quality man he made himself out to be. There were more and more bizarre things coming to light about Michael. For instance, Michael Peterson had collected $347,000 from Nortel, just weeks after Kathleen's death, but when it finally came down to paying the funeral bills, it was Caitlin's dad, Fred Atwater, who laid down the cash to pay for Kathleen's gravestone monument.

Thirty-eight

Fred Atwater was surprised that Michael didn't seem to care enough to get a marker placed on Kathleen's grave. Michael had initially paid for the multiple plots upon Kathleen's death, but later was insisting that the estate reimburse him. Peterson would not release the deed to the plots, which was necessary in order for the family to place a headstone.

So Kathleen's cemetery plot was a mud puddle, and it remained that way for months. Fred Atwater paid the estate $4,100 to cover the cost of the grave site, in order that Michael could get his money. Fred was tired of the months of bickering between Michael Peterson and Kathleen's family. Fred didn't want to see his daughter suffer any more than she had to.

Fred cared about the memory of his ex-wife. He spent months working on Kathleen's headstone monument with a company in his hometown, and the engraving and drawing on the monument was quite intricate. Fred even had a blueprint made, and there was a proposal drawn up, which was sent to Michael for his approval. But Peterson never responded. It took over a year for all the estate paperwork to get shifted around, before Kathleen's family was finally able to place a marker at her grave.

"Michael claimed he was concerned about the headstone. He claimed he visited the grave twice a week,"

Fred recalled. "But there were people who were watching the grave site who said they never saw him there."

There was a laundry list of problems that Michael Peterson had created for Kathleen's grieving family. During his comments to the media, Peterson not only asserted that the city officials were vindictive, he announced that Caitlin had become irresponsible and hateful. Peterson was playing with the media.

Caitlin hadn't really wanted to return to the Cedar Street house, not for any reason, but her father thought she should return there to collect the remainder of her things. Caitlin had left the house just after her mom died, and she had taken only a small part of her belongings. Caitlin had her whole life stored in that house—her trophies, her yearbooks, her childhood diaries—these were things that Fred felt Caitlin had a right to possess.

But Caitlin didn't feel safe going near Michael. When Fred suggested that she request a sheriff escort to take her to Cedar Street, Caitlin didn't like the idea. Caitlin didn't want to anger Michael in any way; she was more concerned that her mom's headstone be taken care of.

"Michael made it impossible for Caitlin to get into that house, unless she was to get a court order," Fred confided. "Because of his threats in his letters, there was such animosity set up, and Michael, in a sense, was blackmailing her."

Fred Atwater had decided, not long after Kathleen's death, that Michael Peterson had a very sick mind. He didn't appreciate the way Michael phrased things, always asserting that if Kathleen were alive, she would have supported his fight against the authorities, insisting that Caitlin should support him too.

Of course it wasn't always the case that Fred could see through Michael so easily. In the beginning, when Michael and Kathleen had first wed, Peterson was arrogant, and very much the breadwinner. Kathleen seemed to be in awe of him, hanging on his every word. And for years, Fred went along with whatever Kathleen's perceptions were, never questioning Peterson and his motivations. Without thinking anything was amiss, Fred would deal with Michael's financial demands, Michael's huffing and puffing about how hard he was working to support all three girls.

Fred would notice that Michael was very free-spending with his money, that Michael liked to play the role of "savior" to his three stepdaughters. He knew that Kathleen was convinced that Michael had "rescued" the Ratliff girls from unhappy lives. Of course Fred never knew how hard Michael had tried, in an insidious way, to discourage Caitlin from paying too much attention to her natural dad. Michael would usually cut Caitlin off, telling Caitlin that Fred's advice was bogus. Michael always contradicted Fred's ideas, acting like he knew better.

As the master of the house, Michael was good at "programming" his flock. It was something that was happening underneath the surface, but it seemed Michael had taken over the whole family, both in mind and spirit. He controlled all of their movements by handling all the household finances. And, even though Michael was no longer making much money from his writing, he was in charge of everything, from family investments to family vacations. He was the ultimate planner.

Peterson was good at hiding the reality of his failing writing career; no one ever fathomed that he was leaning on Kathleen; people never realized that Kathleen had become the family breadwinner. For years, Fred Atwater thought Michael Peterson was doing a good job of raising their patchwork family. Atwater, who earned a Ph.D. from Duke University in physics, who worked as a software developer for huge companies such as Sprint, had been too busy with his career to see through Michael's game.

Not to say there weren't times when Fred had some particular concerns. There was a moment, when Caitlin had just turned seventeen, that Fred and Michael had an argument over the financial arrangements regarding a vehicle. Fred was paying Kathleen monthly child support, and from the time of their separation, the arrangement had worked well. Fred and Kathleen had agreed on a solid financial support system for Caitlin, and Kathleen felt that Fred's payments were more than fair. But then Michael began to interfere.

When Caitlin was seventeen, Michael decided to buy her a new Montero SUV. Within weeks of the purchase, Michael suggested that Caitlin approach her father to ask him to pick up the payments for the new vehicle. To everyone's surprise, Fred refused.

Fred hadn't been consulted about the purchase, and he resented the idea that Michael had used Caitlin as a go-between. It was unfair, Fred believed, for Michael to approach him in that way. If Caitlin had asked her father to buy her a car, Fred would have been willing to do that. In fact, Fred later wound up buying a different SUV for Caitlin when she went off to college at Cornell. But while Caitlin was still living under Michael's roof, Fred wasn't about to pay for something that he hadn't even picked out.

"I just didn't think it was right. Michael was trying to push me," Fred recalled. "I was trying to be reasonable, and wanted to work something out where I would increase Caitlin's child support, rather than pay for specific things that Michael decided to buy. I was talking to Michael on the phone, but he hung up on me. He wouldn't answer the phone, so I went over there and Michael was sitting outside, pouting like a little kid."

As the years passed, there had been a number of financial concerns between the two men. Fred had been
asked to pay for things, and he had been made to look
like the bad guy. But Fred hadn't done anything to deserve that. At one point, Kathleen sent her ex-husband
a memo regarding Caitlin's schooling, about the price of
her private school and school supplies. When Fred calculated the school costs, looking at a record of all his
spending, Fred noticed that Michael was using part of
Caitlin's child support to buy things for Margaret and
Martha. As it turned out, Fred had paid for so many
things that Kathleen hadn't taken into account, she actually owed *him* money.

After receiving a number of nasty letters from Michael,
letters that asserted that Fred wasn't keeping up with his
daughter's expenses, letters that demanded additional
payments, Fred couldn't understand why Michael was acting so cheap and greedy. From Fred's perspective, there
was no good reason for Peterson to be complaining about
money. He honestly couldn't understand the constant
gripes. Michael Peterson was living in a big mansion—he
took ski trips and belonged to exclusive clubs. But for
some reason, both Michael and Kathleen kept trying to
get more money from Fred. Even after he had increased
his child support payments for Caitlin, Fred still felt like
he was being "shaken down."

Fred thought it was strange that Kathleen would go
along with Michael; it seemed she had become materi-
alistic overnight. The way Kathleen had changed, the
way she acted about money, was entirely foreign. But
then, there were so many differences Fred had begun to
notice in Kathleen, especially after Michael and Kathleen became a solid married couple. Michael had
changed his wife's personality so much, that when it
came to personal life decisions, Kathleen didn't have
much of a mind of her own. Kathleen had become a new

person, and the influence that Michael was having overall wasn't always a positive one. Fred noticed that Caitlin seemed to be living in Peterson's "perfect" fantasy world—which he didn't really think was healthy.

There were so many things about the Peterson household that didn't make sense. Kathleen and Caitlin were constantly painting a glowing portrait of their life with Michael. They would talk about the wonderful stepfather Michael had become. Yet things were clearly not all that perfect. Over the years, Fred learned of the notorious problems with one of Michael's sons. And he knew the history of the Ratliff girls, who had a whole series of denials and troubles to overcome.

Fred didn't learn about Caitlin's diary entries until much later, but his daughter would secretly confess that Michael's blood ran hot and cold, that Michael had some sort of split personality. Caitlin would describe Michael as being manipulative. She would reveal that Michael would get mean and nasty, and would fly off the handle for no apparent reason. According to Caitlin, Michael would throw tantrums, exhibit fits of rage, and then expect everyone to forget it, to act like nothing had ever happened.

It wouldn't be until after Kathleen's death that Fred would reflect about his ex-wife, thinking back to the time when they were newlyweds, when they were young, and things seemed free and easy. He remembered the day he learned that Kathleen was pregnant. It was on his thirty-fifth birthday that Kathleen had thrown him a surprise party; she had come down the stairs with a gigantic red ribbon wrapped around her waist, presenting herself as his "present." The couple had tried for so long to conceive that Kathleen and Fred had almost given up. Both of them had careers by then, but they were very excited to start a family.

The Atwaters were living in Maryland at the time, where

Fred was working for the Johns Hopkins physics lab. Kathleen enjoyed being a career woman, and had landed a satisfying position as an engineer for Baltimore Air Coil. Because she didn't want to lose her job, Kathleen returned to work just two months after Caitlin was born. She began traveling for the company quite a bit, so the primary care of Caitlin fell into Fred's hands. And that was fine with him. The hesitant new dad found he truly enjoyed taking care of his daughter. He would feed her, dress her, get Caitlin to day care every day, and he never tired of his new routine. At night, he and Caitlin would play games, and Fred would teach Caitlin all kinds of new things.

As the months passed, Fred became so attached to his little girl, he began to keep a diary for Caitlin. For thirteen years, Fred would chronicle all the important events of his daughter's life.

He started from the beginning, when he and Kathleen fell in love, and wrote about the excitement he experienced in the delivery room, from the minute Caitlin was born. Fred described their happy life, detailing Caitlin's growing stages and the way he and Kathleen developed parenting skills. Fred and Kathleen enjoyed being new parents. They liked the change-of-pace life they lived in Maryland. But a year or so after Caitlin was born, Fred was offered a more high-powered job. The family moved to Durham, where Fred began working as a systems analyst for a company in the Research Triangle.

With Fred's raise in pay, Kathleen was able to become a stay-at-home mom, and they bought a beautiful home on Hermitage Court, in their dream neighborhood, the place Kathleen loved most in the world, Forest Hills. Kathleen, however, quickly grew unsatisfied with the role of mother and housewife. She would soon get a job at Nortel Networks, and her life would become extremely busy.

Somewhere along the way, though, Kathleen had forgotten about romance. The great love that she once shared with Fred, all the romantic evenings they'd had together, just seemed to have disappeared. Even though they were living back in Durham, they couldn't seem to recapture the days when they both were carefree students at Duke. Their marriage had been crumbling over time, but Kathleen was so busy, she wasn't even aware of it.

Before Fred's marriage to Kathleen broke up, Kathleen was living in a state of denial. She knew that Fred did not want to abandon Caitlin, and she felt Fred still loved her, in his own way. And Kathleen had tried, not long after they returned to Durham, to salvage their union. She had given Fred all the devotion in the world, but her time was limited. Fred tried to be patient with her, to allow Kathleen the freedom to work, hoping that she would learn to balance her two lives, that she would pay more attention to him. But when his needs weren't met, Fred found comfort in the arms of another woman.

Fred had talked to Kathleen. He had confessed that he felt isolated from her. Fred explained that he loved Kathleen, but thought she was holding back her emotions. He felt her silence wasn't helping matters. He understood that Kathleen didn't like to talk much. Fred knew that she was a person of few words, but he was having a hard time communicating with Kathleen on any level. His infidelity wasn't all her fault, Fred knew. They both had trouble expressing themselves. But Fred didn't want to keep living that way, completely avoiding each other's feelings.

Fred was willing to try to work things out. He later recalled one fateful night, when he sat down with Kathleen to have a serious "talk" just before they went to sleep. Fred decided it was time to confront his wife, to tell her how unhappy he was. He needed change in their marriage. Fred admitted that he felt emotionally detached from Kathleen. He wanted things to go back to the way they were when they first met.

"I feel like there's nothing here," Fred admitted, pleading with his wife.

"What do you mean?" Kathleen asked. "What is the problem?"

"We're just not connecting like we used to. Don't you feel that?"

"Well, I don't know," she said.

"I feel empty inside," he told her. "There's this big space between us."

When Fred suggested that they go to a marriage counselor, Kathleen wanted no part of it. She was a private person, and she had no desire to share her inner secrets with strangers.

"We don't need to go to anybody on the outside," she insisted. "People should be able to work on their own problems."

Kathleen was hopeful that the trouble between them would just fix itself. But it didn't. And because of the infidelity on his part, the couple decided to separate. The thought of a marriage breakup absolutely devastated Kathleen. She was raised in a very strict household, taught that marriage vows should never be broken. So when Fred filed for divorce, Kathleen stayed locked away at home for months, just crying and moping around, holding on to Caitlin for dear life. By then, Kathleen had been promoted at Nortel Networks, she was busier than ever with work. But she would come home at night feeling sad. To occupy her spare time, Kathleen started doing major remodeling projects around the house.

It wasn't until Michael Peterson came along that Kathleen ever had a smile on her face again. She found that, unlike Fred, Michael was an openly loving person who was able to draw her out of her shell. Michael wanted to be there for Kathleen. Michael wanted to be everything that Fred wasn't.

Fred hadn't wanted any wedding ceremony at all, so Michael made up for that by having a grand wedding at his Cedar Street mansion. Fred hadn't been much of a big spender—he was the type who was happy to spend Sundays taking long walks or bike rides. And Michael would make up for that too. He took Kathleen and the kids on extravagant trips to places such as Southeast Asia. He took them on all kinds of adventures.

Back then, it seemed that Michael Peterson was providing his daughter with a Norman Rockwell family. Caitlin often claimed she had the ideal life. But oddly, after Kathleen's death, most of that facade seemed to peel away.

As Fred began to consider the coincidence between the deaths of Elizabeth and Kathleen, he began to realize that Michael had some kind of demented personality. Michael was acting insane. His attitude was changing from minute to minute. Fred wasn't willing to make the leap, to think that Michael had premeditated anything. At some point, he was convinced, though, that Michael Peterson had lost his grasp on reality.

"When I looked at the e-mails from Michael, where he wrote about the estate, he talked about missing all these items. But Caitlin had a right to have all those things," Fred confided. "Michael was just trying to badger her. He's screaming about missing a hundred thousand dollars, while at the same time, he's taking money and buying all kinds of furniture and crap for the house."

When Fred Atwater did finally go into the Cedar Street house, it was in late 2003, long after Peterson's trial was over. What shocked Fred was all the new purchases that Michael had wasted money on. Fred counted six new couches that were sitting in one of the upstairs bedrooms. He noticed a new large-screen TV in the family room, as well as new pieces of elaborate exercise equipment.

Beyond that, Fred was aware that Michael was spending cash on expensive new suits and Italian loafers, always looking like a millionaire when he appeared at a court hearing or was seen on TV. Fred realized that the Peterson "image" was nothing but a sham, that Michael had gone on a shopping spree to try to impress people. But Michael's antics seemed to be working. The local news always asserted that Peterson was a "successful" novelist, and David Rudolf made certain that the public perception of Peterson's success was at the front of everyone's mind. To everyone in the Triangle region who read the papers or watched the news, it seemed that Peterson was a financial powerhouse.

But to Fred, that perception was crazy, given the fact that Peterson had been soliciting so many people for money. Fred knew that, to help with the costs of his legal bills, Michael had gone to his brother Bill, who had already lent him approximately $300,000.

To the members of Kathleen's family, in the months leading up to the murder trial, there were two sides to Michael Peterson that had become painfully evident.

To the media, Peterson was promoting himself as a wealthy highbrow novelist, a person who had no financial motive to kill his wife. But behind the scenes, Michael was still using every trick in the book to get his hands on Kathleen's jewelry, hoping to pawn it for additional cash.

Thirty-nine

When David Rudolf filed a motion in mid-May 2002, demanding any information police might have collected regarding the death of Elizabeth Ratliff, the entire Triangle region paid attention. Up until that point, the idea that Michael Peterson might be connected to any other death—had not been addressed in public.

Rudolf's motion, filed in the Durham County Superior Court, was demanding information, looking for facts that would exonerate Michael Peterson. The public was informed, through newspaper accounts, that the mother of Margaret and Martha Ratliff had a rare blood disease, that the reports about her death indicated "there were no signs of a struggle." Early news accounts stated that the 1985 death of Elizabeth Ratliff had been caused by "a fall on the stairs."

Elizabeth's sister, Margaret Blair, gave interviews revealing that she had contacted Durham investigators just a few days after Kathleen Peterson's death. Blair admitted to reporters that, while she didn't want to alienate her nieces, she felt obligated to tell police about the strange coincidence between two deaths. Blair believed Michael Peterson was the last person to see her sister alive, and she assured reporters that she was acting out of concern, not animosity. When pressed about the subject, Margaret Blair admitted that she had once tried to gain custody of the Ratliff girls and explained that she had left the matter to "the will of God."

Newspaper reporters addressed the complex issue of Elizabeth Ratliff's death, wondering whether or not any of that age-old information could ever make its way into the trial regarding Kathleen Peterson. In most instances, prior acts were not allowed to be brought before a jury. Even if the prosecutors found evidence that could implicate Michael Peterson in Elizabeth Ratliff's death, such evidence probably wouldn't be admissible.

The inadmissibility of a prior act was a concept many people in Durham didn't agree with. If a man had killed before, and that man was standing trial for yet another murder, most folks in Durham felt that was the kind of information that should be made known to a jury. But the American legal system didn't work that way. At least, not as a general rule.

Regarding the Elizabeth Ratliff death, however, things were more complicated. Her death came into a strange category that might prove to be the exception to the rule.

There was already a famous case on the books in North Carolina that had proven to be an exception, which had set an unusual precedent, and it could provide the loophole that the Durham prosecutors might use. The past case involved Barbara Stager, a woman who had been charged with murdering her second husband in 1988. At the time, Barbara Stager was asserting that she had shot her husband accidentally while he was asleep in their bed.

In that case, North Carolina prosecutors were allowed to introduce evidence of her prior act—because it showed her modus operandi. The two crimes were identical. Prosecutors showed the jury that Barbara Stager's first husband had also died from an "accidental" gunshot wound while he was asleep in their bed. To everyone's surprise, the jury convicted Stager of first-degree murder in the slaying of her second husband . . . and the verdict stood.

But ultimately, the decision about the admissibility of any evidence on Elizabeth Ratliff was something that would be up to the trial judge. Until then, everyone was speculating, and any efforts that the Durham prosecution team might make toward discovering the truth of Mrs. Ratliff's death would remain under wraps.

DA Jim Hardin felt there was a good chance that the Ratliff evidence would be allowed in under 404 (b), a rule that covered the similarity of two crimes. It was the same rule that had been employed in the Barbara Stager case, and he was betting that if he could prove Ratliff's death to be a homicide, the judge would allow the evidence in.

With that in mind, Jim Hardin asked Detective Art Holland and Assistant DA Freda Black to start making calls to Germany, to do background work, hoping to see what they might discover. As they began to track down a long list of people, Holland was astonished to learn that the former army pathologist who had signed off on the Ratliff case, Larry Barnes, had not looked for any signs of foul play.

Speaking to Barnes via phone, Art Holland was stunned when Larry Barnes admitted that all corpses sent to him at the Army's 97th General Hospital, in Frankfurt, were *routinely assumed* to involve death by natural causes.

Larry Barnes said that when he received Elizabeth Ratliff's body, he was never informed by German police that it was a possible forensic case. Barnes explained that back in 1985, he had relied primarily on the "spot judgments" that were made by the German authorities at the scene. Barnes said he wasn't ever trained in criminal work.

During their phone conversation, Barnes referred to the 1985 autopsy report on Elizabeth Ratliff, which stated that she suffered "a bleeding to her brain." But when further questioned by Art Holland, Barnes was forced to admit that he wasn't qualified to provide any opinion. Barnes couldn't say whether Ratliff's bleeding was the result of a stroke, a blow to the head, or a fall down the stairs.

As soon as DA Jim Hardin heard the news about the American authorities and their misjudgment, he gave Art Holland and ADA Freda Black the green light to leave for Germany right away. When they arrived in Frankfurt region, Holland and Black would locate Elizabeth's old neighborhood in Graefenhausen. Amazingly, most of her close friends and neighbors were still there. The first person they sat down to chat with was Elizabeth's former nanny, Barbara O'Hara, who had a new last name, Malagnino. The conversation started off warmly, Freda Black being a down-to-earth woman, and Barbara explained that she wound up marrying the taxi driver, Salvatore, the man who helped her on the day she discovered Liz's body. Barbara's memories of Margaret and Martha clearly showed how much she loved and cared for the girls. She had tried to keep in touch with them over the years, but her efforts were futile. The girls had no memory of her, and Michael Peterson didn't seem to want her in their lives anymore.

After much hemming and hawing, Barbara Malagnino admitted that for years she had suspicions about Mrs. Ratliff's death. The former nanny was not willing to name names, but she had always wondered why the German authorities had been in such a rush on the day Liz died. She had spoken to Amybeth Berner, Barbara admitted. The two of them had discussed an intruder theory. Amybeth had pointed out that Liz still had her boots on, which was unlike her. The two surmised that Liz might have been followed into the house, that she had to have been running away from somebody. At the time, Barbara wasn't willing to believe that Michael Peterson had anything to do with the death, but she was surprised when the American authorities ruled Elizabeth's death an accident.

Barbara seemed uneasy when she talked about Michael Peterson. She seemed somewhat afraid of him. She was unwilling to give the complete details, but she had severed her ties with Michael not long after he became guardian to Elizabeth's girls. Apparently, she didn't like Michael's parenting style. It wasn't that Michael had been abusive, but Barbara muttered something about Michael being rough on the girls. She said he had a hard time potty training Martha, had punished the girls for little things, and he had become reclusive with them, not bringing them out into the community as much.

After Elizabeth's death, Barbara thought Michael had become withdrawn, and Amybeth had agreed. The two women had talked at length about the accident, but Barbara Malagnino couldn't say, for sure, what she really thought had happened. In her heart, she believed it wasn't an accidental fall. She talked about the large amount of blood in the stairwell, and she told Freda Black that if she was needed, she would be willing to testify. It was clear that the former nanny felt uncomfortable talking about Peterson, but Barbara felt it was her duty to tell the truth. Deep down, Barbara always knew the day would come when the question of Elizabeth's death would arise.

While in the Frankfurt region, Art Holland and Freda Black were treated very well by German authorities. The German police said they would be willing to reopen the case, if, in fact, the remains of Elizabeth Ratliff were to prove that a homicide had taken place. The two North Carolina law officials were surprised at how at ease they felt in the foreign country. The German people were so helpful and friendly; most folks were willing to cooperate. Holland and Black were impressed by people's memories of Elizabeth. They found that recollections of Elizabeth Ratliff seemed fairly fresh and vivid.

Even though they were not used to the language bar-
rier and sometimes had to rely on German translators,
Holland and Black were able to quiz a number of people
who knew Elizabeth Ratliff very well. They found it was
not difficult for these people to communicate about Liz.
While many folks had fond memories of Liz and her
girls, they were saddened by her sudden death; some
people had questions and concerns that had never been
answered.

Holland and Black were collecting all the evidence
they could.

As they spent more time in Germany, Art Holland and
Freda Black learned that people never understood why
Liz died so young. Liz wasn't much of a drinker; Liz
wasn't one to use drugs. No one understood how Liz
could have taken such a tragic fall. Beyond that, people
were curious as to why Elizabeth left her girls to Michael
and Patricia Peterson. Some folks recalled that Michael
was the person who orchestrated Elizabeth's last will and
testament; they believed Michael had even written the
will up for Liz, just weeks after George died.

The relationship between Elizabeth Ratliff and
Michael Peterson was quite odd. The two of them were
unusually close friends.

Of greatest interest to Holland and Black was their interview with Tom and Cheryl Appel-Schumacher, who,
after contacting a lawyer, had agreed to talk to the North
Carolina authorities to clear up any misjudgments on
their part. Tom and Cheryl recalled the wonderful party
that Liz had thrown them. They talked about her depression and how, in the days before her death, Liz
seemed to finally be getting over the loss of her husband.
They admitted that they helped clean up the blood in
the staircase on the day of Elizabeth's death, believing
her death was an accident. They couldn't remember for

sure, but they thought that Michael Peterson had helped them with the cleanup.

The Appel-Schumachers were horrified that Elizabeth's death might be deemed a homicide. They insisted that they had not been suspicious at the time. They said they never, in a million years, would have suspected Michael of any wrongdoing. They saw Elizabeth and Michael as nothing more than friends, and they considered Michael and Patricia to be caring and loving people.

The Appel-Schumachers saw their role in the cleanup of the blood as a necessary act. They had not wanted Liz's girls to have any memory of bloody walls. They hoped that they hadn't interfered with justice; they were just doing what was best for the girls.

As they spoke to Holland and Black, the Appel-Schumachers were clearly upset by the details of Kathleen Peterson's death. Like Barbara, they said they would be willing to come to America to testify in the case against Michael Peterson. The Appel-Schumachers promised they would cooperate in any way. But they felt sick to their stomachs to hear about Kathleen in the stairwell with all that blood . . . it was worse than déjà vu.

Before they left the Frankfurt region, Art Holland and Freda Black would have a most alarming conversation with a former neighbor of Elizabeth Ratliff's, a woman from Graefenhausen by the name of Karin Hamm. The neighbor needed to use a translator, but she eventually gave Holland and Black a written statement that said she had seen Michael Peterson "running down the street" away from the Ratliff residence, the night before Elizabeth was found dead.

Forty

Back in the States, another eerie coincidence was making headlines. An award-winning film crew, which had won an Oscar for a documentary called *Murder on a Sunday Morning*, was busy working with David Rudolf and Michael Peterson on developing a documentary for ABC television. The crew, which had flown in from France, told Durham reporters that they'd already spoken to Judge Orlando Hudson Jr., who would be presiding in the Peterson case, as well as DA Jim Hardin. The French crew was asked about the strange connection between the title of their previous film, given the fact that Kathleen Peterson was found dead, allegedly murdered on a Sunday morning. But the film crew found none of that to be amusing.

The award-winning crew, Maha Productions, was given special permission to tape court hearings and the trial proceedings, and were allowed to clip a microphone to David Rudolf. Judge Hudson was in favor of having the documentary made—feeling that it would not compromise the Peterson trial in any way. Having been assured that the documentary would not be aired until after the trial verdict and sentencing, the judge was convinced a documentary would have educational value.

The fact that Kathleen Peterson was alleged to have been murdered on a Sunday morning, turned out to have no particular relevance to the film crew, which would work, almost exclusively, with Michael Peterson and his attorneys, David Rudolf and Thomas Maher. From the outset, it seemed obvious that the documentary filmmakers believed in Rudolf's abilities to convince a jury that there was no real evidence against Michael Peterson. Everyone in the Peterson camp believed strongly in his innocence, and Maha Productions would be given complete access to the accused murderer and his immediate family. They would be allowed to follow Peterson's defense team around for months prior to his trial.

In late October 2002, with Peterson's trial date of May 2003 still way off in the distance, Caitlin Atwater filed a wrongful-death suit that sought compensation for "the pain and suffering of Kathleen Peterson" caused by Michael Peterson's fatal assault. The civil matter would be pursued separately from Peterson's criminal trial. It alleged that Michael Peterson did intentionally, maliciously, and willfully assault his wife, causing her death.

Peterson publicly responded to the civil suit by stating how "saddened" he was about his family being ripped apart. He told reporters that the Durham police had chosen to provide Caitlin with only part of the evidence, which had resulted in a "predictable" action. Peterson felt sorry for Caitlin's pain, the loss of her mother, and her "precipitous" action. He also felt sorry for his other four children, who, having lost a mother, had now lost a sister as well.

Caitlin Atwater's attorney, Jay Trehy, reported that the wrongful-death lawsuit would remain under seal until Michael Peterson's criminal proceedings were concluded. The attorney said that the suit he filed on Miss Atwater's behalf would show "clear and convincing evidence" of malice and wanton conduct on the part of

Michael Peterson. However, to avoid complications, the attorney was not at liberty to discuss any possible motive, or the way in which the alleged murder occurred.

The wrongful-death lawsuit, Caitlin's attorney insisted, was not an attempt to taint the criminal case against Peterson in any way. However, Todd Peterson was publicly enraged by the filing of the civil suit, telling a *Herald-Sun* reporter that Caitlin had been "poisoned" by a one-sided presentation of facts by police and prosecutors.

"If she was interested in the truth," Todd said of Caitlin, "she would have waited until all the facts had come out at trial before making her mind up about what happened to our mother."

Todd was quoted as calling Caitlin's lawsuit a "transparent attempt" to prejudice their father's trial, and he felt that Caitlin's legal action was "inexcusable."

The same day the wrongful-death suit was filed, October 30, 2002, attorney Jay Trehy had knocked on Michael Peterson's front door at 9:00 A.M. Trehy was at the Cedar Street house to supervise a moving company to collect all of Caitlin Atwater's belongings and remove them from the Peterson home. The move took about two hours, and Caitlin, who was about to enter a Durham County courthouse that afternoon, had decided it best to keep her distance.

She would recall her sadness on that day. Having just turned twenty, Caitlin would normally consult her mother about difficult and trying matters. Caitlin had done a lot of soul-searching before reaching her decision to file suit, and she felt that her mom would have wanted her to take action, that her mom would have wanted her to know the truth.

In terms of Michael and Todd's accusations that she had abandoned her family, Caitlin would remind reporters that Michael had essentially "disowned" her months before, when Peterson stood in a court of law and asserted that Caitlin Atwater deserved no insurance benefits from her mother's Prudential policy.

Caitlin and her attorney, Jay Trehy, were conducting an investigation of their own, looking at financial records, checking in with Durham prosecutors, in order to pursue the case. Because of all the stress, Caitlin had taken a leave of absence from her studies at Cornell.

There were too many questions to be answered.

For one thing, Fred Atwater had discovered that Kathleen's Prudential life insurance policy, which she obtained as an executive at Nortel Networks, still had *his* name listed as the beneficiary. Apparently, Kathleen had never signed the paperwork—filled out by Peterson in 1997 after their wedding—that would officially designate Michael Peterson as the sole beneficiary.

Nobody was sure why Kathleen had failed to sign the papers. There was rumor that a call had been placed to Nortel just months before Kathleen's death—that someone was trying to discover the facts regarding her life insurance. There was some technicality that needed to be figured out, and Fred Atwater had become fully aware of it.

It seems there had been a second policy, which Fred and Kathleen had been paying into for Caitlin's college fund, and the payout of half of that policy was made in late 2000 to Kathleen Peterson. Fred had looked at all the insurance papers at the time—he was trying to advise Caitlin—and was totally against the switch of her assets into a high-tech company. Fred felt his daughter was gambling with her future. But Caitlin had been convinced by Michael and her mother to take half the proceeds that had built up—$40,000—and purchase Nortel Networks stock.

Fred Atwater recalled that he was nervous about the Petersons juggling half of Caitlin's college fund. As it happened, just months after the purchase, Nortel stock

plummeted from something like $80 a share to about $2
a share. In the year 2001, Caitlin asked her mom to sell
her Nortel stock at that crazy low rate—losing most of
her $40,000 investment.

It was not long after Kathleen's death, when Fred Atwater studied Kathleen's life insurance policies, that he
realized that Kathleen had failed to sign the paperwork
to designate Michael her beneficiary. Fred was usually
not a superstitious man, but he felt Kathleen's oversight
may have been an omen. In any case, the fact remained
that Michael Peterson, while mentioned in the 1997 insurance policy, was not legally designated as the
recipient of the $1.45 million dollars.

Paperwork had been filed in 1997, designating
Michael Peterson as beneficiary, but the papers were un-
signed. While Peterson's attorneys were asserting that it
was clear the Michael should get the money, it would become a matter for the courts to rule on, and it would be
tabled until after the criminal proceedings were heard.

In the meantime, Caitlin Atwater's attorney would file
a separate claim, contending that if Fred Atwater was not
named the life insurance beneficiary, then the $1.45 mil-
lion should go to Caitlin, that she should be the sole
beneficiary of her mother's life insurance policy, not
Michael Peterson. The claim would mention that under
North Carolina's "slayer statute," if Peterson was to be
convicted of killing his wife, he would be prohibited
from any economic gain.

Forty-one

It would take months, but eventually Margaret and Martha Ratliff would sign a document allowing Durham prosecutors to exhume the remains of their mother. DA Hardin would ask Art Holland to fly to Bay City, Texas, to oversee the two-hour exhumation process of a woman who had been dead for nearly eighteen years.

Because the medical examiner's office in North Carolina had no way of knowing the size or weight of the coffin, or the condition of the remains, arrangements were made through the Durham DA's travel coordinator, John Hutchinson, to fly Art Holland to Texas, and then have him drive back, following Elizabeth Ratliff's coffin to Chapel Hill.

As it happened, the DA's office was watching every dime, expenses were adding up in the case against Michael Peterson, so the coffin was not placed in a separate trailer. Instead, it was placed in an SUV, driven by an employee from the funeral home in Bay City. In order to maintain the chain of custody of her remains, Art Holland had two members from the Durham police as backup. The casket could not be left alone for a minute. The remains had to be kept under guard throughout the twenty-four-hour period it would take to deliver Elizabeth Ratliff's body to the custody of state medical examiner Dr. Deborah Radisch.

Several weeks of planning had gone into the decision to drive the remains. Hutchinson had originally called all the airlines, hoping the casket could be flown back, but ultimately directions were provided from Texas to Mississippi, where the detective and his men would stay overnight, eventually making their way to North Carolina in a slow procession. David Rudolf had sent an investigator from his defense team down to Bay City, so that Michael Peterson would have representation at the exhumation, and the French crew, Maha Productions, had also tagged along to document the ordeal. Everyone was concerned about what they would find in the casket. No one had any idea what degree of deterioration the body would be in.

When Elizabeth Ratliff was delivered to the Office of the Chief Medical Examiner at Chapel Hill on April 16, 2003, Dr. Deborah Radisch was accompanied by a team of medical examiners as the coffin was opened. Among them were Chief Medical Examiner Dr. John Butts and Dr. Aaron Gleckman, both of whom would later testify at the Peterson trial. Also present at the autopsy examination were representatives from the Durham Police Department, the Durham District Attorney's Office, and the law office of David Rudolf.

After the yellow police tape was removed, as the silver-gray metal casket was jarred, everyone stood in amazement. After almost eighteen years, the corpse of Elizabeth Ratliff was entirely intact. Present with her in the casket were several personal items: a white stuffed toy lamb, a metal charm of ballet slippers, a metal unicorn, a seashell, a children's book, *The Little Rabbit*, and a card with a photo of a church in Frankfurt marked "George and Elizabeth Ratliff." Inside the card was a color photograph of their two small girls.

Her wedding gown had yellowed, but the off-white gauzy cotton dress with lace inserts was still completely preserved. Underneath, Elizabeth was clothed in a white full slip, white knee-high hose, and a matching white lace bra and panties. Once her clothing had been removed, the medical examiners noted that her skin had discolored, but everything about the corpse looked immaculately preserved. Elizabeth's hair, her makeup, and her nail polish were all in place. She lay with a soft smile on her face, looking peaceful and rested. The autopsy examination revealed that the embalmed body was in an excellent state of condition, and with the exception of portions of the brain, her internal body cavities were largely complete. It was hard to imagine her body would have been in such perfect shape. It was as though her corpse was speaking.

It was as though Elizabeth Ratliff had something to say.

It would take two weeks for the findings of the new autopsy report to be made public. The public would be shocked to learn that the medical examiners had noted *seven lacerations* to Elizabeth Ratliff's scalp—the same number of lacerations found on the scalp of Kathleen Peterson. The death was ruled a homicide and Dr. Radisch's diagnosis was confirmed by a neuropathology consultation. Medical examiners Dr. Stephen Smith and Dr. Aaron Gleckman would file a report that stated "the inflicted trauma was clearly from a homicidal assault."

In addition to the subarachnoid hemorrhages, there were contusions to Elizabeth Ratliff's left hand and left forearm. So, like Kathleen Peterson, she showed signs of defensive wounds, signs of trying to fend off her attacker. And there were unexplainable contusions to her lips and left eyelid.

When Elizabeth Ratliff's death was ruled a homicide, the local media jumped all over it. Reporters wondered how the two Ratliff autopsies could have had such drastically different results. David Rudolf attacked the Chapel Hill medical examiners for making statements concluding that Ratliff was murdered, asking, "Since when do forensic neuropathologists offer gratuitous comments?"

Rudolf told local newspapers that the new autopsy findings were unscientific. He noted that Elizabeth Ratliff's brain tissue had deteriorated, which, he said, was critical, because the original autopsy exam had concluded that Ratliff died of a stroke. The first autopsy exam, Rudolf reminded the press, had been based on an examination of brain tissue that was now missing. The attorney argued that the publishing of the new findings was inflammatory and outrageous.

But the new autopsy report had also revealed a *linear fracture* at the base of Elizabeth Ratliff's skull, which was associated with one of the lacerations on her left posterior scalp. To the team of North Carolina medical experts, the forty-three-year-old woman had suffered a blunt trauma to her head. It was clear that Elizabeth Ratliff had been beaten to death.

Forty-two

The length of Michael Peterson's 2003 trial would surpass everyone's expectations; it would be the longest-running trial in Durham history. The jury selection process alone lasted from May 5 to June 23—all those weeks being used to whittle down 124 prospective jurors to a panel of 12 and 4 alternates. The main issue for the prosecution was to make sure that jurors understood that a motive was *not essential* for conviction. There was no murder weapon, no eyewitness, and the motive would be speculative.

The case being entirely circumstantial, DA Jim Hardin and ADA Freda Black had mentioned the existence of the new autopsy on Elizabeth Ratliff, noting that the cause of death was changed from accident to homicide. Freda Black would tell jurors that if the Ratliff evidence were to be allowed in, the state would not have to prove that Michael Peterson was involved in Ratliff's death. It was enough, Black would explain, under the 404 (b) provision, that the defendant had been present at an identical crime scene, that the defendant had specific knowledge about how to set up that identical crime.

David Rudolf would tell prospective jurors that Kathleen Peterson fell backward on a step, at the lower part of the stairwell, and split her scalp open. He asserted that Mrs. Peterson had tried to stand up, but had slipped on the bloody floor and had hit her head again, her blood loss causing her death. Rudolf would further contend that the case was going to hinge on forensics. He promised to offer evidence that the police took an hour to secure the crime scene, that police had allowed Michael and Todd Peterson to embrace Kathleen's body and spread blood in the kitchen, the laundry room, on a diet Coke can, and on a couch.

Rudolf also attacked the Durham forensic investigation unit, telling prospective jurors that the unit did not take detailed pictures or notes, had not drawn sufficient diagrams, and could not be counted on for its findings pertaining to the events of December 9, 2001. David Rudolf would continue to characterize the upcoming case as "a battle of the experts," assuring prospective jurors that the defense would show that both deaths were accidental. Rudolf was confident that Mr. Peterson had absolutely nothing to do with either death.

David Rudolf would not say whether Michael Iver Peterson would be testifying on his own behalf, and to prospective jurors, little was known about the life of Michael Iver Peterson. The son of a military career man who grew up moving from place to place, Michael Peterson was indeed known to Durham's upper-crust social circles, but he was a nonentity to the majority of the population. Peterson had never been elected to any political office, and most folks didn't pay enough close attention to know that he had once written a political column for the *Herald-Sun*. In the era of modern, fast-paced living, most people didn't have time to read newspapers, no less novels, so the majority of people in the jury pool had no idea who Peterson was.

As for Peterson's books, it turned out that only a handful of folks were enamored with them. Peterson had a narrow following, mostly among military personnel, but his books had never garnered him much national acclaim. He certainly wasn't a household name. In fact, Michael Peterson wasn't even in the category of certain "noted" Southern authors.

All the efforts that Peterson had made over the years, trying to parlay the name recognition from his books, from his columns, and from his local community involvement, just hadn't worked out for him. But jurors would never hear how Peterson's bids for public office had ended badly; they would never hear about all the rejection letters Peterson had received from editors over the years; they would never hear about the hopeful movie options that had amounted to nothing other than thin air.

Instead, they would be told that Peterson had a wonderful and fruitful existence, continuing his grand writing career at his million-dollar home, where he lived with his wife, Kathleen, who worked long hours as an executive at Nortel. The prospective jurors would be given a portrait of the kindhearted and generous Michael Peterson, who had helped raise five children, and who, along with his wife, was a patron of the local arts.

Days before his trial began, Court TV ran a profile on Michael Peterson, taping him sitting in his vast eleven-thousand-square-foot home, surrounded with trinkets and expensive Chinese artworks. The novelist had collected his thoughts; he was in fine spirits, and was very optimistic about his upcoming case. Peterson sat politely and chatted with a Court TV reporter from his comfortably furnished office, where the homegrown roses on his desk seemed to breathe fresh life into the air.

Down the long corridor, along another wing of the house, the Court TV crew would notice the cheap unpainted plywood that concealed the bloodstained staircase where Mrs. Peterson had died. The Court TV crew was not allowed near the bloodstains, not early on, before the trial started. But they would ultimately take a stroll through the remnants of Kathleen Peterson's blood, before the trial was all over. In the interim, the Court TV reporter was assured that the forensic experts, hired by Peterson, would be able to explain exactly what the bloodstain patterns in the stairwell meant—poor Kathleen, beloved wife, had taken a tragic fall.

Michael Peterson told the TV reporter that he and his wife had the kind of marriage that other people envied. He spoke of his grief for his deceased spouse. His son Todd told Court TV that his father's upcoming murder trial was "incomprehensible." Todd asserted that his dad and his stepmom had "the most loving relationship" he could imagine.

"They never fought," Todd told the reporter, promising that he would be sitting behind his father when the opening statements began. Todd assured the reporter that he, along with the rest of the family, including his biological mom, Patricia, would make their daily presence in court known. They all believed wholeheartedly in Michael's innocence. David Rudolf also participated in the family's Court TV interview, telling the reporter that, while his client was not a perfect man, Peterson's faults didn't mean he was capable of murdering the woman who was "the love of his life."

There was one thing Rudolf was concerned about, he admitted. It was the graphic nature of the autopsy photographs. He would tell Court TV that he expected jurors to have "a gut reaction" when they faced all that blood. But even so, the attorney seemed confident. He was certain he would be able to get people to see beyond that.

Forty-three

On the day of opening arguments, July 1, 2003, two scenarios were presented to jurors in Peterson's murder trial. David Rudolf, who was reportedly paid over $1 million by Peterson, would use high-tech resources—large screens, PowerPoint, an array of expensive audio-visual equipment—to make his case. On the other side of the courtroom were two unpretentious prosecutors, Jim Hardin and Freda Black, who chose to present the facts the old-fashioned way—using charts, metal pointers, and photos mounted on cardboard.

It was a high-stakes trial. Court TV would cover the entirety of it, and before it was over, programs like *Good Morning America* would host Kathleen's family members and *Oprah* would be calling. Amid the high drama, the national exposure, and the public interest, the case had followers arguing for each side. Many onlookers believed that David Rudolf and his team were winning the battle. The defense had poked many holes into the prosecution's case, and there seemed to be so much reasonable doubt.

People who were behind the scenes, those working for the prosecution, and even the presiding judge, the Honorable Orlando Hudson Jr., thought the verdict could go either way. The journalists covering the trial, after sitting through five months of voir dire and testimony, felt that there had been convincing closing arguments from both sides, but were taking bets that Michael Peterson would walk. After the tremendous battle David Rudolf and his team had waged, the courtroom bystanders felt that the best anyone could hope for was a hung jury.

For the defense, there were four men representing Peterson: the notable David Rudolf; Thomas Maher, Rudolf's partner, who was listed among the best lawyers in America; Ron Guerette, a private investigator, who had been to Germany and Texas and back again; and Guy Seaberg, a former prosecutor, who, because of his own run-in with the law, had been disbarred and had moved to Durham, where he was operating various Web sites, including Hizzoner.com.

For the prosecution, there was the elected official, DA Jim Hardin, a lifelong resident of Durham, and the county's top prosecutor; ADA Freda Black, a topgun who handled the county's most violent felony cases; ADA David Saacks, a veteran litigator, who was working on the case in the capacity of researcher, and Art Holland, the lead detective in the case, with twenty-two years of experience on the Durham police force.

From day one, as the drama began to unfold, Jim Hardin opened with what was considered to be an ace: a replica of the alleged murder weapon, a unique fireplace tool called a blow poke, which the public had never seen before. Standing in front of the jury, Hardin reached into a plastic bag and pulled out a four-foot-long hollow brass pole, a hollow fire poker, which he alleged was identical to the possible murder weapon. It was a fireplace tool that had been omnipresent in the Peterson home. Throughout the years, Kathleen's sisters had helped her use the tool to build a warm and cozy family atmosphere, her sister Lori recalling that the fireplace poker was in the home when she visited there in 2001.

The fireplace tool was a gift, given to Kathleen by her sister Candace, in 1984. It was an antique-looking item, a very handy object, which Kathleen kept in her kitchen area. The tool always sat next to the fireplace in the kitchen, and it was useful because it was a blower and a poker all in one. The blow poke, a tool that no one had ever really heard of, was apparently used to fan flames.

Kathleen had built many fires, she had enjoyed the tool for many years. But mysteriously, Hardin alleged, the unique gift, the blow poke, was missing from the Peterson household after Kathleen's untimely death.

"They say it was an accident, a fall down the stairs," Hardin told jurors, "and we say it's not. We say she died a horrible, painful death at the hands of her husband, Michael Peterson."

Jim Hardin then showed the jury two carefully selected photos. He wanted them to see two opposing sides of Kathleen Peterson. From the first photo, the jury could see a very genteel, warm person, a woman with a smile on her face. They could see that she was a woman of substance and presence. Kathleen was a very graceful lady, and her expression was full of charm.

But as the image of the lovely woman faded from view, as Kathleen's beautiful face was removed from the posterboard, the jury would be aghast at the next photo the prosecutor placed in front of them. It was a crime scene photo, showing Kathleen Peterson lying on the bottom of the steps, and the photo was so gruesome, Hardin deliberately shielded it from the courtroom audience, holding it directly before the jury.

The picture was eerie. It showed a bloody and battered Kathleen, her white sweatpants covered with red spatter, her legs spread in an odd position. The picture had a strange look about it; it was almost a still-life representation of horror and gore. Kathleen's body seemed to be oddly propped up against the stairwell door frame, and her battered face was frozen in an expression of sheer agony and terror. The twisted corpse of Kathleen was surrounded by bloody paper towels, bloody rags, and the bloody shoes and socks of Michael Peterson.

Hardin would tell jurors that when the emergency crews first arrived, at 2:48 A.M. on December 9, 2001, the sight of Kathleen Peterson had horrified them. The prosecutor mentioned that at least one person at the scene would testify that the positioning of Kathleen's body at the bottom of the stairs *just didn't make any sense.*

Jim Hardin knew he would be fighting an uphill battle against David Rudolf for weeks and weeks to come. Rudolf had already filed motions to try to stop the evidence from coming in; he had argued that the police hadn't served proper search warrants, that the police had contaminated the scene. Hardin knew that Rudolf was prepared to destroy the credibility of every state witness, that Rudolf was a meticulous defense attorney who had done all his homework. With ABC and other news crews taping, with Court TV airing the event, Hardin would be facing the battle of his career, and Rudolf would be pulling out all the stops.

But Jim Hardin had something that all the experts in the world couldn't truly explain. Knowing that he had to make a striking first impression with the jury, the prosecutor would waste no time in bringing out the worst photograph of all: the image of Kathleen Peterson's shaved head as she was lying on the steel gurney at the medical examiner's office. The photo exposed a large scalp area, covered entirely with bright red wounds. It would be unfathomable to jurors, the sight of the lacerations to Kathleen Peterson's scalp. There were so many slices, and there were jagged type marks that resembled pitchforks.

"They say it's an accident, and we say it's murder," Hardin told the jurors, "and you will have to decide that."

"We say it's murder. . . . " The words would ring in the corridors of the court.

The prosecutor didn't have the actual murder weapon, but he spoke of the blow poke, the gift from Candace, given to Kathleen in the days when she was married to Fred Atwater. The missing blow poke, he said, was identical to the one he held before them. Kathleen's sister had supplied the item to the prosecution. Having purchased a set of blow pokes as Christmas gifts for each of her siblings, Candace had been the person who originally suggested that the blow poke might have been used to cause her sister's death. Candace had brought her own blow poke to Durham, hoping that police might be able to find the missing fireplace tool. But police had searched the Petersons' grounds for days. They had been through every inch of the house on three separate occasions. They had even used dogs to scour the property.

But there was no blow poke to be found. After exhaustive searching, police determined that the blow poke had been removed from the Peterson property.

Jim Hardin wanted jurors to understand that he was not contending the blow poke in his hand was the actual murder weapon—only that Michael Peterson could have used an identical item, causing the severe lacerations to his wife's head.

Hardin would maintain that the primary mechanism for killing was something like the metal pole he held in his hand. Hardin said it was light, hollow, and easily used to inflict the wounds Kathleen Peterson suffered, wounds that had lacerated her scalp without fracturing her skull.

As he spoke, Hardin raised the blow poke high up into the air, swinging it down into his left hand with a striking motion, making a tapping sound. The prosecutor repeated the move a few times, reenacting a beating.

"This case is about pretenses and appearances," the prosecutor continued, changing his tone. "It's about things not being as they seem."

Then Jim Hardin began to unfold the story. He revealed the grandeur of the Peterson mansion, which gave the appearance of a storybook life between a couple who had a happily "blended family." He would tell jurors that these were people who seemed to have it all. These were successful, high-class people, this author and his corporate executive wife, and they seemed to be the quintessential couple. From all appearances, they had the perfect household, the perfect family, the perfect marriage.

"But as the old saying goes," Hardin would tell jurors, "appearances can be very deceiving."

The prosecutor would explain that the Petersons had anything but a perfect home life. Things had gone awry in their household, and by 2001, things had spun out of control. While things looked grand from the outside, things were rotting away at the core. The Petersons had developed a huge appetite for expensive living, Hardin told jurors, and had cultivated a taste for fine things. According to the evidence, the Petersons were able to live well, largely because of Kathleen's salary and benefits during her twelve-year career at Nortel. For many years, the Peterson family had plenty of money coming in, due to the rising profits at Nortel. And as the Internet gained worldwide appeal, particularly toward the end of the 1990s, the potential for greater wealth was always on the horizon.

But then, in the years prior to Kathleen's death, Hardin explained, the Petersons' financial picture would begin to change drastically. And that changing picture was something that Michael Peterson just couldn't tolerate. The prosecutor said that for several years prior to her death, it was Kathleen—not Michael—who had been the primary support for the Peterson-Atwater-Ratliff family. The evidence would show that everyone in the Peterson household—including Michael—depended on Kathleen to bring home her substantial salary and all-encompassing benefit package.

In the years prior to her death, not only was Kathleen carrying most of the financial burden for the family, but she had become overwhelmed by the cost of paying three college tuitions, as well as multiple mortgages on rental properties that the Petersons held, properties that held little equity. Hardin would describe the financial predicament the Petersons had gotten themselves into, telling jurors that, according to the state's financial analysts, by the years 2000 and 2001, Michael Peterson was making no money as a writer. Records would show that because Kathleen Peterson had deferred 80 percent of her income from Nortel Networks in the year 2001, the Petersons had to begin living on credit. They were also forced to liquidate Kathleen's assets.

To help put things into context, Jim Hardin explained that he would be calling a witness, a financial investigator, who would talk about the financial and personnel environment that Kathleen and others at Nortel Networks had found themselves in. By the fall of 2001, the fortunes of Nortel had deteriorated, and as the stock price plummeted, Kathleen Peterson, who had used her deferred income to purchase more Nortel stock, had lost most of her life's earnings.

To make matters worse, Nortel had begun to lay people off in great numbers. There would be evidence to show that Kathleen Peterson was worried about her job, that she was involved in the job-firing process at Nortel, which the company referred to as "optimizing." Hardin would contend that, having fired so many of her employees, Kathleen was aware that her job could easily be eliminated. And Kathleen had confided to her sisters,

Candace and Lori, that she was worried about being fired, frightened that she would join the masses of people who were being replaced by younger people, workers who were willing to do the same job for much less pay.

Because of the state of the U.S. economy following 9/11, in late months of 2001, Kathleen Peterson had become convinced that she would be left with nowhere to go to find employment in the Triangle area. It was unbelievable to Kathleen that all of her years of hard work—after fighting for her engineering degree from Duke, after putting in so much overtime, and forsaking vacation time—her life's work would amount to nothing. Kathleen had lost it all in the stock market. She had listened to her husband's advice, had gambled with her future, and suddenly she found herself being forced to sell her Nortel stock at a ridiculous price. To add insult to injury, even with a conference room named after her, Kathleen Peterson knew that her job was not secure at Nortel. It was clear that no one could count on any loyalty from the company, and if she were to be terminated, Kathleen felt there was absolutely nowhere for her to turn.

For years, Kathleen had been looking forward to an early retirement. She had seen her net worth increase tenfold in the dot-com era—in the age of high-tech mania. But suddenly, at the age of forty-eight, Kathleen found herself in a financial predicament that seemed unimaginable. Kathleen confessed to Candace that she could no longer afford a housekeeper, that she could no longer pay the basic bills around the house. She was forced to use a downstairs shower because none of the master bathroom plumbing was working properly.

Kathleen had taken steps to avoid complete financial ruin; she had signed papers to reverse her deferred payment plan and would be receiving her regular income from Nortel in the year 2002. But even with her annual salary of $145,000, the family was facing too much debt, and with so many more expenses yet to come, Kathleen felt the situation was looking dire.

In fall 2001, Kathleen's *boss* was fired by Nortel. Just days before her boss was let go, he had warned her that her job had been placed on the "optimization" list, and secretly confided that he'd managed to save her job position. It was at that point that Kathleen Peterson developed a sense of impending doom. In the months before her death, Kathleen felt certain that she was about to lose her only real source of income. Nortel Networks was axing everyone who worked around her. Kathleen was taking on more responsibility with each firing, but that would only be a temporary solution for her plight. No matter how hard she worked, Kathleen could see the darkness waiting for her—she had come to the end of the corporate tunnel.

"But Mike Peterson, the creative thinker, the writer of fiction, was able to figure out the perfect solution," Jim Hardin explained. "The solution was to make it appear as though Kathleen accidentally fell down the steps and died. And then like magic—no more money problems. Like magic—with Kathleen's death, Michael Peterson goes from a point where they're having to sell assets and live off credit to survive . . . to having 1.8 million dollars in his hand."

That would be the amount Michael Peterson stood to get, Hardin told jurors, between his wife's life insurance policy and her deferred payment benefits. And that money, of course, would solve a lot of problems. It was a wonderful solution to the financial fire that Peterson had built for himself. But there was only one catch . . .

Peterson would have to kill his wife to get the $1.8 million. . . .

Jim Hardin told jurors about the gamble that Michael Peterson took when he placed the first 9-1-1 call. Peterson was gambling that the police were as dumb as he thought they were. Peterson was gambling that the police would see his wife's death as he wanted them to see it. Peterson had called 9-1-1 to say there had been an accidental fall, and Jim Hardin asked the jurors to listen carefully to the tape of that first call. He would contend that Michael Peterson had selectively given information to the dispatcher, saying that his wife was still breathing—then hanging up.

In the second 9-1-1 call, Hardin emphasized, when Peterson had called again, moments later, suddenly his wife was not breathing. As the 9-1-1 operator continued to ask questions of him, Peterson didn't answer. Peterson was being very cautious about the information he was giving, the prosecutor said, because *he knew the call was being taped.*

A question Hardin didn't raise, but something many people in the courtroom were wondering—especially as the 9-1-1 calls were later played by David Rudolf so jurors could hear the "panicked" voice of Michael Peterson— was why the distraught husband would deliberately hang up on the operator as his wife lay dying.

Peterson had initially reported that Kathleen was breathing.

It would make sense, then, that Peterson would have stayed on the phone with the dispatcher, that he would have wanted to get emergency instructions to try to save Kathleen. It would seem rational, since Peterson was clearly so upset on the phone, that he would do what most people did in an emergency. Most people would hang on the line to wait for help to arrive; they would want to keep the dispatcher on the line to help guide them through an attempt to save their spouses. . . .

Forty-four

David Rudolf began his opening statement by playing the first 9-1-1 call that Peterson made on the night of his wife's death. The defense attorney wanted jurors to hear it for themselves—the voice of a frantic man. Rudolf wanted them to listen to all of Peterson's emotion on tape, asking jurors to decide whether he was evading questions or was a husband in a state of distress.

The defense attorney took the jurors back in time—to 1988—when Michael and Kathleen first met and fell in love. He wanted them to know that in the beginning, when his client met Kathleen Atwater, she was not the high-powered Nortel executive making oodles of money. Back then, Kathleen was a newly separated single mom who was working for Nortel as a technical writer, making $37,000 a year.

It wasn't her money that Michael was attracted to. It wasn't anything like that at all. Rudolf told jurors that Kathleen and Michael had connected in a way that only a few lucky people in the world ever experience. Their love had nothing to do with tangible things; they were soul mates. They were happy living together in a modest house. And when Michael Peterson sold his book *A Time of War*, then he was able to buy the Cedar Street home. This house was *not* a Hollywood mansion; it was just a very lovely, big, old house.

Rudolf pointed to Margaret and Martha Ratliff, sitting behind his client in the first row. He explained to jurors that Michael and Kathleen had raised the girls, that with the death of Kathleen, Margaret and Martha had lost a mother, just like Caitlin had lost a mother. The attorney wanted it known that Michael and Kathleen had worked hard to build a family. They had woven together the strands out of their prior families, and they had created a strong household.

The attorney stressed that what kept the Petersons together for *thirteen* years was their love and strong bond. It had nothing to do with furniture, or any earthly goods. The Petersons liked nice things, sure, but their love for each other was something so great, most people envied it. To prove his point, Rudolf read from an essay Caitlin Atwater had written in 1999, describing what Michael Peterson meant to her mom.

"Michael stopped my mother's tears," Caitlin wrote. "I used to sit at the top of the stairs, leaning through the banister, and listen to my mother sob every night for a year after my father left. But Mike was able to restore her strength and confidence, and to show her that she could find true love. From the beginning, I was in debt to Mike in my heart and mind, for bringing back my mother's happiness."

Rudolf continued reading Caitlin's essay, making certain that the jury heard the loving feelings Caitlin had toward her stepdad. So, it wasn't only that the Petersons were in love—they were also good parents. The Petersons took care of each other and their children with pride. They had the kind of bond that no one could deny. Their love couldn't be faked. Their relationship couldn't have been more perfect. Michael and Kathleen were so in tune with each other.

The defense attorney painted an image of Michael and Kathleen as being very affectionate with each other.

In early December 2001, the couple had already gone out and bought their Christmas tree, and the weekend Kathleen died, they had been out dancing at a holiday party, until very late on Friday night. On Saturday, December 8, they had been celebrating a call about a potential movie deal. Michael's books had yet to be made into movies, but Rudolf explained that wasn't unusual. That was the way things went in Hollywood. Regardless, the Petersons were still excited at the prospect of a movie production, and they had reason to celebrate.

The two of them had decided champagne was in order, and that night they had made dinner and had settled in their cozy family room to watch a romantic movie, *America's Sweethearts*. Their son Todd had stopped by with a friend at about 9:30 P.M., and he had witnessed the Petersons drinking champagne and wine. The Petersons seemed happy and content. There was nothing unusual going on.

Not long after Todd and his friend left the house, at 11:08 P.M., Kathleen received a call from a coworker. It was Helen Preslinger calling from Ontario about a meeting that Kathleen was flying up to Canada to attend. The phone records had logged the call, Rudolf explained, and Preslinger would report that when she spoke to Kathleen, she could hear Michael in the background. Preslinger could hear no fighting going on, no tension in Kathleen's voice.

"Kathleen didn't say she had to get off the phone," Rudolf told jurors. "It was a completely normal conversation."

According to Rudolf, at around midnight, Kathleen and Michael had gone out to the pool, which was their habit, so he could smoke his pipe and she could sneak a few cigarettes. Then, somewhere in the vicinity of 1:45 to 2:00 A.M., Kathleen had excused herself to go upstairs to get some sleep. She wanted to be bright-eyed for a conference call she was expecting the next morning.

And that was the last time that Michael had seen his wife alive.

The defense attorney told jurors that on the night she died, Kathleen Peterson had a blood alcohol content of .07—just one point below the legal limit. He also pointed out that Kathleen had Valium in her system, which was not a good mix. The two substances together had what Rudolf called "a potentiating effect," explaining that "each one makes the other more inebriated."

David Rudolf told jurors, "It was a particularly bad combination for Kathleen Peterson, because she had been having headaches and dizziness for weeks. And she was wearing flip-flops, and she was climbing a narrow and steep and poorly lit stairway, a stairway that was made out of oak, hardwood, without any kind of floor covering."

David Rudolf would describe how upset his client was when he found his wife at the foot of the stairs. He explained that Todd and his friend Christina had pulled up to the house at the same time the EMS and the Durham Fire Department had arrived. And, as expected, Rudolf would attack the quality of the police work in the case, suggesting that Durham police had allowed the scene to become altered and contaminated, while they were "looking for red flags" at the same time.

"Police had reason to think the worst of Michael," the attorney told jurors, explaining, "the reason, just to put it bluntly, is because Michael Peterson had been criticizing the police for years."

Peterson was one of those people—for better or for worse—who said what was on his mind. In his newspaper columns, Peterson wrote about the problems he had with the way the Durham police conducted their business. Rudolf claimed there were twenty or thirty different columns Peterson had written criticizing the police. He read from a sample 1999 column, where Peterson had complained that the police were doing little to fight drug dealers, calling them "incompetent." In that column, Peterson had written that in Durham "the chance of a criminal getting caught is only slightly better than getting hit by lightning."

In September 2000, Peterson had accused the Durham police of manipulating the crime statistics. In March 2001, Peterson had criticized the police for minimizing gang problems in Durham. The list went on.

And because of all the years of criticism, Rudolf asserted, the Durham police had developed what he called "tunnel vision" against Michael Peterson. Rudolf would argue that it wasn't hard for them to look at all the blood at the scene, the altered and contaminated scene, and assume the worst about Michael Peterson. His client became the suspect, Rudolf asserted, merely because he had blood on him. But Michael Peterson had been holding his deceased wife. Of course there would be blood on his clothes. Yet the police took him, like a suspect, and put him away in a room, and they wouldn't let him talk to his own son.

"Can you imagine?" Rudolf asked.

The police conduct was particularly offensive, in Rudolf's view, after Dr. Kenneth Snell, the state medical examiner, had arrived, and had then formed an opinion about what he personally observed at the scene. The medical examiner had found that Kathleen Peterson's death was a result of her head hitting the stairs, that it was an accident. And to impress jurors, Rudolf read aloud from Dr. Kenneth Snell's report:

"Probable cause of death, closed head injury, due to blunt-force injury to head, due to a fall down the stairs" was what Snell had written.

In Rudolf's opinion, because of the tunnel vision of

police, because of the bias they were operating under, the die had already been cast against Peterson from the moment police arrived on the scene. The defense attorney would virtually tell jurors that once the indictment was obtained, the police went on a witch-hunt, looking for evidence that supported their view, ignoring any evidence that didn't. Rudolf would state that the Durham police had indicted first—then had gone out looking for evidence to support their indictment.

But Rudolf's view seemed out of sync. There were many things Jim Hardin had talked about in his opening statement, things that, with common sense, added up to murder. Hardin had said that when EMS had arrived at the scene, they had seen Michael Peterson standing over his wife, covered all over with blood. Hardin had said that Peterson was barefoot, that his shoes were bloody, sitting next to his dead wife. And he would offer a reason as to why Peterson would have taken his shoes off—the luminol testing, done by Durham police as they processed the scene, showed there were bloody footprints leading from the stairwell, through the kitchen, to the laundry room.

Durham investigators would later testify that Peterson's bloody footprints—had been invisible to the naked eye. The luminol, a chemical used to highlight the presence of blood, had picked up Peterson's steps, and they had documented a path that went through the dining area, to the kitchen counter, into the laundry room, and back to the stairwell. Those invisible bloody footsteps, the investigators would testify, looked like "rabbit tracks."

Hardin had also spoken about the massive amount of blood all over the walls. Some of the blood in the stairwell was over six feet high. And there was cast-off spatter outside the stairway that was ten-feet high. Hardin had shown the jurors the crime scene photos, and he had described all the blood that was on Kathleen, under Kathleen, and below Kathleen—*blood that was all dry.*

Based on the evidence, the jurors learned that Kathleen Peterson had been dead for some time, that there would be evidence to prove that she had been deceased long before EMS workers had arrived.

When David Rudolf addressed that issue, he would assert that after Kathleen Peterson had fallen, she had been lying at the bottom of the steps for some period of time. But Rudolf would contend that no one could say exactly how long Kathleen had lain there.

Her head had hit the steps and had split open "like a pumpkin," Rudolf contended, which caused the massive loss of blood. The drawings and diagrams made by Dr. Deborah Radisch, he would tell jurors, were misleading. Rudolf explained that Dr. Radisch hadn't done it on purpose, but she had drawn diagrams of the splits in Kathleen's head that made them look wider than they actually were.

In short, Rudolf wanted jurors to know that his team of experts, including Dr. Henry Lee, would testify that the lacerations on Kathleen Peterson's scalp were more consistent with a fall. The defense attorney would assert that because Kathleen Peterson had suffered no brain contusions, because she had suffered no brain swelling, no internal hemorrhages, no skull fractures, the physical evidence supported his client's innocence.

"I mean, can you imagine somebody beating somebody over the head, whacking them as hard as they can, trying to kill them," Rudolf asked, "and there's no skull fracture, there's no brain contusions?"

Rudolf went on to talk about the blood spatter, about the expensive replica Durham police had built of the bottom of Peterson's stairwell. He asserted that the tests conducted by Agent Duane Deaver, the blood spatter expert of the State Bureau of Investigation, were inaccurate.

Rudolf took cheap shots at Deaver's work, going so far as to point out that the tests Duane Deaver conducted were done with blood from the Red Cross.

The attorney never mentioned that the blood Deaver obtained from the Red Cross was already dated, that the blood had a shelf life, that Duane Deaver hadn't used any blood that could have possibly saved a life.

Rudolf showed a video of Deaver's tests in which the expert used a sponge, putting blood on it, to discover how the cast-off blood might have gotten into such strange places along the Peterson stairwell. The defense attorney attacked Deaver's methods, and he contended that the amount of blood in the stairway, as horrific as it might seem, wasn't consistent with a beating. Rudolf had a completely different explanation as to how all that blood splattered along the Peterson stairwell.

"You all have seen dogs shake water off, and it goes all over," Rudolf told jurors. "Well, that's what happens with blood as well. Hands or clothes coming in contact with the wall. Or coughing up blood. Or sneezing blood. That's what causes all the blood spatter that you'll see."

Regarding the autopsy photos, Rudolf insisted that photos could be "misleading," that they could express a point of view "designed to show something." He implied that prosecutor Jim Hardin had tried to shock people by showing them such gruesome photos. He told jurors that with his display of harrowing photographs, Jim Hardin was trying to *haunt* them.

Forty-five

Someone with blood on their bare feet had walked from the hallway where Kathleen had been found dead to the utility sink in the laundry room. After hearing over eleven police witnesses testify about their findings at the scene, jurors would listen to the words of evidence technician Eric Campen, who, along with two other members of the Durham police, had documented a nearly invisible trail of bloody footprints.

Crime Scene Investigator Campen told jurors that the trail was only visible when investigators sprayed the floor with luminol, a chemical that reacted with traces of blood, a chemical that emitted a blue-green glow, showing blood that had been invisible to the naked eye.

The faint footprints led from the utility sink in the laundry room, to the kitchen sink and the refrigerator, and finally, to a cabinet where wineglasses were kept—wineglasses that were identical to the *two used glasses* found next to the sink on the night of Kathleen's death. Jurors would later learn that, regarding the two wineglasses, only one contained fingerprints—from Michael Peterson. The other glass on the kitchen counter had no identifiable fingerprints at all. Jurors would later discover that the prosecution team had found a broken crystal wineglass, which they had paid $30 for an expert to repair.

As prosecutors continued to build a case against Peterson, it was becoming clear what their theory was: Peterson had taken one or two wineglasses out of the cabinet, had poured a bottle of wine down the sink, and had tried to create the appearance that he and his wife had been drinking heavily. Rudolf would make much of the fact that there were "partial" unidentifiable fingerprints on the second wineglass. Rudolf would show the jury two liquor bottles—Chambord and cognac—taken from the Peterson home, asking why they hadn't been tested for fingerprints. But the fact was, on the night of Kathleen's death, there would have been no reason to process liquor bottles that were tucked away in another part of the house.

Rudolf would question police relentlessly, wondering why they had not checked more closely for fingerprints, implying that their work was sloppy and shoddy. But when prosecutors entered that broken crystal wineglass into evidence, it could not be explained by anyone. It was, perhaps, shattered in a struggle. But without witnesses, the broken crystal glass remained a mystery.

No matter how hard Rudolf attacked the police, arguing that the evidence was not absolute, that the bloody footprints didn't mean anything, that Peterson was caressing his dead wife, that his shoes and socks had already been off before police arrived, there was no way to get around another fact—a partial footprint from Michael Peterson's shoe was evident on the back of Kathleen's sweat pants. Peterson had stepped on his wife, and Durham police had taken photos of the footprint, which clearly showed the impression of the bottom of an athletic shoe, in blood, on Kathleen's hind leg.

After twenty-one days of testimony, and thirty prosecution witnesses, jurors heard from another special agent from the North Carolina State Bureau of Investigation, DNA expert Mark Boodee, who testified about the mix of saliva he had detected on a can of diet Coke seized by police that night. The DNA expert would tell jurors that the Coke can, found on the patio area just outside the Peterson home, tested positive for saliva that came from the defendant. The expert would also tell jurors that *DNA from other individuals* had been found on that diet Coke can.

For jurors, the prosecution case was no longer seeming like a bunch of smoke and mirrors. Even though prosecutors did not have a weapon, even though they could not prove that anyone had helped stage the scene, prosecutors had produced the blood evidence, they had introduced photos and videotape of the bloody walls and stairwell, and graphic images showing that the victim, Kathleen Peterson, was battered. Among all of that evidence, the diet Coke can seemed less significant, yet the fact that it held partial bloody prints, and DNA with mixed saliva, seemed highly suspicious.

Of course there was no evidence to support what Todd Peterson might have known, or what he might have done, on the night of Kathleen's death. Todd Peterson had refused to give any statement to police. He was featured on Court TV and local news as being a supportive son, as someone who was fighting for his father's good name. Todd expressed his feelings of love for his dad, describing Michael as a normal, fun guy who would spend time hanging out at the house watching TV sporting events.

Reporters would later discover that Todd Peterson had his own strange Web site, which was in direct conflict with Rudolf's characterization of Michael Peterson as the role-model, as the perfect dad to a set of well-raised children. While Todd Peterson sat in court every day dressed to the nines, looking very clean-cut, very *GQ*, it turned out that he was running a web site, www.Futazi.com, which offered tips to high school students on everything from kissing and foreplay to ideas about bodybuilding and proper application of makeup. On the site, Todd had introduced himself as "Roman Croft," showing before-and-after photos of himself in little boxer shorts. Todd's site had a strong emphasis on sex, and included pornographic images that were certainly not appropriate for the young teenage demographic he was targeting. Some of its content was highly pornographic and quite offensive.

It was on August 6, 2003, weeks into the trial, that things in Michael Peterson's world really began to heat up. Dr. Kenneth Snell would take the stand to tell the jury that he had made an error in his initial report. The medical examiner would testify that, because he was initially unable to see the amount of lacerations to Kathleen Peterson's head, he had misdiagnosed the cause of death. Dr. Snell would explain that he had watched Dr. Deborah Radisch and other forensic pathologists perform the autopsy at the medical examiner's office in Chapel Hill, and then had realized that "some instrument" could have created the lacerations to Kathleen Peterson's scalp.

One of the strongest witnesses for the state, Dr. Snell told jurors that he had changed his initial findings of "accident" and had ruled Kathleen Peterson's death a *homicide.* With Kathleen's matted hair out of the way, Snell had witnessed seven lacerations, and the medical examiner had changed his opinion completely. Kenneth Snell testified that, because of additional evidence, it was "routine" for information from a field report to be revised.

The same week that Kenneth Snell testified, *People* magazine had reported on the Michael Peterson murder case. Even though the case against the Durham novelist had been largely overshadowed by the sensational Scott and Laci Peterson case, *People* would report details about the mysterious Michael Peterson. The magazine presented a shimmering image of Michael and his wife on the night Kathleen died, a couple who popped champagne corks in celebration of his latest movie deal. The magazine made Peterson seem very Hollywood, very successful, and described Michael as "a doting husband who often surprised his spouse with gifts of valuable jewelry and silk scarves." Without taking sides, the article presented Peterson in a rather positive light, noting that the North Carolina murder case had divided the members of Durham's "close-knit upper crust."

But the *People* article missed the mark. The magazine had appeared on newsstands too soon. In fact, it appeared the very week that the most explosive information of the trial was being entered into evidence.

On August 7, Judge Orlando Hudson Jr. ruled that prosecutors would be allowed to introduce evidence to prove that Michael Peterson was bisexual, that pornographic photos of men and suggestive e-mails retrieved from Michael Peterson's computer were relevant to show why he might have beaten his wife to death.

After objections from the defense, which argued that Peterson was e-mailing a male prostitute because he was doing research for a book about "gays in the military," Judge Hudson ruled that the pornographic evidence would be presented. Because the defense had made contentions about the Petersons' idyllic marriage, the defense had opened the door. The e-mails were very specific regarding Peterson's intentions: he wanted to pay for sex, he was willing to have an escort come to his home while his wife was busy at work, and he wanted the business of his alternative sex life to be discreet.

When Judge Hudson made his ruling, Michael Peterson sat behind the defense table, reading an e-mail he had deleted on December 8, 2001. From the stunned look on his face, it was clear that the novelist had no idea that experts had been able to undelete all of his previously erased e-mails.

The e-mails entered into evidence contained explicit requests for sex from Michael Peterson to a male escort, who called himself "Brad." Prosecutors had circulated Peterson's e-mails to jurors, proving that Peterson was looking for sexual relations outside of his marriage. They were able to show, through numerous e-mails to the young male escort Brad, that Peterson had spent months trying to arrange to pay for sex with the young man.

Brad, apparently, was an active member of the U.S. military, who had been called to serve after 9/11. The e-mails indicated that Peterson was willing to wait for Brad, that the e-mails from Peterson weren't just a happenstance request for sex. Prosecutors had evidence of exact prices to be paid, of exact times and dates being set by Michael, and most importantly, they were able to show that Kathleen Peterson, on the night of her death, most possibly had gained access to information about Brad because Peterson had a file in his desk with printouts of Brad's escort service, complete with nude pictures of Brad with a big hard-on.

Prosecutors were able to question Helen Preslinger, who testified that she heard Kathleen ask for her husband's e-mail address on December 8, 2001. Preslinger was aware that on that night, Kathleen had gone into her husband's office just after 11:08 P.M. Preslinger had sent an e-mail to Kathleen, it was something Kathleen needed for their conference call the next morning, but the e-mail had never been opened.

Prosecutors would speculate that while Kathleen had waited in her husband's office that night, looking for the e-mail from Helen Preslinger, it was also possible that she might have gained access to the information on her husband's computer, which, according to state computer experts, had been deleted by someone on December 8, 2001, and again on December 11, 2001. What Kathleen Peterson might have discovered that night, in addition to the file in his desk regarding Brad, was a print-out of *hundreds* of photos of explicit male porn images, and the following list of the favorite sex sites that Michael had downloaded:

www.hardnstraight.com
www.MarineMeat.com
www.smutserver.com
www.sleazydream.com
www.youngstuds.com
www.pimpserver.com
www.fistingzone.com

Forty-six

Durham assistant district attorney David Saacks presented the case regarding evidence of Michael Peterson's sexual preferences to be allowed into court. Saacks talked about the possibility of a "love triangle." He would tell Judge Orlando Hudson Jr. that even if there weren't a financial motive to commit murder, there certainly could have been an argument between Michael and Kathleen on the night she died, because there was a folder of graphic e-mails written by Michael to another man, which could prove to be an explanation for what happened in the Peterson household on the night in question.

Saacks would make comments about the e-mails and male porn photos retrieved from Peterson's computer, asserting that it would have been easy for Kathleen to put two and two together. The Durham prosecutor stated his belief that Peterson's bisexuality "could possibly go to motive." After the prosecution team won a victory, David Saacks later told the *Herald-Sun* that the prosecution had proof that "Peterson engaged in homosexual relations with two other men" *before* he married Kathleen Peterson.

"The fact that we brought the pornography into the trial was to corroborate that this is where Peterson's interest was," Saacks confided. "The main thing was to show proof of marital infidelity because it was a possible motive for murder, but also because it would bust what the defense brought up in the opening statement about this being the ideal marriage and them being soul mates."

Jurors would soon learn that Peterson had a file in his desk drawer that included a packet of e-mails to a male escort, Brad. Police had seized the file, which was somehow mixed in with Kathleen Peterson's important tax documents and her check stubs, and prosecutors had reason to believe Kathleen Peterson had found the file folder. They surmised she might have looked through her husband's desk while she was waiting for her e-mail from Canada.

Because Durham police had witnessed Michael Peterson very busy working on his computer—on the night of his wife's death—the computer was seized and an expert was hired by the state. Todd Markley would later testify that Peterson had used a program called Quick Clean to delete 2,500 pictures from his computer. The expert would testify that hundreds of Peterson's files were deleted during the week of Kathleen Peterson's death, including 216 files that were erased the day before Mrs. Peterson died, and 352 files that were deleted two days after her death.

According to the computer sleuth, during the week of his wife's death, Michael Peterson had tried to delete everything from his computer altogether, and then had selectively reloaded certain programs and e-mails back onto his machine.

The expert was an employee of an Ohio-based company called CompuSleuth. He would testify that his company not only found deleted pornographic photos and suggestive e-mails, but had found e-mails written by Michael Peterson regarding his financial worries as well. The numerous e-mails were entered into evidence, and regarding his financial troubles, Peterson's words were read aloud for jurors to hear.

In one of the e-mails, written days before Kathleen's death, Michael talked about "poor Kathleen," who was "undergoing the tortures of the damned" at Nortel Networks. According to Michael, Nortel had already laid off forty-five thousand people. He believed that his wife was a "survivor," and thought her job would remain intact, but he mentioned that she was experiencing "monumental stress," having to work under such negative conditions.

In another e-mail, Michael spoke of the financial difficulties being suffered by his sons, Clayton and Todd. He informed relatives, including his ex-wife, Patricia, that Clayton and Todd were both living in debt, paying high interest on credit cards, explaining that he was "worried sick about them." Michael expressed to one relative that he was "sorry as hell to have to come begging," but he was hoping that the person could offer $5,000 a semester in assistance toward Martha Ratliff's college tuition. In separate pleas to Patricia, Michael requested that his ex-wife take out a $30,000 home equity loan to help with the cost-of-living expenses for their boys.

When the bisexuality of Michael Peterson was entered into the trial, the genteel ears of Southern ladies and gentlemen in the courtroom perked up. Some of Kathleen's family members weeped. It was too embarrassing, too humiliating for them to see Kathleen's private life being dragged through the mud. From the explicit nature of Michael's e-mails, it was obvious that he was not only an adulterer, but he was perhaps more homosexual than straight. The thought of Kathleen's marriage being a sham, especially when she was paying for everything, and taking care of everyone, was all the more hurtful to her sisters and to Caitlin.

Michael and Brad had begun communicating in late August 2001. They had spoken on the phone. They had discussed their likes and dislikes. And Michael had checked out Brad's Web site, which, from the looks of it, made Brad seem like a superstud. Michael wondered if Brad had ever considered going into the porn business and suggested that Brad contact a porn king in Palm Springs.

In an e-mail written from Brad, dated August 31, 2001, Brad asked Michael for more specific details about the gay porn king. The porn king apparently owned a Palm Springs resort, where he auditioned young men for possible film roles. The following morning, at 3:36, Michael had written back to offer a full report about the "major figure" in the male porn industry, who had gotten started by "paying Marines to jack off on film."

Michael suggested that Brad go to the Internet to look up the history of the man and his resort, and was he intrigued to learn that Brad would consider the possibility of doing porn films. Because Brad was such a strapping, beautiful, blond hunk, at least from looking at pictures of him on his Web page, Michael felt Brad fit the USMC profile that the guy in Palm Springs was looking for.

Michael suggested that Brad go to Palm Springs and audition for a part in an all-male porn film. From Brad's reviews, posted on his Web site, it was clear that the young military stud would fit right in with other soldiers and sailors who had done those kind of flicks. It was good money; it was easy money. Michael thought that Brad would be perfect, that he could make it "big time." He explained that the Palm Springs porn king took pride in "discovering macho young guys—mostly Marines."

In the meantime, Michael wanted Brad to come up

to his house. He wanted the young man to see the gorgeous place, where he could give Brad more information about the porn business, if that was of any interest. Michael said that he himself had always wondered what his life would have been like as a porn star, stating that his "Cecil B. DeMille moment" had happened many years prior, when Michael was a "poster boy" for the marines, having had his face plastered on walls in every recruit office across America.

In a subsequent e-mail, Michael said he would be happy to help Brad get started in any "career change" he might be considering, whether it was the porn movie business, or a new start in education. At one point, the young soldier had mentioned his interest in becoming a dentist, and Michael offered to introduce him to friends who could help Brad gain admission to one of the colleges in North Carolina. Michael said he had friends and connections everywhere, and he was willing to befriend Brad in any way.

Michael was offering friendship, not because he was looking for a discount. He understood that Brad needed to earn a living. Michael was happy to meet with Brad for "straight-on business," without any strings attached. Michael said he was looking forward to meeting a "fuck machine," and offered to fuck Brad "for the set price."

Brad wrote back immediately, telling Michael how "cool" he sounded, telling Michael that he was used to being a "top," but would let Michael "bang" him, assuming Michael was "man enough." Regarding Michael's remarks about having "plenty of money," Brad joked that if Michael had extra cash to throw around, he would appreciate Michael donating it to the "Poor Private's Foundation," since he was still a private, "albeit, private first class."

The two of them had plans to meet on Wednesday, September 5, 2001. Michael had a meeting to attend in the early part of the evening, and Brad was about to be flown out of the area, but Michael would be willing to meet Brad in an airport hotel to "give a soldier a send-off."

But the meeting never happened.

Brad was unable to return Michael's message of September 2, because as it happened, the soldier's flight plans had changed and he had taken off at 6:00 A.M. the next day. And then, without question, the 9/11 terrorist attacks had impacted Brad's life immensely. Because of the red alert, Brad had been placed on guard duty around the clock, every day. He finally wrote to Michael on September 30, explaining that he'd been so crazy on the job, he hadn't made time for any calls, and he hadn't hooked up with any clients. Brad apologized for not getting back in touch sooner, writing to say he had returned to Raleigh briefly and was now headed to Fort Bragg for additional guard duty.

Though the two men never did find the time and place to hook up, their e-mails were conclusive evidence of Peterson's sexual secret, and prosecutors called Brad to the witness stand to testify. They wanted the young soldier to identify Michael Peterson as the man whom he'd spoken to, as the man he made sexual arrangements with. Unwilling to go before the court without being given statewide immunity from prosecution, Brad had hired his own attorney, Thomas Loflin III. The media whirled into a feeding frenzy around Brad, and his attorney was insisting that Brad's identity remain veiled, since he was still on active duty, serving in the army reserve.

As it turned out, Judge Hudson refused to shield Brad's face or identity from the press. The feisty judge said that giving the young man immunity in exchange for his testimony was a big enough concession, and said he wasn't about to make any "deals" with "Brad," who was no different from any other witness in the case.

The next day, prosecutor Freda Black questioned Brent Wolgamott, aka Brad, and asked him about his male escort business. The young man, with a crew cut and a wide smile, had worn a navy blue blazer with brass buttons; he had dressed the part for his fifteen minutes of fame. He seemed only too happy to have his say on the witness stand with national camera crews fighting to get pictures of his face.

After being granted immunity, Brent "Brad" Wolgamott waived his Fifth Amendment right, and told the court that he charged $150 an hour for his services. He bragged that his client roster included doctors and lawyers, and told Freda Black that most of the men whom he would see would have "their time" with him and then go back to their "happy-hubby lives."

"And what type of services did you perform?" Black wanted to know.

"Oh, well, that's pretty broad," the soldier said, smiling.

"Did it involve sexual activity?"

"Sometimes it does."

"What types of sexual activity?" Black asked.

"Oh, well, just about anything under the sun," the young man testified, laughing and shaking his head.

When David Rudolf had a chance to cross-examine the witness, he asked questions that tried to show how Kathleen Peterson would have been *aware* of her husband's bisexuality. Rudolf implied that Kathleen most likely *accepted* her husband's double life, that Kathleen was probably not bothered by it.

But Kathleen's family knew better. They knew Kathleen was devastated by her first husband's affair, and there was no way in the world that Kathleen would have tolerated Michael having lovers, gay or otherwise.

The twenty-eight-year-old Wolgamott had never met Michael Peterson, had never seen him face-to-face, until the day he appeared in court. The young man claimed that he was no longer a male escort, testifying that he was a college student working hard at trying to make something out of his life. Wolgamott tried looking over at Michael Peterson during his few hours on the stand, but the young man couldn't catch Peterson's eye. In terms of being able to comment about what Kathleen Peterson might have known about her fifty-eight-year-old husband's homosexual desires, the former male escort had no idea.

He described his clients as being "predominantly straight with minor homosexual tendencies," and said that he would have no way of knowing what went on in the Peterson household, explaining things never got that personal. He testified that "there were never any romantic relationships involved," never any highly personal exchanges with any of his clients.

Forty-seven

Before blood analyst Agent Duane Deaver was able to testify in open court as a blood spatter expert, he faced a barrage of questions from David Rudolf, who was challenging the expert's credentials. Rudolf tried to diminish the blood expert, he tried as best he could to rattle Agent Deaver, who had been analyzing bloodstains at crime scenes since 1988.

The defense attorney didn't want the jurors to hear Agent Deaver's findings. Rudolf used his best efforts to stump Agent Deaver, to muddy the waters, to mock the special agent, claiming that Deaver wasn't *qualified* to be called as an expert because his experiments were flawed. In fact, Rudolf's argument against Deaver's testimony would last so long, that the electric power in New York City and parts of the Northeast would have time to go out and be restored again.

David Rudolf tried relentlessly to persuade the court that Deaver was not "proficient" enough to testify in Michael Peterson's murder trial. However, after all the endless hours spent outside the presence of the jury, Judge Hudson would ultimately declare that Agent Duane Deaver, who had testified as an expert in over sixty cases, who had been involved in over five hundred criminal cases during his career, would be heard.

From the moment he took the stand, the state's star witness was bombarded with demands for credentials. In an attempt to sway the jury, to get the jury not to pay too much credence to Deaver's findings, Rudolf was able to get Deaver to admit that he hadn't published any books or scholarly articles, that he hadn't earned any advanced degrees. The blood spatter expert was put on the hot seat by both David Rudolf and Thomas Maher, and he was verbally assaulted for not having "scientifically valid" opinions.

The defense attorneys had already argued, unsuccessfully, that Deaver's opinions should be thrown out. Now, with the agent on the witness stand, they would try to make his findings appear "unreliable." Agent Deaver would be forced to justify each of his experiments step-by-step.

When Special Agent Duane Deaver was finally able to give his opinions to the jury, he pointed out that his blood spatter findings took a great deal of work. On December 9, 2001, Deaver had spent five hours analyzing the stairway, and he showed jurors his findings, using a model of the stairway in the Petersons' home.

At the scene of a murder, bloodstains could literally point to the killer, and by analyzing their shape, size, and position, Deaver had been able to figure out, not only where the assailant stood, but also how many times he had swung the weapon. As gruesome as it was, Agent Deaver's testimony moved forward. As the blood spatter marks began to fit into the crime scene like the pieces of a jigsaw puzzle, the SBI agent's testimony would captivate the courtroom.

This is the crux of what the jury learned:

1) Kathleen Peterson was assaulted in the stairwell by someone who was wielding a blunt object. Deaver cited

a "cast-off" bloodstain on a wall nine feet above the stair-well to support that finding.

2) Kathleen Peterson was struck at least three times, and while her head may have struck the stairs when she fell at some point, there was evidence that the victim was beaten as she was standing. There was one bloodstain that indicated that her head was battered twenty-seven inches above the stairway. Deaver concluded that Kathleen Peterson was in "various positions" when the attack occurred.

3) Michael Peterson had to be standing or crouching near a blood source—either his bleeding wife or a pool of her blood—when a great force was applied. There were eight tiny drops of blood found on the inside of Peterson's khaki shorts, and drops of blood were found on his Converse All Star sneakers as well. Agent Deaver explained that tiny specks of blood could only be created by someone using a great amount of force, that only when blood is projected forcefully, does it break into much smaller drops.

4) Evidence existed that someone had smeared blood in the stairwell, that luminol testing showed an effort to clean up, that one of the steps had been wiped clean. Luminol was a reagent that reacted with the iron found in hemoglobin. A widely used reagent, luminol could locate blood that had been diluted 12,000:1. Agent Deaver testified that there was evidence that the blood on Michael Peterson's shorts was "diluted," as if someone had tried to use water to wash the blood out.

5) Two of the steps in the stairwell contained blood-stains, transfer stains, made by something metal with a hook on the end. The blood marks had similar characteristics to the blow poke tool, the fireplace tool that could no longer be located in the Peterson house.

6) Deaver used bloody mops, wigs, and sponges to re-create the blood spatter patterns on the Petersons'

stairwell. He worked with an identical replica of the staircase, and he explained his findings in the courtroom, using the perfected miniature-scale model of the back staircase to point out the exact measurements of the blood on each step and riser.

7) There was no blood found in the mouth, nose, or nasal passages of Kathleen Peterson during her autopsy. Deaver's opinion was "there was no mechanism for expirated blood," meaning there was no blood in Kathleen Peterson's passageways to support the notion that she had coughed or sneezed any blood.

8) Deaver concluded that there were three "points of impact" that were made in space. His tests proved that blood spatter patterns on the walls in the stairwell could have only been created when Kathleen Peterson's head was struck "in space," not from hitting any surface. In order to trace the origin of the blood spatter, Deaver had used a common "stringing technique," whereby he marked the walls with strings, to find out how far each blood source was from each wall.

9) There was "no significant alteration of bloodstains" in the area of the Peterson stairwell. In Deaver's opinion, the "stairwell was in good condition," the scene was not contaminated, and therefore an accurate investigation was possible.

10) There was blood evidence to support that Kathleen Peterson was beaten to death while she was standing, faceup, and facedown. Kathleen Peterson's death was not consistent with a fall. The blood spatter expert had been able to trace back, from each bloodstain mark, exactly where the victim and assailant were standing when each blow was delivered. According to Deaver, the assailant stood outside the stairwell, and as Kathleen Peterson was on the twelfth step of an eighteen-step climb, the assailant began beating her with something like a fireplace tool.

Forty-eight

Jurors were sent home early, during lunch recess, on the day Duane Deaver's testimony concluded, so that the attorneys from both sides could engage in a hearing. The defense team's battle was a concerted effort, and they were good at presenting a united front. However, the attorneys for Michael Peterson had something horrible lurking: the relevance of the death of Elizabeth Ratliff.

Rudolf and Maher had argued that the latest autopsy findings on Elizabeth Ratliff should not be entered into evidence, telling the court: "It is literally impossible at this time, eighteen years and thousands of miles removed from the death of Elizabeth Ratliff, to determine her true injuries."

Now in a separate hearing, the subject of Kathleen Peterson's death halted for a moment. In the middle of the trial, the harrowing death of Martha and Margaret's mother—who had been properly buried, exhumed, and buried again in Texas—had come before the court. Rudolf and Maher implied that the death of Elizabeth Ratliff would only bring chaos to jurors, that jurors already had too much information to sort through. They wanted to keep the focus on Kathleen Peterson alone.

Rudolf told Judge Hudson that because it would be impossible to re-create the scene, he objected to having people brought in from Germany to try to recollect Elizabeth Ratliff's death. Rudolf doubted that any witness would be able to articulate what might have happened so long ago, and objected to the prosecution's attempts to "refresh" old recollections. Rudolf wanted to remind the court that this was a case about the death of Kathleen Peterson. There was no evidence against Peterson regarding the death of Elizabeth Ratliff. Rudolf felt he shouldn't be in the position of having to defend a whole different case.

But Judge Orlando Hudson Jr. ruled that the deaths were "sufficiently similar" for the testimony about Elizabeth Ratliff to have bearing in the trial. Prosecutors had argued successfully that the 1985 death would demonstrate "intent, knowledge, and absence of accident." As the judge made his decision, the usual smile, the usual smug expression, completely disappeared from Mr. Peterson's face. Peterson held his forehead in his hands, shaking his head, his eyes giving away a shadow of disbelief.

It was unclear whether Peterson was acting or reacting. All throughout his trial, Peterson had been jovial. Peterson had been really good at hiding his emotions. Even during the awkward times, when his sexual e-mails were presented, Michael Peterson seemed to have his act down pat. He would enter the court each day, dressed up like a peacock, and smile to the cameras and the onlookers in the courtroom. His entourage behaved in a very smug, confident manner, often joking and laughing when the jury wasn't present. The only ones who weren't smiling very much were the Ratliff girls. During every court recess, Peterson would go over and whisper things to the girls, as if to assure them that everything was going to be okay.

The Ratliff girls would nod, they would sometimes smile at Michael's private remarks. But the girls didn't seem to grasp the pathos, didn't seem to understand the deep catastrophe of this culminating event. For most of the trial, they seemed to be under Michael's watchful eye. Even as the evidence about the death of their mother came forward, they would stare blankly at the people who had come from Germany to testify. When their mother's friends took the stand to speak of their concern for Elizabeth's "baby girls," neither Margaret, who had turned twenty-one, nor Martha, who was just nineteen, showed any visible reaction.

Cheryl Appel-Schumacher would be the first of many to testify about the death of Elizabeth Ratliff. She and her husband, Tom, had been flown to the United States by the prosecution, and they had dodged reporters awaiting them at the airport. The couple had not wanted to be part of the media circus, but they had agreed to testify. They were not sure what they could offer, but they would provide details about the death scene, in order that the truth be known.

Occasionally wiping tears from her eyes, and often choking up, Cheryl Appel-Schumacher told jurors about the large amount of blood that she and her husband cleaned up after Elizabeth's body was moved. Cheryl testified that the blood stretched from the top of the landing to the bottom of the stairs, and she would break down sobbing as she described using a bowl of water, a rag, and some soap, cleaning each portion of the wall, bit by bit, constantly changing the bowl of water, as it turned bright red.

Cheryl testified that Michael Peterson "took charge" during that very difficult time, which hadn't surprised anyone, because Michael had "come to the rescue" after George Ratliff died, helping Liz manage all of her military affairs.

Cheryl Appel-Schumacher spoke of Elizabeth's daughters, who were then ages three and four, insisting that all of Liz's friends had felt that the Petersons were the right people to be the girls' guardians. Cheryl had vague recollections that "there was some suspicion that things were not as they seemed," but never did she or her husband suspect Michael Peterson of any wrongdoing. Cheryl had a memory of neighbors mentioning an absence of "footprints in the snow" around the back of the house, but she testified that she herself had never questioned the authorities when they ruled Elizabeth's death an accident.

When Tom Appel-Schumacher took the stand, he confirmed his wife's statements regarding Peterson, and then went on to describe the great amount of blood in Elizabeth Ratliff's home. Tom told jurors that there was a lot of blood up and down the staircase wall, and there appeared to be blood "spattered in different places around the foyer area." He said that he and his wife had "spent hours" cleaning up all the blood "so that the children would not see it."

Another witness, Billie Allen, had been flown in from Germany to testify about the floor-heating system in Elizabeth's former home. Allen had become the current resident of Elizabeth's house, and she testified that the house had a special type of floor-heating system, that it had heating tubes that ran under the floors. Prosecutors later pointed out that the floor-heating system would have accounted for Elizabeth Ratliff's body being warm on the morning she was found dead.

During her brief court appearance, Billie Allen handed prosecutors a doctor's note on Karin Hamm's behalf, which stated that Hamm had recent surgery and could not travel to the United States. Jim Hardin still hoped to introduce an English translation of the statement Karin Hamm had given to Art Holland months prior—in which she reportedly saw Michael Peterson hurriedly leaving Ratliff's home the night before her body was discovered.

To the defense attorneys' chagrin, Judge Hudson ruled that Karin Hamm's written statement—about what she saw from her daughter's bedroom window on November 24, 1985—was not admissible in court. As it happened, there was no German translator available to fly into Durham, so at the last minute, Karin Hamm's statement was pulled.

Not that it mattered. The prosecution had a long list of people who came forward to tell the jury about their personal suspicions regarding the death of Elizabeth Ratliff. People flew into Durham to say that Elizabeth's death had caused them emotional pain, that they had accepted the "official report," which ruled her death an accident, primarily because the military was involved in the investigation, and they felt it was not their place to question protocol.

Those who testified about the discrepancies at the scene, about the mistakes made, about the suspicions and the fabrications of Michael Peterson, included: Dr. Larry Barnes, former army investigator Steve Lyons, Margaret Blair, Barbara O'Hara Malagnino, and Amybeth Berner.

Amybeth Berner told jurors that she had "questions and concerns" about Elizabeth Ratliff's death from the moment she entered the house, testifying that back in 1985 she had called it "a crime scene" and wondered why the authorities hadn't investigated the sudden death fully.

In an attempt to censor any extraneous remarks from each Elizabeth Ratliff witness, the defense insisted on holding hearings outside the presence of to the jury. Even though these hearings were broadcast nationally on Court TV, witnesses would be prevented from detailing the most juicy elements to the jurors.

For instance, in one hearing, Amybeth Berner would

tell courtroom observers that she had come to believe, over time, that Michael Peterson was the prime suspect in the death of her friend Elizabeth Ratliff. Berner would also testify, outside the jury's presence, that back in Germany, Peterson had once bragged to her about his "connections" in the CIA, claiming that he could have someone killed.

The statement about Peterson being in the CIA would become a theme—others would bring up the issue privately, because for years Peterson claimed he held a job as a "government consultant." Of course, it turned out that there was absolutely no truth in Peterson's claims, that there was no evidence that the man ever held any full-time job after his stint with the marines.

However, Peterson had bragged to many folks about his "involvement" with the CIA. He had a library full of books about the CIA; he wrote novels involving fictional characters in the CIA; he was obsessed with the CIA, the FBI, and all forms of special government agencies.

Nonetheless, Amybeth Berner's testimony about Peterson's possible CIA connection was cause for laughter from the defense table, with Peterson leading the way. His defense team's reactions were clearly meant to make Amybeth Berner look like she was a dreamer, like she was just making things up.

"Michael told me he was in the CIA at some point," Amybeth Berner testified at her hearing, "he said he murdered someone while he was in Vietnam, and that concerned me."

Forty-nine

In many ways, the case had become a tale of two sisters. There were the Ratliff sisters, Margaret and Martha, who were standing by their legal guardian, the man they called Dad, Michael Peterson. There were Kathleen's sisters, Candace Zamperini and Lori Campell, who had been waiting for twenty months to see justice, who, after seeing the evidence, had become convinced that their brother-in-law had killed their sibling. And there were Elizabeth's sisters, Margaret Blair and Rosemary Kelloway, who had been misled at the time of Elizabeth's death, and had been told that Elizabeth only suffered a small loss of blood behind her ear.

Now all three sets of sisters would sit on opposite sides of the courtroom, each in her own private hell, each in her own state of denial, disbelief, and despair. The Ratliff girls were not speaking to any of their aunts—not Margaret or Rosemary, not Candace or Lori. It was as if the girls blamed their aunts for coming forward, as though the Ratliff girls felt their aunts were all part of this great conspiracy that had been launched against Michael Peterson.

When state medical examiner Dr. Aaron Gleckman testified before the members of the jury, explaining that Elizabeth Ratliff's death was not due to a medical condition or a fall, that her death was a result of a "homicidal assault," the reality hit home with Liz's sisters. They weeped as the results of the autopsy were explained, and they were subjected to graphic comparisons between the two deaths, photos being shown of the seven lacerations to the scalps of each murdered woman.

Following Gleckman's testimony, Dr. Thomas Bouldin, a UNC neuropathologist, testified about disturbing findings regarding Kathleen Peterson. Bouldin would tell jurors that "red neurons" were present in Kathleen's brain, which was proof that she had experienced a decreased flow of blood to her brain for approximately two hours before her death. Kathleen's sisters hung their heads and quietly sobbed as they thought of Kathleen lying helpless in her own blood, awake and fighting for her life, for a good part of that time.

As for Michael Peterson, none of it seemed to faze him. On the day the evidence about Elizabeth Ratliff began, Peterson donned a fresh red carnation on his lapel, as if there were some special message he was sending to the universe. Michael Peterson was great at throwing kinks into the trial. He had certain things up his sleeve, and he would continue to make accusations behind the scenes. It was clear from the looks on their faces that his brothers, his sons, his few friends, and, of course, the Ratliff girls completely believed in him.

Peterson and his defense team were wired with microphones throughout the trial. They all believed wholeheartedly that the jury would have much reasonable doubt in their minds. There were so many errors that police made; there was no tangible proof prosecutors could offer. There was no way a jury could convict him—could send a man to spend the rest of his life in prison—without being absolutely positive that he was guilty.

And the jurors, the twelve members and the four

alternates, were looking over at Peterson with favorable
expressions. From looking at their faces, it was obvious
that the jurors felt sorry for Peterson's flock, that some
of the female jurors seemed to dwell, particularly, on
Margaret and Martha Ratliff, who, having lost their
other parents, would be losing the only parent they
had left.

But the jurors seemed to shift their emotions. They
certainly had harder expressions on their faces after they
heard the testimony of Candace Zamperini. For months,
Kathleen's sister had driven from her home in Virginia
to be present in the Durham Superior Court. Candace
was a well-dressed, well-spoken woman, who sat in the
front row behind the prosecutors. She was often seen
holding Caitlin's hand, or offering a shoulder for her sister, Lori, to lean on.

Candace wanted justice. She wanted her sister to be
able to rest in peace.

From the evidence already presented, jurors had seen
lacerations, bruises, and scrapes. In all, there were thirty-
five wounds covering Kathleen Peterson's body, and
there was the crushed thyroid cartilage Kathleen suffered, which showed attempted strangulation. Before
she testified, Candace had been forced to sit through
months of testimony that would attempt to exonerate
Michael Peterson. She would suffer his endless laughing,
his whispered snide remarks, and his angry glares when
the jurors weren't present.

But now, just after Labor Day weekend, it was her turn.

Holding the brass fireplace tool in her hands, the blow
poke that she herself owned, Candace told the jury that
the blow poke had become a "fixture" in Kathleen's
home. Candace said she had bought the tool for herself,
and had given the identical item to each of her siblings
at Christmas in 1984. Candace had seen the item in her
sister's home over the years; she had even used it, recall-

ing Thanksgiving 1999, when she and her sister decided
to light a fire to make things festive as they prepared the
holiday dinner.

Candace showed the jury three pictures of Kathleen's
home, pointing out the blow poke, which was always
sitting in the background near the fireplace. Jim Hardin
then offered the blow poke to the jurors, so each of
them could hold the hollow item. Two of the jurors actually gripped it and swung the blow poke, as if they were
pounding something.

Then Candace, who was fighting back tears, told jurors about a trip that she and her sisters made to Fort
Myers, Florida. The family had joined up for a reunion
in May 2001. It was a visit to see their mother, Veronica,
and Candace and Kathleen were roommates, sharing a
bedroom as they had when they were little girls growing
up together.

Candace testified that, while in Florida, she and Kathleen "talked for hours" about their lives, each giving away
secrets. During their conversations, Kathleen had talked
about the stress she was under at work. Kathleen said she
was spending twelve-to-fourteen-hour days at her job, that
she was unhappy having to lay off so many employees, and
yet she felt she had to "stick it out to the bitter end." Kathleen confided that she "would not have a job by the end of
the year." She expressed concerns about having to pay college tuition for three children, and she complained that
she no longer had any time for herself. She was feeling
run-down and having headaches, yet she had no time to
go to a doctor. For the first time, ever, Kathleen had confided that she felt exhausted and tired, that she had been
drinking and taking Valium because things were so dire
at home.

Kathleen talked about the falling price of Nortel stock,
and she explained that she had lost her life's blood in
the stock market. Kathleen talked about the looming

expenses at her home, and she admitted she no longer could afford the upkeep. There was water damage from a leaky roof, and also $10,000 in termite damage. There were major plumbing problems, there were bats in the attic, the problems seemed endless, and Kathleen couldn't afford to fix any of it. Kathleen confided that she wanted a smaller home, but she said Michael wouldn't consider that possibility.

Candace told jurors that her sister "felt sick that nothing was turning around" at Nortel, and cried tears about losing over $1 million in stock prices, which were continuing to fall. Candace explained that she tried to console her sister, that she had suggested that Kathleen look elsewhere for a job. But that didn't seem to be a viable option for Kathleen. Kathleen had climbed to the top of the ladder at Nortel, and at her age, she felt she wouldn't be hireable at the same salary elsewhere.

Hours later, as Candace went through the events surrounding her sister's death, describing the blood on the walls in the Peterson stairwell, explaining her attempts to clean up the blood, she told jurors about spraying Windex in the stairwell, about her desire to hide the horrific scene from other family members.

"I found blood running down my arm," Candace testified, her voice weakening. "I just really remember reaching my arm up and spraying the cat picture."

And with that, Candace Zamperini broke down in tears. As she sat on the witness stand in her black suit and pearls, the woman tried to compose herself. She made every effort to keep her head held high, but the court had to take a brief recess. Candace found herself being led away by her husband, Mark, and her sister, Lori. She had been whisked out of the courtroom so her tears could no longer be visible.

When Candace took the stand again, she was grilled by David Rudolf. The attorney asked questions pointing to Candace's initial belief in her brother-in-law's innocence. He asked Zamperini to explain why she made statements to police, early on, about what a wonderful marriage her sister Kathleen enjoyed with Michael Peterson.

But, in her final remarks to the jury, Candace testified that whatever opinion she ever had of Michael Peterson, whatever support she had shown him early on, was a result of misguided thoughts.

"Sitting here today, I have no idea who Mike Peterson is, none whatsoever," she testified. "Who he held himself out to be, and who he's turned out to be, I have no idea who he is."

Fifty

It would be ten weeks into the trial, after jurors heard testimony about "thousands" of blood spatters at the scene, after they had been shown haunting photos of the Peterson stairwell, that the defense team would make a curious decision. David Rudolf, Michael Peterson, and the rest of his group thought it would be best for jurors to head to the mansion; this way, they could see the blood in the stairwell for themselves.

The jurors were getting much more than they bargained for. Having given up their summer vacations, having listened to cross-examinations and all kinds of varying opinions, suddenly this group of good citizens found themselves being driven over to Forest Hills, escorted by bailiffs and attorneys from both sides. The eight women and four men of the jury, along with their four alternates, became solemn as they were driven up the long and winding driveway. They surely would have been impressed with their immediate surroundings, if it weren't for the fact that they were being led directly to the back stairway of the Peterson house. At Rudolf's request, this staircase had been kept boarded up, and preserved since December 14, 2001.

As the stairwell was being opened, no one could have anticipated the mystic vapor that would exude from behind the plywood. There was that smell of death, that smell of decay, dull and faint, but discernible. No one said anything at the time, but the odor, which the jurors endured, just seemed incomprehensible.

Even though everyone remained silent, even though not a word was spoken at the house, the scene in the stairwell looked like a horrible nightmare. The jurors scanned the narrow staircase, which, until then, had disturbance from external air only once, when Dr. Henry Lee had examined it. As the jurors looked at the scene in person, the totality of the blood was disturbing. There was blood on the woodwork, on the walls, and on the famous black-cat poster. It was blood that had rotted over time, it had turned brown, yet the blood made its way down the wall in so many unusual patterns.

It was a stark contrast from the front stairwell of the house, which was a white spiral work of elaborate architecture, sitting in the middle of a room that was large and lofty. Jurors would catch a glimpse of the beautiful antique tapestry hanging beside the front stairwell—a medieval print that had been purchased by Elizabeth and George Ratliff on their honeymoon—which they had heard some brief testimony about.

But it would be in the back staircase—that the jurors hesitated. It was there that the phantasm of Kathleen in crimson blood, the image of her mangled body, had become all the more accessible. From within the house, the stairwell lent itself to a sense of bitter struggle. It had become eerie—like a vault that entombed Kathleen Peterson's shrieks—her death cries.

Yet it must not have occurred to Peterson or anyone in his camp that the jurors would be struck by the inconsistency they faced. In Peterson's view, the amount of dried blood seemed to support the claim that his wife had fallen down the stairs. And Peterson's lawyers had anticipated that jurors would agree. Rudolf and Maher were convinced that once the jurors saw the actual scene, they would observe the physical confirmation of Kathleen's tragic fall.

But the odors in the place were oppressive and the sight of all that dried blood conjured images of torment. The scene was morbid. To some, the mansion seemed like a haunted place, and the echoes of Kathleen and Elizabeth, both tortured spirits, no longer seemed to be so completely abstract.

Fifty-one

In a demonstration for the jury, famed expert Dr. Henry Lee dropped red ink on a white poster to show how the diameter of blood spatter could increase with velocity. The arrival of Dr. Henry Lee had brought out additional media, the courtroom was jammed, and jurors seemed mystified by Dr. Lee's grace, by his easy smile. Dr. Lee's opinion covered two days of testimony, September 15 and 16, during which time the forensic expert found many things wrong with the state's case.

Henry Lee, with a Ph.D. in biochemistry, had built the Connecticut State Police an internationally recognized laboratory. His fame had gone global with his 1995 testimony in the O.J. Simpson trial, and he would be deemed America's top forensic scientist. People had driven from all parts of the Research Triangle hoping to have a chance to meet him.

Dr. Henry Lee signed copies of his books. His signed autographs.

The man was a legend.

The crime scene analyst would spit up gobs of ketchup to underscore his point that Kathleen may have coughed up blood, testifying that there was "too much blood" for anyone to be able to make exact determinations about what happened in the stairwell. He testified that it was possible that the bloodstain patterns had been caused by

Kathleen Peterson shaking her hair, by any variety of motions.

"We have to look at the totality, everything, before we jump to the conclusion that this was a beating," Dr. Lee told jurors. "To reconstruct, you have to look at the totality. You cannot look at one isolated pattern and make a picture."

According to Henry Lee, Agent Duane Deaver's blood spatter experiments were nothing more than "child's play." Dr. Lee found Deaver's work to be rather useless, stating that it would be impossible for anyone to re-create the stairway scene in a laboratory.

"In your opinion," Rudolf asked, "is the bloodstain evidence consistent with a beating death?"

"No," Lee said. "Inconsistent with."

Dr. Lee focused on the outside of the stairwell. He testified about the three "points of origin" in space, saying that the blood source could have come from anywhere, from someone's head hitting a surface, from someone coughing. Lee explained that, in his view, a point of origin was not necessarily a point of impact.

He testified that anything could have created the blood spatter, that the three points of origin did not mean that a beating had occurred. Dr. Lee disagreed with Agent Deaver's opinion that the particular spatter on the wall—in the corner of the stairwell—came from someone beating Kathleen Peterson with some sort of blunt object.

Dr. Henry Lee disagreed with all of Duane Deaver's opinions. Looking at an enhanced photo of the crime scene, Lee recognized a "swipe mark" in the stairwell, but claimed the swipe mark didn't indicate any cleanup of the area. If there had been an attempt to clean up, Lee testified, the person had done "a lousy job."

Regarding the blood droplets found inside Peterson's shorts, again, Dr. Lee had a different view. Henry Lee stood up in front of the jury to illustrate the possible ways blood spatter had gotten in the inside leg of Peterson's shorts, pointing out that Michael Peterson was "a skinny guy, with not too much meat."

Dr. Lee testified that because Mr. Peterson was wearing "baggy shorts," because there was a lot of space between the flesh and the fabric, "any configuration" could have caused the drops of blood. Mr. Peterson's walking on a step, his sitting down—Lee said there were a lot of possibilities.

"Based on your education, and your training, and your experience, and your own observations and findings in this case," Rudolf asked, "do you have an opinion to a reasonable degree of scientific certainty as to whether the totality of the evidence in this case from the scene is more consistent with an accident?"

"It's more consistent with an accident," Lee testified.

Later that afternoon, under cross-examination, Jim Hardin was able to get Henry Lee to admit that the "points of origin" that Agent Deaver located were each origins for blood that were created "out in space." Nevertheless, Dr. Lee would contend that locating a point of origin did not necessarily equate a beating.

Prior to Lee's testimony, a neuropathologist, Dr. Jan Leestma, had testified on behalf of the defense. Dr. Leestma told jurors that he believed Kathleen Peterson's death had been the result of an accidental fall. Like Dr. Henry Lee, Dr. Jan Leestma was being paid $500 an hour to testify about his opinion. In essence, Dr. Leestma told jurors that Kathleen Peterson had suffered two falls, causing four impacts. However, when Jim Hardin asked the hired expert to explain exactly how that might have occurred, Leestma told Jim Hardin to ask a blood spatter expert, or a biomechanical engineer, for that answer.

"So I'm asking you, since it was Dr. Leestma's opinion that she had two falls and four impacts," Hardin said to

Dr. Lee, "as the blood spatter expert, can you please explain to this jury the sequence of events about how that happened?"

"With all due respect," Dr. Lee answered, "I can't really give you the sequence of events. I cannot. I don't know exactly which one fall is first or second."

"Well, in fact, Dr. Lee, you can't even say that all those lacerations were caused by falls, can you?"

"I did not say that."

"Well, that's what I want to understand," Hardin pressed, "you can't say?"

"I cannot say that," Lee responded.

"You can't say that all of those lacerations were caused by falls?"

"I don't know," Lee testified. "That's outside the area of my expertise."

By the time Jim Hardin finished with his cross-examination, Dr. Henry Lee's testimony wasn't seeming quite as worthy as his reputation. A recently retired commissioner of public safety in Connecticut, a coauthor of definitive books on forensics, Dr. Henry Lee had spent hours on the witness stand, had been a showman, had flung ketchup and red ink, but he hadn't convinced the courtroom observers. He was smooth. He was fun to watch. People gawked at Dr. Henry Lee. But not everyone was sure he had the right opinion.

Regardless, the forensic man was still treated like a star. The folks in Durham read articles about him with fascination. The local papers drew cartoon caricatures of him. Dr. Henry Lee had been so comfortable on the stand, so confident in front of the TV cameras, he had even brought some levity to the situation. Throughout his testimony, he had managed to crack a few jokes.

Caitlin Atwater, however, would later confide that Dr. Lee's attitude bothered her. She couldn't understand Lee's theory that there was "too much blood" for the death to have been a beating, yet not too much blood for a fall. She realized that the man was highly respected, but Caitlin felt his opinion didn't make sense. Caitlin was upset and offended by Dr. Lee's courtroom performance.

"I understand he was trying to be personable," she later confided. "But the people in the courtroom were laughing about my mother's blood."

Fifty-two

The "Perry Mason moment" of the trial happened just days after Hurricane Isabel hit the East Coast, which had created disaster areas in Virginia, Maryland, and Delaware. It had shut down the trial proceedings, having caused power outages and uprooted trees in Durham. In the aftermath of the storm, as people in North Carolina were trying to get their lives back on track, the Peterson trial came back into session, and David Rudolf called Detective Art Holland to the stand to introduce a striking piece of evidence.

"Did you ever ask us if we had located the blow poke?" Rudolf wanted to know.

"No, I didn't," Holland testified.

"Did you just assume that it was gone?" Rudolf asked.

"Gone, or put up somewhere," Holland told the court.

Unbeknownst to Art Holland, David Rudolf had held an exparte meeting with Judge Hudson on a Sunday, whereby Judge Hudson was brought to the Peterson mansion, in order that Rudolf could show him a blow poke that was lying against an obscure wall in the garage. Judge Hudson signed an order allowing the attorney, along with photographers and the French documentary crew, to film the blow poke in the condition and location that it had been found. He told them they could move it, and ordered them not to destroy the item.

Judge Hudson, however, had no way of knowing that David Rudolf had brought the blow poke into the court-room had hidden it behind the defense table. When the defense attorney brought out the long, cylindrical item, whipping it out in front of the jury in a clear plastic wrapper, the prosecution had no chance to object. Even though no foundation had been laid as to who found the item, even though there was a question as to the au-thenticity of the item, Rudolf shrewdly insisted in a bench conference that he couldn't reveal the circum-stances under which it had been found. Rudolf said it would violate attorney-client privilege.

Durham police had pulled three search warrants look-ing for the murder weapon. They had combed the Peterson house and property, inch by inch, looking for that blow poke. But now, prosecutors were in a position. Jim Hardin decided not to argue in open court, he did not want to give any weight to the newly found piece of evidence. The courtroom had gone numb when Rudolf had produced the blow poke—everyone was visibly shocked—but Jim Hardin decided to just let the testi-mony go forward.

As the defense attorney wielded the brass tool, which had no drop of blood or dent mark on it, he would point out the cobwebs and insects that were covering the fire-place instrument.

"Have you ever given any thought to what would hap-pen to an item like this," Rudolf asked, "if it were used to beat someone to death?"

"Probably be mangled up," Holland responded.

"See any dents in there? Even like a tiny indentation?"

"It doesn't appear to have any dents," Holland ad-mitted.

The stealth unveiling of the blow poke was allowable

under North Carolina law. Judge Hudson had signed an order allowing the defense team to take it into custody. But Rudolf's attempt to enter it into evidence appeared to surprise Judge Hudson, who had stated in his order: "In the event the Defendant wishes to introduce the blow poke into evidence, or conduct any forensic testing on the blow poke, the Defendant shall inform the State of the existence of the blow poke."

David Rudolf had not abided by the rules of "reciprocal discovery." The defense attorney claimed that his decision to bring the missing blow poke into court was something he had thought of "last minute." Rudolf claimed that he hadn't shown it to prosecutors beforehand, because he just wasn't sure that he was going to present it.

The newly discovered blow poke, revealed just as the defense was wrapping up, would threaten to unravel the state's case. Suddenly the state's theory that Peterson had killed his wife with a blow poke made less sense to everyone. Here was a blow poke that the Durham Police department had overlooked, the supposed murder weapon in the case, and it was there for everyone to see, in perfect condition.

Even though the origin of the blow poke remained a mystery, both sides knew that when the case would go to the jury for deliberation, there would be this fireplace tool they would have to deal with. It was an exact match to Candace's blow poke, which prosecutors had claimed was the murder weapon.

Perhaps David Rudolf had pulled off more than a "Perry Mason moment"; perhaps he'd pulled off an "O.J. moment." With the existence of the blow poke, everything that had come before, even the testimony of Dr. Henry Lee, with his ketchup and blood spatter analysis, didn't seem relevant. The presentation of the blow poke, which had been missing for twenty-one months, was very much like the famous glove from the O.J. Simpson trial, which, unfortunately, didn't fit O.J. Simpson's hand.

To the courtroom audience, to the members of the media, the entry of the brass blow poke into evidence, complete with cobwebs and bugs, made things look quite bad for the prosecution. In the circumstantial case, the state had gambled on what they *thought* had been the murder weapon. For months, the prosecution had hung their hats on the "missing" blow poke, repeatedly indicating that the hollow item was the perfect tool for murder. But suddenly it seemed that the prosecution's theory was bogus.

Facing a full-capacity crowd in the gallery, David Rudolf made the most of the turnaround in the case, grabbing the "missing" brass blow poke as he launched into a 3½-hour closing argument. As part of his impassioned speech, Rudolf played a tape of Jim Hardin's opening statement, reminding jurors that Hardin had boasted that the state had pinpointed the murder weapon.

Rudolf argued about the state's "tunnel vision."

Rudolf attacked the state's motive, telling jurors that the prosecutors had "trotted out the old standbys" of sex and money, claiming that, in reality, the Petersons' five-year marriage was in great shape, both financially and romantically. He claimed that the combined net value of the Petersons at the time of Kathleen's death—the mansion, other income, and rental properties—was almost $2 million. He told jurors that at the time of Kathleen's death, not even her sisters had a negative word to say about Kathleen's relationship with Michael.

In terms of the physical evidence linking Michael Peterson to a homicide, Rudolf insisted that, while he couldn't explain exactly how Kathleen sustained lacerations to the back of her head during a fall, it wasn't necessary to know how a "freak accident" might have happened. All the jury needed to focus on was the belief that a freak accident *could* have happened.

As for Elizabeth Ratliff, Rudolf reminded jurors that Judge Hudson had ruled that before the jury could consider her death, they first would have to find that her death was a homicide, and also have to find that Michael Peterson was the perpetrator. Then, with a great sense of spirit and pride, David Rudolf stated that there were at least ten reasons to acquit Michael Peterson. "In this age of David Letterman," Rudolf told jurors, there was a "top ten list" for them to consider. Jurors could acquit his client if they believed even one of the items on the list, and he flashed his list on a big screen. The jurors were free to read along as Rudolf stated his reasons as to why they should acquit his client.

Here was David Rudolf's "Top Ten" list:

1) The missing murder weapon wasn't missing—and it wasn't used to commit a murder.

2) There was no credible motive—and you don't decide to kill your wife for no reason.

3) Michael and Kathleen Peterson were happily married, with no history of violence—and spousal abuse didn't generally start with murder.

4) Michael Peterson's grief and shock were sincere—and no one at the scene disagreed with that.

5) Kathleen Peterson's injuries were not consistent with a beating. No skull fractures + no other fractures + no traumatic brain injury = no beating.

6) The bloodstain evidence was not consistent with a beating, and the state's "real" expert did not dispute this.

7) The information and documentation from the scene was not reliable. Garbage in, garbage out.

8) The state relied on junk science and ignored the limitations of real science.

9) The state relied on emotion, guess, and conjecture.

10) The state's investigation suffered from *tunnel vision*. Indictment first—evidence afterward.

Fifty-three

"We're not dealing with the average individual here," Freda Black told jurors. "We're dealing with a fictional writer. He is a person who knows exactly how to create a fictional plot."

The beautiful, dark-haired Freda Black, who was presenting the first half of the state's closing argument, was not one to mince words. She began by using the words, "soul mates." Then she read from a set of wedding vows, telling jurors how little those vows meant to Michael Peterson.

"Did he honor her? Did he keep her?" Black asked. "The answer to those questions is no."

The prosecutor described the "unnatural positioning" of Kathleen Peterson's body, the pair of wineglasses, one with Michael's fingerprints, a bottle of Windex that was strangely out of its place, as well as the broken crystal wineglass—all of which led prosecutors to believe that the defendant had killed his wife and then staged her death. She told jurors that Peterson was "acting" when he placed calls to 9-1-1, assuring them that Peterson wasn't truly shaken up when he called for help, implying that police soon realized they were dealing with a calculating murderer.

"If he's really a grieving spouse," Black wondered, "why did Officer McCallop see him checking his e-mails on his computer while he was in that study? Would you be checking your e-mails if your spouse was lying out in the hallway with blood everywhere?

"Did you notice that one of the e-mails was sent at three thirty-six A.M.?" she asked. "Is it okay for Kathleen Peterson to be sleeping in the marital bed while Michael Peterson is up e-mailing Brad?"

Freda Black disputed Rudolf's claims that the state's expert witnesses did not give accurate information, that the state's experts had made assumptions that were outside their area of expertise. Black said that all of the state's witnesses—from forensic pathologist Deborah Radisch to blood spatter expert Duane Deaver—were seasoned North Carolina officials who had no reason to misstate their findings. Black reminded the jury that any misinformation state witnesses might offer in a court of law would jeopardize their job. These professionals were unlike defense witnesses, who were highly paid to offer their testimony.

"The defendant is so arrogant that he thinks that all these people would risk their reputations, their integrity, jobs, and freedom for him," she quipped. "*He's that important?* I think not."

Black spoke highly of the local police, of the medical examiners, of all the witnesses for the prosecution, assuring jurors these experts were trustworthy. She told jurors that once this case was over, the defense team's hired witnesses would be long gone, but the hardworking team of experts in Durham would still be right there to testify in the courtroom, fighting for justice in much-less high-profile cases.

"They might not appear on *Larry King Live* or Court TV," she said, alluding to Dr. Henry Lee. "But you know what? They are tried and true, because they work for our state."

Black told jurors that Michael Peterson had tried to

sell his staged, trumped-up story, not only to the authorities, but to his family. "And in this courtroom, he's tried to sell it to you," she emphasized, "a fictional plot.

"Part of that plot," Black said, was the "dramatic discovery of what defense claimed was the missing blow poke."

Freda Black questioned the timing of the appearance of the insect-covered blow poke, and said it could have easily been bought by someone on eBay. She told jurors that the item could have been purchased anytime after the fact, suggesting that it wouldn't have taken long for cobwebs and dust to develop on the blow poke entered into evidence by the defense.

She questioned whether the item that the defense entered was actually the original item from the Peterson household. Freda Black covered all the bases. She told jurors that even if the defense exhibit was the blow poke that belonged to Kathleen, it was of little consequence.

The state had never claimed to have found the actual murder weapon.

"We have never told you that we were absolutely certain that it was the blow poke that killed Mrs. Peterson," Black asserted. "You've heard we believe it was something of the sort."

Black also concentrated on the similarities between the death of Elizabeth Ratliff and that of Kathleen Peterson. Both women were about the same age. They had similar facial features and similar bone structures. The prosecutor said that the list of similarities between the two deaths—which included timing, modus operandi, and financial gain for Michael Peterson—should be considered in their totality.

"Do you really think that lightning strikes twice in the same place? Do you?" she asked jurors. "This defendant knew the blueprint of how to make this look like an accidental fall, because it had worked one time. And he tried to make it work again. But it didn't."

As District Attorney Jim Hardin continued the closing argument, he used a simple posterboard to make swift points to jurors. A soft-spoken man, the prosecutor immediately discounted the defense theory that the victim died from a fall.

Hardin asked that the jury use their logic, their common sense, telling them there was just too much blood in the stairwell, and too many injuries to Kathleen Peterson, for her death to have been caused by a fall. Hardin insisted that the defense "theory" was counterintuitive, that "it doesn't fit right here in your gut."

"Do you really think the defendant was at the pool?" Hardin wondered. "Does the defendant really spend several hours in the winter, wearing shorts, by the backyard pool, as his wife lay dying inside? Doesn't that strain credibility? Who in the world is going to stay outside that long? I submit to you that the defendant wasn't out at the pool. He was in the house, committing this horrible act."

Jim Hardin held up an autopsy photo for jurors, urging them to remember the pain Kathleen Peterson suffered as they considered the evidence against her husband.

"A picture is worth a thousand words. But if these walls could talk, what would they say?" Hardin asked. "Kathleen Peterson is talking to us through the blood that is on the wall. She is screaming to us for truth. And for justice."

Hardin would argue that no reasonable person could look at the story detailed in Mrs. Peterson's autopsy and conclude that she had just clumsily fallen down the stairs. No one could deny the horrible reality: the combination of the fractured bone in Kathleen's neck, her facial wounds, and the deep lacerations to her head.

And then there was something else that Hardin pointed out—the absence of wounds on other parts of Kathleen Peterson's body. If Kathleen Peterson had fallen down the stairs, Hardin reminded jurors, there would have been bruises to obvious places, to her larger body parts. But there weren't.

"Common sense tells you this was a beating. This wasn't a fall. This is a horrible way to die. It must have taken her a long time to die. She's fighting for her life. That's why there's so much blood," Hardin insisted. "He assaulted her. She went down. He continued to assault her. That's when premeditation formulated.

"Thirty-eight injuries, ladies and gentlemen," the prosecutor continued. "How in the world does someone get *thirty-eight* injuries over their face, back, hands, and wrists by falling down some steps? Even if there were two falls? That makes absolutely no sense.

"This is not a whodunit," Jim Hardin insisted. "If you find that this was murder, there's only one person who could have done it—Michael Peterson."

Fifty-four

Profile of a sociopath

In the 1830s, this disorder was called "moral insanity." By 1900, it was changed to "psychopath." More recently, the term used is "sociopath," also known as "antisocial personality disorder." A sociopath has an outstanding capacity to charm and seduce followers. Because the sociopath appears to be "normal," the sociopath is not easily recognizable as being deviant or disturbed. While many sociopaths are mind-manipulating cult leaders, the traits of the sociopath can also apply to one-on-one relationships. Note: the below traits of the sociopath are based on the psychopathy checklists of H. Cleckley and R. Hare:

*Glibness and Superficial charm. Language can be used by them, without any effort, to convince their audience. They are captivating storytellers who exude confidence.

*Manipulative and Conning. They see their self-serving behavior as permissible and never recognize the rights of others. They appear to be charming, yet are secretly hostile and domineering.

*Grandiose Sense of Self. They must be the center of

attention. They use their own fantasies to create an *us-versus-them* mentality.

*Early Behavior Problems. They usually have a history of just "getting by" through conning others. They have problems in keeping friends and exhibit aberrant behaviors such as cruelty to people or animals.

*Pathological Lying. They create a complex belief about themselves and their abilities, and it is virtually impossible for them to be truthful on a consistent basis.

*Shallow Emotions. They show what seems to be joy and love, but it is more feigned than real. They are outraged by insignificant matters, yet completely unmoved by what would upset a normal human being.

*Poor Behavioral Control and Impulsive Nature. They alternate small expressions of love with acts of rage and abuse. They believe they are all-knowing, yet have no concern for their impact on others.

*Irresponsibility. They are not concerned with ruining other people's lives and are indifferent or oblivious to the devastation they cause.

*Promiscuous Sexual Behavior and Infidelity. They engage in sexual acting out of all sorts, usually kept hidden.

*Parasitic Lifestyle. They make all-encompassing promises without having a realistic life plan. Their opulent lifestyle is supported by donations and gifts from those who are pressured to give, through fear or guilt.

*Lack of Remorse, Shame, or Guilt. They have a deep-seated rage at the core. To them, the end justifies the means, and nothing stands in their way.

Fifty-five

A favorable omen for the defense came when the jury composition had been changed, last minute. Three jurors were dismissed, replaced for varying reasons, and in an unexpected turn of events, one of the alternate jurors brought on board was a male nurse, leaving the final jury of twelve with three nurses in the deliberation room. The public speculated that the new makeup of the jury might very well cause a problem. The alternates, perhaps, hadn't been paying as much attention. People surmised that the deliberations would be more difficult than anyone had first realized.

As jurors were considering the charge of first-degree murder, they sorted through dozens of exhibits, multiple photos, transcripts of testimony, and, of course, the set of identical blow pokes. On day two of deliberations, court clerks had been asked to bring them a boom box and the cassette tape of Peterson's 9-1-1 calls. Also on day two, jurors requested a transcript of Jim Hardin's opening statement, in which the prosecutor first mentioned the blow poke as the possible murder weapon.

Since opening statements could not be considered evidence, Jim Hardin was able to argue that successfully that the transcript would not be provided. David Rudolf, however, argued, "if the jury wants to look at the prosecutor's opening statement to see what he did or didn't prove, that's appropriate." Rudolf insisted that Hardin wanted to "run from his opening," and he asked Judge Hudson to inform jurors about Jim Hardin's objection to their being given a transcript. His request was denied.

The fact that jurors wanted to review Hardin's remarks, the fact that they were examining 9-1-1 tapes, along with the identical blow pokes, did not bode well for the state. Clearly, the jurors wanted to check to see just how specific Jim Hardin had been when he spoke about the murder weapon in his opening remarks, which meant they had a question about the credibility of the state's case. Media reports surmised that the jurors wanted to see what the prosecutor had promised, to see what he did and didn't deliver.

If jurors were counting on the blow poke as *the* weapon, if they were counting on the state to prove it, the jury could vote not guilty based on that alone. The jurors had a lot to think about. Since they were not given the option of convicting Peterson of the lesser offense of second-degree murder, they had to find him guilty of first-degree, premeditated murder, or let him walk as a free man.

On the third day of deliberations, the defense team sat in the courtroom, looking somewhat glib. Michael Peterson sat with his whole team, all of whom seemed to be awaiting a verdict in their favor. Michael, in fact, felt comfortable enough to slouch down in a courtroom seat that was marked for the district attorney, the defendant resting his head on the back of the chair, his designer loafers propped on the courtroom railing. David Rudolf was also kicking back, having slipped on a pair of white headphones, listening to an eclectic mix of music on his iPod player.

While the jurors continued to mull over Peterson's fate, giving no hint that they were reaching a decision, prosecutors were cautiously absent from the courtroom.

Jim Hardin, Freda Black, and David Saacks remained in their sixth-floor offices of the Durham County Courthouse, trying not to second-guess themselves. The team had already decided, if there was a hung jury, they would try Michael Peterson again. They had already made initial preparations about which witnesses to call. They decided they would be able to retry the case with a much shorter witness list, and knew that they would focus on the "red neurons" present in Kathleen's brain, scientific proof that she had been dead for two hours *before* Peterson made his 9-1-1 calls.

Behind the guarded wall of the deliberation room, the jury of seven women and five men had come to a standoff. They were split, six to six, and for two days the jurors honestly thought they were never going to be able to come to an agreement. The jurors had studied the lacerations on Kathleen's skull. They had examined the blood spatter on the inside of Peterson's shorts. The jurors could see, from photo exhibits of the crime scene, that there was blood on top of dried blood on the wall of the stairwell. Yet, when they first began deliberating, five of them were undecided, four thought Peterson was guilty, and three thought he was not guilty. It wasn't until the end of the third day that everyone came to believe Mrs. Peterson had died as a result of a beating. But then, the trouble was, the jurors could not agree as to whether or not the beating had been an act of premeditation.

Their arguments went back and forth. The jurors were sometimes crying, sometimes fighting, as they reexamined the autopsy photos. Late in the afternoon, day three of their arguments, the jury was split, ten to two, with two people still believing that Michael Peterson was not guilty.

Those who felt Peterson was guilty had taken the position that a) Michael stood over his wife, watching her as she bled to death, or b) he had gone back into the stairwell to finish her off. Either way, ten of the jurors felt convinced that his actions were premeditated, because there was evidence that Kathleen had managed to stand on her own two feet after his initial attack.

But the other two jurors would have to think about it. They needed to find evidence that met all five aspects of first-degree murder: premeditation, malice, cause, deliberation, and intent. The twelve jurors agreed to go home and sleep on it.

It was on October 10, 2003, in the midmorning of the fourth day, when the jury had reached a unanimous decision. Everyone scrambled into the courtroom, Michael Peterson having his family huddled around him as the manila envelope was handed to the court clerk Angela Kelly, who read the verdict aloud:

"We, the twelve members of the jury, unanimously find the defendant, Michael Iver Peterson, to be guilty of first-degree murder."

Peterson's brothers, Bill and Jack, looked completely stunned. His sons, Clayton and Todd, just stared off into space. Margaret and Martha Ratliff wrapped their arms around each other and sobbed. Hearing their cries as handcuffs were placed on his wrists by deputies, Michael Peterson turned to the two girls, telling them, "It's okay, it's okay."

Michael Iver Peterson was immediately sentenced to serve the mandatory *life in prison without parole*, he was led away from the courtroom, and whisked to the Nash Correctional Institution, located about seventy miles from Durham, where he would spend the remainder of his natural life. There he would join another infamous prisoner, former Carolina Panther Rae Carruth, who was still serving his prison term of eighteen years, for having plotted to kill his pregnant girlfriend, Cherica Adams.

Peterson's lawyers said they planned to appeal Peterson's conviction on at least two grounds: the judge's decision to admit evidence about Peterson's alleged homosexual conduct, and the testimony about Elizabeth Ratliff's 1985 death in Germany.

"Frankly, I don't understand the verdict," a very solemn David Rudolf said, speaking to reporters on the courthouse steps. "I am very, very, very disappointed."

Throughout the weeks and weeks of testimony, Michael Peterson had taken extensive notes on legal pads. It turned out that the novelist had a *book deal* waiting for him over at the HarperCollins publishing house. However, the deal was contingent upon Michael Peterson's being found innocent, and thus was immediately withdrawn.

Bill Peterson, speaking to reporters on behalf of Michael's family, spoke of the "complete and utter demoralization" of his brother, insisting that Michael Peterson was innocent. Bill Peterson told the media that because prosecutors had focused on "gay porn" during the trial, they had prevented the defense from putting Michael on the witness stand.

Patricia Peterson gave a brief statement to reporters as well, speaking of the solidarity felt by the Peterson family, of their sheer and complete belief in his innocence, regardless of what the jury had determined. To prove her devotion to Michael, Patricia told the media that Michael "did not participate in the act" of Kathleen Peterson's death.

"This is about the death of a mother," Patricia told a TV news team. "This is about children losing their mother, and possibly losing their father. It is an unconscionable loss for every one of those children."

When the verdict was made public, screaming head-lines read:

GUILTY: PETERSON GETS LIFE IN WIFE'S KILLING. And to every-one's chagrin, there was even more information that family members came forward to tell, which revealed se-crets about Peterson's "alter" personality.

Michael Peterson's sister, Ann Christensen, called re-porters from her home in California to say that her brother, ten years her elder, had a volatile temper, which was often directed at the women in his life.

"It's not just anger," Christensen told news reporters, "it cuts you to the bone."

Kathleen Peterson's sisters, Lori Campell and Can-dace Zamperini, also came forward after the verdict. They revealed to *Herald-Sun* reporters that Michael was a controlling husband who "flew into rages around the house."

Candace Zamperini explained that Kathleen had hid-den the "trouble" in her marriage from the family, and in an interview with Court TV, Candace referred to a diary that Caitlin had written, three entries of which were so upsetting, she couldn't bring herself to finish reading them.

"I hope that someday other people can read what life was truly like with Michael Peterson in that house," Can-dace told reporters. "He did verbally abuse people and control things."

In an interview with Court TV, Lori Campell revealed that Michael's temperament was erratic. Lori told news reporters that she was aware of an "incident" that oc-curred when her sister was on a trip with Michael in Paris. According to Lori, Kathleen alleged that Michael had hit her, just after their belongings were stolen on the Metro. Kathleen explained that Michael had gone out and bought her an expensive purse, in an attempt to "make up."

"He became angry and he took it out on her," Lori told media. "I admired her and looked up to her. Kathleen was an intelligent woman. But she didn't leave him."

Kathleen's sister Lori would also state that she never believed for a minute that her sister had fallen down the stairs. Upon learning about Kathleen's death, she recalled, the first words out of her mouth were "He did this to her" and "He didn't love her."

Elizabeth Ratliff's sister, Margaret Blair, had confided to members of the prosecution that Michael Peterson allegedly beat his English bulldog, that she had seen Michael hurt the family pet, watching the bulldog's eyes become bloody. Blair told Durham prosecutors that she had witnessed the incident, and she had gotten "the biggest white fluffy towel" she could find, so she could comfort the poor dog.

Elizabeth's former nanny, Barbara Malagnino, alleged that back in the early days, she had seen Michael Peterson beat his pet, Bud, a basset hound. Malagnino further alleged that just after Elizabeth's death, Michael Peterson had "scraped the nose" of one of the Ratliff girls, rubbing the girl's face in urine on Mrs. Ratliff's wooden floor.

Kathleen's first husband, Fred Atwater, and daughter Caitlin would confide that on 9/11, the day of the U.S. terrorist attacks, they had been informed that Kathleen was in the emergency room being treated for a head injury. Fred and Caitlin were told that Kathleen had hurt herself by diving into the swimming pool, but they could never get a straight answer from Kathleen about what happened. Upon reflection, they felt the story Michael had told them never really made sense. Kathleen was not a big swimmer. She was the type to wade into the water slowly. . . .

And on the steps outside the courthouse, after a press conference was held by Jim Hardin, Freda Black stated that the passion in her closing argument had stemmed from the significance that the case held for victims of domestic abuse all across the world.

"I was speaking for women," Black told reporters. "These were two female victims of domestic violence."

Fifty-six

Many people who watched the trial had become armchair analysts. Among them were amateur observers, well-read attorneys, Court TV addicts, as well as members of the Peterson clan, who used obvious code names on message boards, who seemed to thrive on gossip and speculation. In the final days of the trial, a majority of these outside observers expressed an overwhelming opinion that Michael Peterson would be found not guilty. They seemed certain that Peterson would walk, that he would be acquitted.

The jurors held a press conference to talk about the verdict, claiming the Elizabeth Ratliff evidence had not influenced their decision. As for Henry Lee's testimony, jurors said it was "irrelevant." When asked about the blow poke, jurors said they didn't know what the murder weapon was, but they were convinced that Michael Peterson had beaten his wife to death, using some kind of blunt object.

But jurors didn't know, nor did courtroom observers or Court TV junkies, about one of the most interesting details that was never presented during the case. People had no clue that DA Hardin had been contacted by a U.S. attorney about a recent sale out of Kennebunkport, Maine. The call was regarding the sale of two blow pokes. . . .

THE VOICE OF JIM HARDIN

"Before our closing arguments, I received a phone call from a lady in Kennebunkport. She told me that a man by the name of Michael Peterson had called her and ordered three blow pokes. She said they'd shipped two of them to him, that he had given them his credit card. Peterson would have received them just after Rudolf had placed the defendant's blow poke into evidence. Maybe he wanted to give them as gifts. I don't know. But the woman from Maine faxed down the order form to us, and we have it in the vault.

"I don't know where the blow poke the defendant entered into evidence came from, but I can tell you one thing, it wasn't in that garage because we certainly would have found it when we executed the last search warrant on June 27, 2002. I gave specific instructions for every inch of that house to be measured. I was in that garage, several other people were in that garage on a couple of occasions, and that blow poke was not there."

"I think every aspect of this case was calculated. Every aspect from the defense, from the media leaks, which started with an accident theory, saying that she was drunk, high on Valium. Then they float the intruder defense out there, and then come back to the accident defense. Everything they did, in my opinion, was calculated from the inception.

"From Peterson's perspective, he had this mapped out in his mind. It was just so apparent to me, with the 9-1-1 calls, how selective he was with his information. Then he was selective with the officers when they got there, about how information was provided, essentially through Todd, so he was protected. He wanted some information provided, to give them something so they would continue to believe it's an accident. But I believe that was all calculated.

"Mr. Rudolf tried to put a lot of things in front of the jury that either he wasn't going to prove, or he couldn't prove, and he did that by design, that's my opinion. That's all done to *confuse the jury. Basically, Rudolf, throughout the trial, was testifying without presenting evidence.*

"People are going to say that I staked myself out on that blow poke, and I probably did, as it turned out, more than I wish I had. But Rudolf made a tactical error on his part, he staked himself out when he talked about the loving relationship, saying they were soul mates. We were very pleased that he had done that. It opened the door for us. We had a lot of Brad information, the computer information, and when he talked about their idyllic relationship and how Peterson had no motive to harm her, he opened the door wide enough for a Mack truck to drive through.

"For me, Dave Rudolf tried this case like he tries every case. He's got a playbook. And that playbook includes attacking the prosecution, sometimes attacking the victim, and pandering to the press. Rudolf was constantly in front of the media talking about things I believe he cannot ethically talk about. He was giving constant interviews, two or three a day, while the case was going on. I don't think you're ethically entitled to do that.

"I have no idea why Peterson downloaded a hard copy of Brad's Web site with all the reviews people had given Brad about their 'encounters.' For some reason he had downloaded this, along with e-mails, and all this pornography was in a desk file with some of Kathleen's important papers. These sexual materials were in there with Kathleen's Nortel records, with her November benefits sheet, with tax bills that had to be paid, with some phone bills. They were things you would have to attend to within a month.

"In my mind, it all goes back to, if she loses her job. Think about her precarious job situation. She was about to lose her job. Kathleen had been able to survive a couple of rounds of firing, but then her immediate supervisor was terminated. She had been placed on the 'optimization' list just before her boss was fired, and then she had been taken off the list. But personally, I think she was aware that if her boss was being terminated, she was next on the chopping block.

"It's our view that Kathleen would have had significant deprivation of oxygen to the brain. You've got the two-hour period before those red neurons could develop, so she had to lay there for at least two hours bleeding and dying. And during that period of time, there were a succession of assaults. There was the initial assault, and, in our view, there was another assault, because of the blood spatter on top of cleanup.

"Obviously, we had to piece things together. Obviously, Peterson didn't want to talk with us about it, but you look at his situation. He had just lost an election. They're in a horrific financial situation. She's on the verge of losing her job. Personally, I think all those stressors were coming to a head. And I think that when she found out that he was having extramarital relations, or at least attempting to have them, I think she told him to hit the bricks.

"As for Michael Peterson, I think he's an evil person, and, at his core, is a psychopath."

Fifty-seven

THE VOICE OF FREDA BLACK

"*When the family first came into our offices, they basically expressed their disbelief that this really was a homicide and that Michael committed the crime. Candace and Lori were the first to have a discussion with us, and they made a specific request to know what evidence we had. We were leery to tell them all our evidence, because they didn't know us, and they weren't in our corner yet.*

"*Jim and I told them some things about the blood spatter evidence, and offered them an opportunity to look at the autopsy pictures. And when Candace looked at them, she cried. A few weeks later, she had a conversation with Art Holland, and with Dr. Radisch, and Candace called to let us know that she felt satisfied that her sister had been murdered.*

"*A friend of Lori's, a guy named Dennis, had told her that he had sexual relations with Michael. And Lori wasn't sure if it was true, but she was hopeful that if it was true, that maybe it was just a onetime thing. She told me she didn't want to worry Kathleen about it, so she made the conscious decision not to tell Kathleen. When we contacted this fellow, he said he would refuse to testify. He had hired a lawyer, and we decided he wasn't going to be worth it. It was going to be a big ordeal to get him up here, and we had Brad, who would cover that category.*

"*Their suggestion that this was some type of revenge, because*

Peterson had been critical in his newspaper articles, that people would have framed him out of revenge, the average citizen would find it hard to believe. Most of the people who testified didn't even know who Michael Peterson was. How would they come up with an idea to frame somebody that they don't even know?

"Mr. Peterson is not O.J. Simpson. He's simply not that important of a person. They tried to use the idea that we framed him, you know, that there was contamination of the scene. Peterson was so arrogant that he thought we would risk everything by framing him. But why would we want to do that? It's an unbelievable allegation to think that people from all these different agencies would risk everything they work for in the legal process.

"The only picture that we consistently got of Michael Peterson was that he and his wife appeared to have a solid relationship. We heard that from all the people who knew them, which made us believe that if there were really bad things going on in that home, it was going on behind closed doors, that Kathleen was not telling friends and family everything, which was not surprising to me.

"Kathleen was the type of woman who would have found it embarrassing and humiliating to admit she was being mistreated. A woman of her stature and position, to be willing to put up with what she was probably having to put up with, whether it was the anger, whether it was the demeaning comment. I would think that because his ego was so big, Peterson didn't fathom that this woman was supporting him and his children. He probably didn't let his mind go there.

"Kathleen probably didn't confide in anyone. We tried to find someone who was her best girlfriend, but we never found that person. We tried to find out who her best friends at work were, but we kept coming up on a dead end. I think Michael mesmerized what little spare time she had. And if you think about the lifestyle she had, you know, if she wasn't at work, she was either at home cooking or just doing all the things that it takes to run a household that big. There were the parties that she hosted, and she took care of the girls. So where was she going to have any extra time to even have a best girlfriend?

"Rudolf showed different pictures and videos of items in their house, trying to prove that they weren't poor, that they weren't hurting for money. Rudolf showed the video over and over again, he showed still pictures and certificates of authenticity, trying to show that all of the Petersons' material possessions were worth a lot of money.

"One of the items they showed was something that dated back like a zillion years ago. It was a figurine or something supposedly from an ancient Chinese Dynasty. And they showed a certificate of authenticity, which stated the object was purchased in May of 2002. But all I could think was, why is he buying expensive artwork when he's supposed to be paying lawyers? To me, it's just a show of his selfishness. Here he's going to go to trial for first-degree murder, and he's got bills to pay, but Peterson goes out and buys a luxury item.

"When we were executing the final search warrant, I went into the house with the men from the police department, and, I mean, the house was not kept up well. There were trash cans overflowing with garbage. There were items of linen just laying in the closet. It was definitely not very tidy, and he'd been living there with the children since he'd gotten out on bond. I really don't believe he wanted to clean the house. I don't think that he cared about anything in the house, and whether it was clean or not.

"We were there in June, and the primary reason we were there was so we could take measurements to have a carpenter reconstruct a portion of the staircase. We also had FBI come with us to take some fiber samples, because there was a fiber in front of one of Kathleen's fingernails. We believe that she had her hands on her head, to try to fend off blows, and in the process, some of her own hair came out, and some other fiber ended up under her nail. But as it turned out, we weren't able to match that fiber.

"We always believed that Mr. Peterson got rid of the weapon. One key reason was because of this perfectly round spot of *blood that was found outside the front door of the house. Now, according to what Mr. Peterson told EMS when they got there, he had not really gone outside, except perhaps to look out the door. But Duane Deaver explained that because of the roundness of that spot, it had come from a source that was perpendicular to the pavement. As opposed to something coming off clothes or shoes, it was a blood drop that came off an item."*

Epilogue

Two years after Kathleen's death, long after the Peterson mansion was placed on the market, all of its contents having been picked over during a public auction, Kathleen's grave was well-kept with flowers, and someone had anonymously left a loving poem, entitled "If Tears Could Build a Stairway." By the time Michael Peterson had turned sixty, he had begun serving his time in prison. He was happily teaching illiterate inmates how to read and write, and also giving television interviews proclaiming his innocence.

Then for some reason, out of the blue, members of Peterson's support group decided to propose a new theory to explain Kathleen's demise. Some people found it impossible that anyone would continue to fight for Peterson. Others felt Peterson's supporters were hanging on because of yet-to-be-disclosed book or movie deals, because of the continuing national TV coverage; the Michael Peterson story was ready to be aired on *Dateline NBC*, and there was an upcoming ABC documentary, a promising TV event to air as a three-part series.

Whatever the reason for the public outcry from Peterson supporters, the explanation they were offering, the new theory about how Kathleen Peterson died, was something that boggled the mind.

In a letter written to DA Jim Hardin on December 5, 2003, Larry Pollard, a respected attorney and former neighbor of Michael Peterson's, suggested that the murder case be reopened. Pollard, along with Nick Galfianakis, another respected attorney in Durham society, were spreading the word that the deep gashes to the back of Kathleen Peterson's head had been caused by the talons of an owl.

The letter mentioned owl attacks, stating that the neighbors had seen "owls hunt at night." The letter gave eleven "points of evidence" that supported the theory of an "owl strike," noting that the number and shape of the wounds to Kathleen's head were consistent with talon marks.

"We have owls in our neighborhood that have been out there for years," Pollard wrote, "and were indeed out there, on the night Kathleen Peterson was found dead." Larry Pollard told the district attorney that the reopening of the investigation regarding Kathleen's death was "morally, legally, and ethically, the right thing to do."

Jim Hardin sent a reply to the letter, stating firmly, and politely, that the owl theory was "not credible." To the *Herald-Sun*, Hardin would not only squelch the validity of the theory, the DA would call the owl attack concept "one of the most ridiculous things I've ever heard."

Unexpectedly, the hardworking prosecutor had been named one of the top "Ten Lawyers of the Year" by *Lawyers Weekly USA*. The esteemed publication gave Hardin the nod, specifically because of his brilliant and undeterred work in the five-month trial against Michael Peterson.

Nick Galifianakis would tell *Herald-Sun* reporters that the "owl theory" was not going to go away. He hoped to try to convince a judge to exhume Kathleen Peterson's body, to test her scalp for "owl DNA." Both Galifianakis and Pollard were planning to file a "motion of appropriate relief." They would claim that, if their owl theory could gain the attention of a local judge, theoretically, a new trial could be ordered for Michael Peterson.

In courthouse circles, the owl theory drew grins from people. Certain skeptics would speculate about mysterious owls, pointing out that there were no owl feathers, no path of blood left behind. Others would call wildlife experts to discover that owls had rarely been known to attack humans. Any rare attacks that did occur happened only during nesting season, in the spring and summer months.

When the owl theory became public, Caitlin Atwater was not quite as angry as other members of the family. She found a moment of humor in it, and took it in stride, unlike her aunt Candace, who had written a scathing letter to the *Herald-Sun*, furious that the paper would dignify such nonsense by printing stories about an owl.

"No bird, animal, reptile, or alien from outer space attacked my sister," Candace wrote. "A man, not an owl, flew across the Atlantic and is tied to the awful deaths of two dearly missed women.

"Please do not dignify any further efforts to try to portray what happened to my sister as anything other than cruel murder," Candace insisted. "Please use your journalistic influence to support solutions and safe havens for women who suffer from domestic violence."

Caitlin might have still been too young to understand the harsh reality of her existence. She had never seen Michael hit her mother; she didn't really want to think about it. She had known him to throw temper tantrums, had watched Michael once hit Margaret with a camera case—it was a swipe he took at Margaret Ratliff—really, no big deal. It was something Michael would do, just strike out for little reasons, for stupid things, but he wouldn't really physically hurt anyone. It was more like an attempt to humiliate someone. . . .

Of course Caitlin was a survivor. She would find the strength to carry on. She still had Fred's shoulders to lean on, as well as her aunts, uncles, and cousins. And Caitlin still had her friends, plus her schoolwork at Cornell. She believed in herself and was determined to succeed, to make her mom *proud*. She would no longer speak to her former brothers and sisters, who had mocked her during the trial, who had taken a wrong turn somewhere. Clayton, Todd, and the Ratliff girls still believed in Michael's story and protested his innocence to the media. The brothers and sisters she once had were forever gone from her life. She hoped that one day they would find truth, that they would open their hearts and minds.

In a hearing before Judge Hudson, in January 2004, Caitlin Atwater won a victory regarding her civil lawsuit: the criminal judgment against Michael Peterson would be binding in her wrongful-death suit. For the pain and suffering Michael had caused her mother, for taking her mom's life, Caitlin would be awarded monetary damages. The amount would be determined at a later date. However, Thomas Maher had taken over as counsel for Peterson's appeal, and Maher would argue to the court that if he was able to get the murder verdict overturned, the acquittal might negate the civil ruling as well.

For all it might be worth, Caitlin would have to wait for Michael's lengthy appeal process to come to an end before she could collect any compensation whatsoever. And as it happened, Michael Peterson had already filed a request to be declared "indigent." Because that request had been granted, Caitlin stood to gain no compensation directly from him, but she still would be entitled to the proceeds from her mother's $1.45 million life insurance policy.

Caitlin would not let herself become upset by any court ruling, by a crazy owl story, or by her stepdad's mockery of the legal system. She wanted to remember the good times, the times when she played as a child in the wooded neighborhood of Forest Hills. She recalled many happy times, growing up in the Peterson house, and told a funny story about a night when a bat flew over her head. It happened back in the summer of 2000, when she felt something swoop over her ear in the middle of the night.

Caitlin had run over to Margaret and Martha's room, and the three girls were freaking out, running all over the house, realizing that bats were flying all around them. They laughed about it later, but at the time they were frightened, finding bats everywhere—in the hallway, on the stairs. The creatures seemed to be coming in through the vents. She recalled Michael catching a few bats in a shoe box and taking them outside. She remembered how zany she and her sisters felt; they had huddled together in one room and had put towels under the doorway, hoping that no dark-winged attacker could possibly squeeze through.

The next morning, when the exterminator arrived to find that the Petersons had a whole bat colony living in their attic, no one could believe it. The family was told that the creatures had built-in radar systems, and, unless the entire house was evacuated and exterminated, the bats would keep flying back.

Caitlin would look back on it and remember her mother's laughter. She recalled the jokes they all made about their crazy family, about having bats in their belfry. It seemed like an eternity had passed since that hot summer day, when a colony of bats, like the evil that lurked in the Peterson mansion, could no longer call the place home.

UPDATE 2013

NEW PERSPECTIVE: THE TV INTERVIEWS

If all the world is a stage, then Michael Peterson should win an Oscar. In his eight years behind bars, he's perpetuated a portrait of himself as a falsely accused man—an innocent man—who loved his wife more than words. If nothing else, Peterson has put on an astonishing performance. Along the way, he's convinced his supporters that: (A) There was never any murder. (B) The judicial system did not allow the jury to hear the full story. (C) The case brought against him was the result of a vendetta.

To the many doubters of Peterson's guilt, his claims have been taken seriously. Of course, his staunchest supporters, his two sons, Todd and Clayton, and his adopted daughters, Margaret and Martha Ratliff, believe that Michael was falsely convicted from Day One. His daughters, in particular, were visibly shaken when they learned their father would live out his days in a prison uniform. Humiliated and dejected, the girls cried openly in the courtroom on the day Peterson was sentenced to serve life without parole.

At least for some, the question has remained: Is Peterson guilty? After all, how could the genteel Michael Peterson, a man of literary prowess, a man with an illustrious past, be capable of carrying out an act of intentional murder? How could this polite Southern gentleman have brutally beaten his wife, have strangled the life out of his beloved Kathleen?

To hear Peterson talk about it, he's "not sure" what really happened to Kathleen that night. All he knows is that he found her at the bottom of the stairs.

But how did she get there?

Could it have been too much liquor? Could it have been the flip-flops she was wearing? Could it have been an owl?

Peterson couldn't be sure.

As fate would have it, in March 2009, just weeks after Peterson lost his last appeal, I sat down and spoke with the novelist at the Nash Correctional Institution for an interview I was conducting for my TV series *True Crime*. I was shocked that he agreed to see me, especially having known about my book. But then, I guess he figured that any publicity was good publicity.

As I watched him emerge from behind bars, I wondered why Mike Peterson, clad in his brown prison uniform, seemed kind of happy to see me. Maybe he was bored. Maybe he just wanted someone to vent to. Or maybe—since he'd lost his last chance for an appeal—he knew he had nothing left to lose. Whatever the case, he certainly seemed chipper. For a man doing life without parole, he had an air of confidence about him (or maybe arrogance?) as he approached the cameras.

He looked older and gray, and I watched him smile as they removed the handcuffs and escorted him to a simple plastic chair. We spoke in pleasantries for a while, just some basics about my camera crew and how well we were being treated by the prison guards, blah-blah-blah.

As the microphones were being hooked up and the camera lights were being adjusted, I told him about the recent interviews I had conducted with two of his supporters, former North Carolina Congresssman Nick Galifianakis, and author David Perlmutt. Peterson seemed encouraged by that.

"I know I'm not guilty," he told me. "It's very difficult for me to accept the fact that I am a *prisoner,* a convicted *murderer.*" (There was a slight pause.) "Well, that's just nonsense."

"You believe this was an accident, a fall down the stairs?" I asked.

"That's what I've always believed. That's what I thought. I mean, people would say, 'Well, how do you know she fell down the stairs?' Well, you know, you come in. You've been drinking a lot, she's been drinking a great deal. You find somebody at the bottom of the stairs. 'Hmmm. I *guess* they fell down the stairs,'" Peterson quipped.

"So that's what, you think, happened?" I pressed.

"I don't know what happened. But I know that I didn't kill Kathleen. I loved her."

Our interview lasted ninety minutes, and most of it ended up on the cutting-room floor. In our time together, there were some curious tidbits I learned from Peterson himself, about what kind of life the couple had inside their beautiful mansion. For one thing, Michael told me that Kathleen died in his arms. He was somber as he recalled the moment when she took her last breath.

He spent time reminiscing about the good old days, talking about the strong bond he and Kathleen shared and their circle of friends who still supported him. It struck me as peculiar that he seemed more interested in talking about himself and his false conviction than memorializing his lost soul mate.

But if Peterson was so utterly innocent, then *why,* on December 8, 2001, when he found his wife "still breathing" at the bottom of the stairs, did he hang up on the

911 operator? It seemed odd that anyone calling for emergency help would hang up on the lifeline.

Even odder was the fact that when Peterson called 911 again, just moments later, he suddenly had a new story to tell the dispatcher: now Kathleen was NOT breathing.

Hmmm.

Strange that Peterson would make two 911 calls—each of these was short, and each ended with him hanging up the phone.

"Where *are* they??" he yelled at the operator, anxious for help to arrive. "She stopped breathing. Please, *please*, would you hurry up?"

When the paramedics arrived at the scene, they found a grieving Michael Peterson, kneeling over his dead, bloody wife. Michael was extremely distraught at the time, so much so that the first responders had to force him away from her body.

Apparently, Michael couldn't bear the thought that his wife was dead. She was his soul mate. She was everything to him, and he elaborated about that during our prison interview. "One of the things you've talked about is how often you would mention Kathleen's name," I said.

"Yes. I want to talk about her. I *adored* her. She was wonderful. She was just the most fabulous person," he said. "I laughed, we laughed, and, you know, that's the thing that always got me. I mean, nobody ever, *ever* could come [and] say, 'Oh, we heard you and Kathleen had a fight.'"

And that was true.

Not one of their kids had ever seen them fight.

And their friends? Well, most of them were jealous of the loving relationship that Michael and Kathleen shared. It was a marriage to be envied, to be emulated, to be celebrated.

Or, so it seemed. But then, no one knew about all the hidden money problems the couple actually had.

The Petersons were drowning in a great deal of debt. They were even considering moving out of the mansion to keep the kids' college tuitions going. In the meantime, they were busy keeping up appearances, buying Christmas gifts and attending fund-raisers. They were carrying on—as if all was well with the world.

However, in the fall of 2001, the sky was falling for Michael Peterson because the dot-com bubble was bursting, and the problem of the economic downturn in America had affected the Peterson household. By December of that year, things only seemed to be getting worse. Indeed, Kathleen was quite scared. She was terribly worried about losing her high-powered job at Nortel Networks. Michael knew the communications company was faltering, and Nortel employees were being laid off in droves.

If Kathleen got the ax, it would not bode well for Michael Peterson.

Without Kathleen's income, there was no breadwinner in the house. Michael had been good at pretending he was climbing the literary ladder, that he was on his way to becoming the next Tom Clancy. In reality, Peterson's illustrious writing career had hit the skids years before.

Yes, he wrote a newspaper column for *The Herald Sun,* but that paid a measly sum. It was something he did for the bragging rights—not for the paltry income. And then there were also his unsuccessful runs for office. In 1999, Peterson lost his bid for mayor; in 2001, he lost his bid for a city council seat.

By 2001, it seemed Michael Peterson had no viable income.

Of course, there was always the outside chance that one of his books would bring in cash from the sale of film rights. But having been down that road before, Peterson *knew* those kinds of film deals were few and far between. He also knew that even when a deal was struck, the author was typically paid a small "option fee," which in 99 percent of the cases was an amount not much greater than $1,000.

Perhaps that's why it seemed hard to believe that Michael and Kathleen were supposedly celebrating the sale of the "movie rights" to one of his books on the night she died. At least, that's what he claimed they were doing, even though there was never a film made based on any of Peterson's books—before or after—Kathleen's death.

Nonetheless, drinking and celebrating seemed to be a big part of the Petersons' lives, so I asked him about it.

He admitted, "We did a lot of drinking. That's true."

"So you enjoyed socializing?"

"Oh, loved it. To be honest, Kathleen and I would find almost anything to celebrate" (he smiled). "We drank an awful lot of champagne" (he smirked). "It was one of our favorite things to drink."

"Sometimes . . . sometimes we'd go and buy wedding cakes sometimes at the bakery," he said. "And we'd come back and eat it (the wedding cake). We'd celebrate *all* the time."

They bought wedding cakes for no reason? Really?

Peterson sat with a straight face, telling me that.

Okay. So they were big into celebrating. And they were celebrating his "success" the last night she was alive.

"I know it's difficult, but I have to ask you about that night . . . and what happened?" I finally said.

"Okay. Well, we had sex. She took a bath. We came downstairs. She started to cook. It was a—a—pasta thing, in the kitchen," he explained. "And then we—uh—you know—went into the family room and watched the movie. And then the movie ends.

"And then we go into the kitchen with our wine glasses, and when you walk into the kitchen, there's the phone and it was an answering machine, and it was blinking.

"Uh, so—I picked it up and I listened, and it was a message for Kathleen that she had a conference call in the morning," Peterson said.

In fact, Kathleen did receive a call that night. It was from a coworker in Canada, and Kathleen learned that she needed to get a file e-mailed to her immediately. The problem was, Kathleen had left her work laptop at Nortel, so she decided to ask Michael for his e-mail address. She went into his private office to retrieve the attachment.

Police records show that Kathleen got an e-mail at Michael's e-mail address at 11:53 P.M., but the attachment was never opened.

Michael would later claim that he and Kathleen had gone down by the pool around midnight to have a nightcap. He said the two of them often hung out by the pool to unwind at the end of a hard day. According to Michael Peterson, his wife left the pool area to head off to bed. This happened somewhere between 1:45 and 2:00 A.M. As for Peterson, he stayed outside to enjoy a cigar for about a half hour after Kathleen left.

"And then I went in the house, and in the back porch, the kitchen, there's a sink area there. Her glass was there, and, uh, I put mine down," Peterson recalled.

"And then I was walking around to go lock the house up. And then, as you go around, there's a back staircase. And she was lying on the back staircase."

"And—I—uh"—he breathed a sigh—"that's where—Well, that's where everything both begins and ends."

Actually, Michael Peterson was right. For Kathleen, everything had ended.

For Peterson, the ambulances were outside his door, a fire truck was there, and police were waiting outside the house—until Detective Art Holland arrived at about three in the morning.

Art Holland, a seasoned homicide detective, would take over the investigation. He would be in charge of the crime scene investigation, or CSI, and all that goes along with processing the scene of a crime. As it happened, Detective Holland was on site when the first medical examiner, Kenneth Snell, came by the house to perform an exterior examination of Kathleen's head. And without the benefit of seeing her skull wounds after her head was shaved, Dr. Snell initially ruled the cause of Kathleen's death as *accidental.*

"Was there any doubt in your mind, when you walked in that stairwell, as to what happened?" I asked Holland.

"Because of the volume of blood and the other items that were situated around her body—you—you had bath towels, you had paper towels—you had—you had Michael Peterson's shoes. You had Michael Peterson's socks. I mean, *that right there* brings up a red flag," he said.

"Why, if—if a man just found his wife deceased at the foot of the steps, why—why would he even *think* about taking his socks and shoes off," Holland wondered, "unless he was trying to clean up the crime scene? And that was kind of obvious at the time—that something wasn't right."

Holland said he was cautious, that he wanted to be careful about the way he approached the grieving widower that night. But still, he had a job to do. He had hoped Peterson would cooperate and talk to him about what had happened.

But Michael Peterson kept silent.

"I explained to him that we needed to investigate it further and because of the circumstances that I would have to obtain a search warrant," Holland recalled. "I wasn't pointing my fingers at him at the time. I just knew that the scene needed to be processed so we could determine how she died."

"And how did he react to that?"

"He was quiet. It was like he was speechless. He was kinda, like, shocked that we were gonna process his house as a crime scene."

"When you executed the first search warrant, what was the first thing that struck you as being out of the ordinary as you're going through the Peterson house?"

"It was obvious that he had tried cleaning up," the detective said. "You could have just walked and looked in the stairwell and seen blood spatter over [the] top of where he tried wiping blood off that north wall."

The dried blood on the walls, the bloody "swipe marks" in the stairwell, along with the tiny blood spots on Peterson's shorts, were just the obvious things CSI noticed as they first began their process. But later, when they used the chemical luminol, which allows police to see blood that's normally invisible to the naked eye, a whole new level of deception became evident.

"When you spray luminol, it reacts," Holland explained, "and when we did that, we saw footprints leading from the stairwell to the washing machine.

"Then the footprints went back to the kitchen, leading to the area of the sinks in the kitchen. I mean, there were just so many indicators of a clean-up."

* * *

I was curious about what was running through Michael Peterson's mind during the CSI process. Since he thought police were working against him, I wondered exactly how he might explain the ways the police were able to frame him.

"I was a wreck during this period, I really was," Peterson confided. "We were all just in this incredible grief, and there was at least fifteen, twenty, Durham police officers, lawyers from them—bam, bam, bam! They had come to execute the search warrant—timed *perfectly* for the wake," he said.

"You were a public figure in Durham, certainly. For all intents and purposes, you were very famous when this happened to Kathleen. So it became a huge media circus—a lot of gossip going on in town?" I asked.

"Yeah, and then it became a trial. It became a circus," he recalled. "But the overall tragedy, the loss of Kathleen"—he shook his head—"that lost focus.

"She left center stage," he continued. "It all became a matter of warring sides. Who's gonna win this thing? You know, is it gonna be the prosecution, Mr. Hardin? Is it gonna be David Rudolf? And that's what *these things* turn into. I mean, they become *entertainment* TV. They become Court TV."

He droned on and on about his *Herald Sun* column, about the police being biased against him, so I later approached Art Holland about the subject to see what reaction I'd get.

"For him to say that it was a conspiracy, that the city was after him. . . . That crime scene was *mine*," Holland insisted. "And I didn't care if it was the governor, the mayor— whoever lived in that house—would have gone through the same thing that he went through."

* * *

To the media, to his supporters, Michael had always maintained that he would never have done anything to harm his wife. As for his kids—his blended family—they all supported Michael, and they publically defended him . . . *at first*. But then, Kathleen's only biological child, Caitlin, had gone to the DA's office to read the autopsy report. It was that autopsy that turned Caitlin from being one of Michael's biggest supporters—into his worst enemy.

By standing up to Michael, by accusing him of murder, Caitlin was outcast by the rest of her half siblings. But Caitlin had seen evidence of the seven lacerations to her mom's head; these were cuts that went clear down to the skull. Caitlin also saw evidence of the bruises Kathleen suffered to her hands and face—signs of a struggle— defensive wounds. And in addition to all that blood spatter, and the pool of blood her mother was drenched in, Kathleen's cartilage in her throat was broken as well, which pointed to strangulation.

"Caitlin went to the DA on her own, right?" I asked Peterson.

"Yeah. Caitlin changed her mind. But to *me*, I cannot believe that deep down, Caitlin really believes I hurt her mother," he insisted. "She knew better than that. She knew us too well. She never saw us fight. She never saw anything. She never knew anything but love and happiness and fun."

"What about the bisexuality?" I asked point-blank. "Did Kathleen know?"

"Yes. Of course, she knew," he said. "It was just not a major factor in our—our lives. I mean, it had nothing to do with *love*. People get very upset when you say something like that. But there's love and then there's sex, and"—he shook his head—"that's what *that* was.

"I'm stunned," Peterson continued. "I thought certainly all my children knew [about the bisexuality and adultery]. I can't believe they didn't know."

Hmmmmmmm. . . .

"Let me ask you this. What happened in Germany?"

Peterson took a moment to think. "You mean the night Elizabeth McKee Ratliff died?"

"Yes."

"Okay," he said, with his eyes looking down. "At no time was there ever, *ever,* was there any question, suspicion, *anything,* about this being anything other than a natural death.

"Uh . . . the German police didn't see any [blood]. The American police didn't see any [blood]. The doctor didn't see any [blood]," Peterson assured me. "Why didn't somebody *say* anything at the time? Why didn't they say, 'Oh, this is a suspicious death'? But nobody ever raised this . . . until—you know—Kathleen died."

"But that's not true," I reminded him. "Amybeth Berner was *there,* and she saw a lot of blood. She said she saw blood going up the stairwell. She testified about that in court."

"Amybeth Berner is now 'recalling' something that no one else ever saw," he insisted.

"No, actually, I spoke with Bruce Berner as well, her husband. He was there that night, remember? And he saw all the blood too, you know. And Amybeth took him up the staircase."

To that, Peterson had no answer. Instead, his face went limp.

It was as if Elizabeth's mysterious death didn't exist to Peterson. Somehow, in his thoughts, Peterson dismissed the death of Mrs. Ratliff; he had utterly tucked it into a cobweb in his mind.

Funny how, just after losing the trial, Peterson's attorney, David Rudolf, also dismissed the Elizabeth Ratliff homicide as being *irrelevant*.

"I think the Ratliff evidence was a nonissue in the state's case," Rudolf told reporters. "I mean, basically, they were able to establish that Mike Peterson had been with her [Elizabeth] the night before she was dead, with blood around."

A nonissue?

Mr. Peterson was the last person seen with Elizabeth *before* she was mysteriously *"dead, with blood around"*?

Mrs. Ratliff was found in a pool of blood—in a mess of blood—in a stairwell. There was so much blood that Cheryl Appel-Schumacher, a dear friend of Elizabeth's, was called to the Ratliff home on the day of her death. Cheryl was there to help clean up all the blood, and she recalled that horrible day in vivid detail when she took the witness stand in Durham.

"The highest point on the wall I had to clean was above the light switch at the top of the stairs, when I was standing," Appel-Schumacher told the jury. "And that was a different kind of cleaning because those were very little, tiny dots. Almost like if you took a paintbrush—a child's paintbrush, preschool paintbrush—and you flicked it.

"That was the kind of spray of blood, spotted blood, that was at the top. And that was the only place that seemed like that," she testified. "The rest [of the stairwell] as you came down, the side of the wall was more circular, or like a teardrop. As you came down, the [blood] spots were bigger."

What a strange coincidence that two women— Elizabeth Ratliff, in 1985, and Kathleen Peterson, in 2001—were both found dead in a stairwell, with nearly identical injuries to the scalp, in a pool of their own blood, and Michael Peterson was the last person to have seen each of them alive.

Elizabeth Ratliff was not Peterson's wife, but there's evidence to suggest that he was in love with her—and perhaps the two had had a short affair. Certainly, the fact that she willed her two children to his care is proof that the two were closer than "just friends."

And there's more.

In an interview with Amybeth Berner that I conducted years after the trial, she confided something about a financial motive that Peterson may have had regarding Elizabeth McKee Ratliff.

When George Ratliff died, Elizabeth Ratliff was awarded $250,000 in insurance money.

"And who was handling that money for her?" I asked Berner.

"Michael. She specifically told me that money—that she didn't want to touch it. That was put away for the girls' schooling."

"What's your theory about what happened on the night Elizabeth was killed?"

"I think she questioned him [about] where her money was," Berner said. "And my hunch is that he probably took that money and had moved that money, and Liz questioned him. And—that—enraged him."

Enraged, indeed.

Was Peterson living off other people's money?

It sure seemed like it.

The prosecution at trial said the novelist had "a million reasons to kill."

For him, it was *all* about the money.

Kathleen had a life insurance policy worth $1.4 million. She had about $400,000 in deferred salary and stock options from Nortel. A couple million dollars would go far to fund Peterson's lifestyle, especially since the house was fully paid off and the kids were out on their own.

"Michael Peterson stood to gain a lot of money if the accident theory prevailed," Freda Black later said. "He stood to gain life insurance. There were stock options. There was a lot of financial motive, we believe, that would have caused him to have the motive to kill Kathleen."

"What about the e-mails between Peterson and the male escort? Would that be motive? That he wanted to hide his double life?" I asked.

"They [Peterson and Brent Walgamott] were communicating back and forth about each other and about what they might like to do together, and how much it was gonna cost," ADA Black said. "It was very specific."

Freda Black had questioned male escort Brent Walgamott on the stand. She had handed the jury copies of the e-mails that went back and forth between Peterson and Walgamott, showing the two men had made a specific plan to meet in nearby Chapel Hill.

It was a plan that never materialized, but it was certainly documented.

"Right there, in the top drawer of that desk, were those e-mails between Michael and the male escort," Black explained. "We believe she found them that night."

"And she confronted him?"

"We believe she confronted him and he lost his temper. We had established through a lot of people who knew him that he had a *horrible*, violent temper, at times. And we believe that he just lost it."

Black had asked the jury in her closing statement: "Do

you *really* believe that Kathleen knew that Mr. Peterson was bisexual?"

It was a question that rang in everyone's ears.

The sarcasm in Black's voice was unmistakable.

Turns out that no one on the jury believed Kathleen would have tolerated adultery of any kind—not based on the testimony they heard throughout the trial.

I later confirmed that was the jury members' attitude when I interviewed Kelli Cogan, one of the twelve jurors who convicted Peterson.

"Was there anybody on the jury who thought *maybe* he was innocent?"

"There was not one person who ever said, 'I think this man is innocent' ever," Cogan said. "It was just a matter of putting 'one plus one' together. And that 'one plus one' equaled 'guilty.'"

Still, in the wake of the conviction, there were Peterson supporters who had come up with the strange theory of an owl attack. It was a "murder" theory concocted by Peterson's next-door neighbor Larry Pollard, who just didn't want to believe that Michael Peterson was guilty. In fact, Pollard was so utterly convinced an owl had killed Kathleen—he used his ability as a lawyer to file motions for a new trial, to no avail.

Nonetheless, the owl theory had to be considered. It had received so much media attention—and had been the butt of so many jokes, so—I asked Peterson to give me his thoughts about it.

"There's an owl theory out there. Do you give it any credence?"

"Well, I don't know," Peterson said. "I *do* know that the owl is every bit as realistic as that *ridiculous* blow poke thing."

Peterson was referring to the mysterious murder weapon, the hollow fireplace tool that had somehow disappeared just after Kathleen's death. When he spoke about the "blow poke," it was interesting to watch his body language shift. Watching him, I felt it was as if he'd practiced talking about the poker so many times, Peterson actually was able to mimic having an imaginary blow poke in his hands.

He made a gesture as if he was blowing through an imaginary object, and another gesture, as if he was *beating* something with the imaginary blow poke, mocking the idea that such an object could be used to kill someone. Peterson even went so far as to say that he was surprised a blow poke wasn't found *inside* Elizabeth Ratliff's exhumed coffin. In other words, the prosecution, in his opinion, would go to any devious and unethical lengths to convict him.

"The only thing I know is that *I* didn't do anything," Peterson insisted. "And I guess basically, still in my heart and mind, I'd like to believe Kathleen fell down the stairs—but nobody buys that one," he said. "Except, maybe I'm the last holdout [for the accidental fall theory]. But I don't know. As far as an owl, I don't know."

THE BOMBSHELL:
A NEW TRIAL

Psychologists have often talked about a person's ability to create a new reality for themselves. In Michael Peterson's case, it's obvious that he has convinced himself—and a growing number of supporters—that he did not commit any crime, ever, in his life. Indeed, Peterson's girls believe so completely that he was convicted of a crime he did not commit, they have managed to "forget" that Michael was the last person seen with not one, but *two* women who died at the bottom of a staircase: their mom and their stepmom.

Perhaps Michael Peterson's lifetime of spinning tales has worked in his favor. After all, Peterson is a master at manipulating history. As a case in point, let's recall his Purple Heart, a coveted award he bragged about, and then used to help parlay himself into a successful war novelist.

For years, Peterson claimed his Purple Heart was awarded from heavy Vietnam combat. His radio operator stepped on a land mine and was killed, and Peterson, allegedly, was badly injured by flying shrapnel. However, the truth came out when Peterson ran for the mayor of Durham and his war records were examined. Suddenly the novelist was forced to admit that he had *never* been awarded a Purple Heart.

To local news reporters, Peterson explained away the

false claim by saying the memory of the war had been "too painful" for him. Without blinking, Peterson sheepishly admitted that his "war injury" came, not from flying shrapnel, but from having been injured in a jeep accident in Japan—long after his Vietnam days had ended.

Talk about a fiction writer who truly believes in his fiction.

But that could explain why, from Day One of Kathleen's murder investigation, Peterson came to view himself as a victim of a corrupt justice system. This became Peterson's nonstop theme: because he'd been a critic of local law enforcement, he was now the target of a bogus witch hunt.

It was a theme used by his defense team in the courtroom, over and over again, with the result expected to be a "not guilty" verdict for Peterson.

Could there have been any truth in the defense team's claim? Was there some kind of conspiracy to convict the novelist?

Well, maybe yes, and maybe no.

Though no one could prove it at the time, it turns out that back in 2001, someone inside the State Bureau of Investigation (SBI)—one of the state's bloodstain experts, Agent Duane Deaver—had falsified his credentials. He had provided "misleading testimony" to the Peterson jury, perhaps to "fit" his *theory* that this was murder.

It was on December 15, 2011, when Judge Orlando Hudson, the superior court judge who originally heard the case, ordered that convicted murderer Michael Peterson would be released on house arrest. Judge Hudson told a packed courtroom that Peterson would be granted a new trial because back in 2003, during Peterson's first trial, Duane Deaver, the key bloodstain witness for the state, had misled the jury by embellishing his credentials—and had given *false testimony* in court.

Deaver's tainted expert testimony resulted in a strange twist of fate for Michael Peterson. Lo and behold, after losing all of his appeals—after grabbing at straws and owls and anything and everything that could free him from prison—suddenly Michael Peterson was being given a new chance.

Agent Duane Deaver was investigated at the request of Attorney General Roy Cooper, a request that came after the 2010 landmark exoneration of a wrongfully convicted North Carolina man named Greg Taylor. Taylor had been convicted on blood evidence, largely because of the testimony by Duane Deaver, who told a jury that there was blood on Taylor's truck, when, indeed, it might have been *mud* on Taylor's truck. No one will ever know if it was mud or rust, or what the crime scene evidence revealed. But the fact was, Deaver's testimony provided the only single piece of physical evidence connecting Taylor to the murder.

Because Deaver's SBI lab test on Taylor's truck had come back *negative* for blood, because Deaver *lied* on the stand and testified that the sample on Taylor's truck came back *positive* for blood—all of Deaver's cases now came into question. Naturally, that would lead to the subject of retrials.

Of course, the instant Greg Taylor was exonerated in February 2010, high-profile attorney David Rudolf filed a motion to grant Michael Peterson a new trial. Rudolf argued, in essence, that Deaver, under oath, had distorted the facts and had exaggerated his experience in bloodstain analysis. To prove his point further, Rudolf hired a top forensic expert, who wrote in a sworn affidavit that Duane Deaver's testimony at the Peterson trial was, essentially, junk science.

Deaver was not "a neutral scientist seeking facts,"

Rudolf told the court, but rather "a tool of prosecutors more intent on winning convictions than seeking the truth." *[Duane Deaver had] a longstanding practice of fabricating evidence of guilt,* Rudolf wrote.

[Deaver was] tailoring his testimony to whatever the prosecutor wanted or needed him to say, committing perjury *in order to advance his primary goal: to secure the conviction of the person on trial,* Rudolf asserted.

In January 2010, Duane Deaver was fired from his position as the head of the bloodstain analysis team at the SBI. Having heard even more damning information about Deaver, which stemmed from an official audit performed by a former senior FBI official, David Rudolf decided to pursue the matter with his own investigative team in order to learn just exactly *who* Duane Deaver really was.

Rudolf's investigators discovered that Duane Deaver's training in blood spatter analysis was sketchy. It consisted of just *two* training courses that were taken way back in the 1980s. Deaver had done no course work since then. He had never been a part of any forensic organization. He had not kept up with any written protocols or scientific methodology in the field.

When Rudolf's national expert reviewed Deaver's work in the Peterson case, the man said that Deaver's blood experiments "lacked the required elements of basic science."

In the wake of the landmark exoneration of Greg Taylor, all of Deaver's cases would be looked at again, and all of his work would be considered highly questionable—at best. A domino effect was already in motion, and Peterson was at the top of the heap.

Indeed, Rudolf argued to the court that Deaver's experiments, performed in preparation for Peterson's trial, almost seemed like child's play. In one experiment, Deaver took a Styrofoam head and dropped it to the floor. In another, he took a bloody sponge and attached it to a four-by-four board. Deaver also experimented by stomping his feet in a pool of blood.

It was all so—*unscientific.*

Every experiment that Deaver performed regarding Kathleen Peterson's death, Rudolf's expert later said, "had no relevance to the case, and *proved nothing.*"

So it was on December 15, 2011, just after six in the evening, that Michael Peterson emerged from prison. Helicopters flew overhead as Peterson was greeted by an onslaught of local media outlets. He was being treated like the celebrity he always wanted to be. When the novelist smiled and hugged his four children, and his new grandchild, Dorian, the cameras flashed. He looked like the luckiest man in the world.

Like a rock star satisfying the paparazzi, Peterson headed over to the microphones and TV cameras to reassert his innocence and hint that his new trial would have a new outcome.

"I have waited over eight years—two thousand nine hundred and eighty-eight days, as a matter of fact— believe me, I counted—for an opportunity to have a retrial," Peterson said.

"I want to thank Judge Hudson for giving me the opportunity so that I can vindicate myself, and prove my innocence in a *fair trial* this time," Peterson went on. "I want to thank all of the people who supported me all over the world. Is it possible for me to express my gratitude? What I want to do now, though, is spend time with my family and my children, and certainly at a later time, I'd be happy to talk with everybody and share more."

"This is one of the happiest days of my life," Todd Peterson told the *News Observer.* "I never, ever thought he would get out. So this is a massive surprise."

Support from all over the world?

Really?

Was Michael Peterson really that much of a worldwide concern?

Sure, Peterson had support from his ex-wife, who flew in from Germany; and, yes, he had support from his sons and adopted daughters, who'd flown in from other parts of the country. But Peterson seemed to have confused his support system with a worldwide effort to exonerate him. Who did Peterson think he was? Some kind of martyr?

Then again, the novelist did have a large handful of vehement supporters, one of whom would allow Peterson to stay at his house while he awaited his new trial. And, not surprisingly, just a few months after his release from prison, Peterson's attorney filed a motion requesting that the novelist be relieved of having to wear that pesky electronic monitoring bracelet.

However, that request was denied by the court.

With a bad taste in his mouth, Michael Peterson still spews venom.

Yet, he can just about taste freedom.

For now, the snake is inside the basket.

And the snake charmer is still at his game.

A special bonus
for fans of real-life crime dramas . . .

Keep reading for an excerpt
from Aphrodite Jones's *New York Times* best seller

Cruel Sacrifice

Available from Pinnacle Books!

Prologue

It was a freezing cold day in the dead of January when the three girls got to New Albany. They left Madison right after school let out that afternoon, and had lied to their parents about their plans for the night. No one knew they were on their way to Louisville, more than fifty miles away from their quaint Indiana hometown.

All Toni knew was that they were going to a punk rock concert, but first they had to make a quick stop in New Albany. Soon they'd be crossing the Ohio River and the state line, and they'd be on their way.

"Did you tell her yet?" Laurie asked Hope on the ride down.

"Tell her what?" Hope asked, playing dumb.

When they pulled up to Melinda's house on Charlestown Road, everyone was silent. Melinda opened the door, she already had her trench coat on, but the three stepped inside for a few minutes just to warm up. Of the four teenagers, Laurie was the oldest, the only one with a car and a driver's license. Although she was just seventeen, she seemed to be in control of things. Anyone who knew her for even a short time knew that Laurie had an attitude problem, that she tried very hard to be different, to be daring, that she desperately wanted to be accepted, and that she wanted her friends to follow her example.

Melinda was a very different type of person. While Laurie's demeanor was quiet and mysterious, Melinda was hyper and seemed excited to see them. Even physically, Melinda was the opposite of Laurie in every way. In contrast to Laurie's hard square jaw, chunky body, and cropped head of bleached hair, sixteen-year-old Melinda had a seductive smile, a perfect figure, and a thick head of flowing light brown curls. Melinda wore more conventional teen clothes; Laurie was a "punker," usually dressed in solid black clothing. Hope and Toni asked if they could borrow some of Melinda's clothes to wear for the night, and the four girls followed each other upstairs.

No one else seemed to be home so they made themselves comfortable in Melinda's bedroom, sorting through her array of shoes and jeans, admiring her closetful of jackets, and eyeballing her purses on the inside door. They looked over some of her T-shirts, piled neatly in a stack of milk crates, and inspected her collection of tapes, mostly bubblegum music like New Kids On The Block, Paula Abdul, and George Michael. There was the usual teenage paraphernalia hanging on Melinda's walls: family photos, stuffed animals in various nets, posters of idols, including a few of Elvis in *Jailhouse Rock.*

Toni picked out a pair of shoes and slipped them on. Hope found a pair of Melinda's jeans to wear and some shoes to match.

"This is the knife I'm going to use," Melinda said gleefully as she reached in her purse and pulled out a big old kitchen knife.

Melinda said she was going to scare Shanda with it. She had Shanda's number and address written down on a piece of paper and she decided to call there one last time before they took off, just to be sure Shanda was home.

Nobody said a word. They stayed there giggling and primping for about a half hour, carefully appraising themselves in front of Melinda's mirror.

Even though Laurie had never met Shanda, Laurie knew all about Melinda's plan to scare Shanda, to beat her up, to "teach her a lesson."

Melinda kept trying Shanda's number and hanging up on the machine. All the while, she was busy filling the other two girls in. Hope and Toni were both age fifteen. They were impressed with Melinda's cool talk, her cursing, her bravado, and her story. It didn't take long for Melinda to conjure up an image of Shanda, the cute little girl she hated with such a passion. Shanda was a blond; she had a nice butt; she wore tight jeans and too much makeup. Shanda was a copycat, she was trying to look like Melinda. She was wearing the same kind of shoes, the same hairstyle. She was, Melinda told them with disgust, a slut.

As they listened to Melinda rage on, Laurie got a little bit antsy. She knew the history all too well—Melinda was a lesbian, and Shanda was stealing away her girlfriend. Melinda wanted Shanda out of her life. But Laurie was sick of hearing it. She just wanted to get going.

The four left a few minutes later, and Laurie had Hope take over the wheel. Hope only had a learner's permit, but Laurie trusted her. Melinda had a piece of paper with the words "Capitol Hill" written down, and she was looking for Shanda's dad's house in nearby Jeffersonville. She knew it was near Jeffersonville High School somewhere but she couldn't figure out where the street was. They pulled into a McDonald's and Hope and Toni went in for directions. While they were there, they ordered some Chicken McNuggets.

Capitol Hills Drive, they learned, was a tucked-away street in a middle-class subdivision. It was getting pretty close to dark by the time Hope parked the car about a half a block away from Shanda's house. Melinda told Hope to go up to the door with Toni and introduce themselves as friends of Amanda.

"Just say Amanda wants to see you," Melinda whispered.

At the front door, they discovered the doorbell didn't work so they knocked, and Shanda came to the door, opening it in the full view of her stepmother Sharon and her father, Steve.

"Is Shanda here?"

"I'm Shanda," the wide-eyed girl told them.

"Do you want to come with us and meet Amanda?" Hope asked.

From inside the house, Steve Sharer asked his daughter who was at the door. Shanda said it was "friends." But Steve saw that these girls didn't recognize Shanda. He heard them ask for her. Shanda told her dad she was only going to step outside to talk to them for a minute, and she closed the door behind her.

The girls told Shanda that Amanda was waiting at a deserted place called The Witches' Castle. They asked Shanda if she would like to ride out there with them.

"Not right now, cause my parents are awake," Shanda said in a hushed voice. "Come back around midnight and I'll go. And be sure to have Amanda with you when you come back. Keep her with you. Have her spend the night with you or something . . ."

When Shanda went back into the house, she told her father that it was just some girls who wanted her to go to the mall. They argued briefly about it. Shanda told her dad to calm down, and ultimately he did. Since he had divorced her mother, Steve generally saw Shanda only on the weekends. He wanted his little girl to be

happy. He must have realized he was getting nowhere
by arguing with her that night.

In the meantime, Hope and Toni went back down the
road to Laurie's car and explained the situation to
Melinda. At first, she was mad because they didn't manage
to lure Shanda out of her house. The two girls assured
her that they could come back and get Shanda later, and
they headed for Louisville to hear some music.

It took them a while to find the place where the concert was being held, the A-1 Skate Park. It was a place
where skateboarders hung out, really just a warehouse
with skate ramps where skaters could show off their various maneuvers. On Fridays, punk rock bands played
there, and people used the concrete as a dance floor.

The minute Hope pulled up at the park, a bunch of
young men approached the car and one of them started
flirting with Melinda. Laurie wanted to get some booze,
and the guys said they'd lead them to a nearby liquor
store. The girls followed them in their car through the
Louisville streets, only to wind up in the back parking
lot of a deserted school. Once there, the guys tried to
intimidate them by bumping into Laurie's car, but eventually the four girls made it back to the skate park. They
stood in line to get tickets to the concert.

As it turned out, after about ten minutes, Hope and
Toni decided they had enough of the loud music, the
heat, and the slam dancing. Toni saw Melinda pinch a
girl on the butt and thought it was time for her to get out
of there. She and Hope asked Laurie if they could wait
for them in the car, and Laurie handed over the keys. As
soon as they walked outside, they met a couple of cute
guys who introduced themselves as Jimmy and Brandon.

Melinda and Laurie stayed at the slam dance concert
for at least two hours, so there was plenty of time for the
four teens to get to know each other outside in the car.

As the jam box blasted loudly in the backseat, Jimmy and Brandon were both making advances.

Hope and Toni must have gotten comfortable with them quickly because after a few kisses, Toni suddenly blurted out, "The two girls that we're with are planning on killing somebody tonight."

Part One

The Ordeal

One

It was going to be a very busy and hectic weekend over at the Sharer house. Steve had his father-in-law, his dad, and a few other relatives staying over to help take a wall down in the living room to enlarge the space. On top of that, there was his wife Sharon, his stepdaughter Sandy, and his daughter Shanda, all crowded into the tiny home.

It wasn't too long after Hope and Toni left when the phone rang. It was a neighborhood girl who invited Shanda to a party, and even though he was hesitant about letting his little girl stay out late, Steve agreed to let Shanda go, provided she be home by 10:30 P.M. He reminded her that they were going to be tearing that wall down early the next morning and he needed her help.

It was after 11: 15 P.M. when she waltzed through the door, and she had her friend Michelle with her. Shanda asked if she could stay over.

"Look, we're going to be cramped for space," Steve insisted.

"Please, Dad?"

"No."

Steve called the girl's mother and arranged for her to pick Michelle up. A few minutes later, he decided he was too tired to wait for the woman to arrive. He told the girls there was some pizza in the kitchen and said they could watch TV for thirty minutes. Then he turned in.

They must have watched until almost midnight, and Steve finally came out of his bedroom.

"Cool it. Turn it off. Let's hit it," he told them, meaning it was time for lights out. For Steve, that was it for the night. He fell asleep and never heard the door close when Michelle left.

Across the bridge over in Louisville, Melinda and Laurie decided they had enough of the concert. When they came out of the skate park and found Hope and Toni making out with some guys in the car, they figured it was a good time to use the nearby pay phone to make a few calls. They were gone a good long while. They'd called Shanda's house a few times but all they got was the answering machine. They called Amanda, too. When they returned to the car, Toni was waiting outside.

Hope was still in the car with Brandon so the three girls went next door to Long John Silver's to use the restroom and kill some time. Once Brandon was gone, Hope got the car started, and Melinda told her to drive back to Shanda's; but on the way out of Louisville, Hope got confused and was driving in the wrong direction, heading toward Tennessee.

While they circled the interstates, Melinda discussed her plans.

"God I can't wait to kill her," Melinda shrieked with glee.

She mentioned the knife and explained that she intended to tease Shanda with it. She said that she thought Shanda was cute, that she'd like to have sex with Shanda, that she was going to run the knife up and down her stomach and play with her.

It took them a while to figure out the interstates but they finally made it back to Shanda's. Melinda wanted

Hope and Toni to go back up to the door but Toni was refusing. No one could persuade her. Even Hope tried to get Toni to go but she said it was too cold out, that she was freezing. Melinda couldn't go herself because if Shanda saw her, she'd get scared. Melinda had threatened her many times; she was not a face Shanda wanted to see at 12:30 A.M.

Eventually Hope and Laurie agreed to go. Melinda got down on the floorboard in the backseat. Before she got out of the car, Laurie helped cover Melinda with a red blanket and handed her the knife. She and Hope went up the driveway and disappeared behind Shanda's house.

As the two girls got around the corner, they saw some guy coming out of Shanda's house, a young guy. He was saying goodbye to Shanda. They ducked behind Shanda's garage for a minute. They knew the guy probably saw them out of the corner of his eye but he took off in his truck just seconds later. They were nervous about approaching the side door, but Shanda made it easy for them. She was right there waiting.

"Hi, are you going to go with us?" Hope wanted to know.

Shanda seemed glad to see them. Laurie was a new face, but Shanda wasn't concerned about that. She just wanted to hear what Hope had to say about Amanda. Hope told her that Amanda was waiting for her at The Witches' Castle. Amanda wanted her to come out. The three talked for about five minutes. Hope was having trouble convincing Shanda that she should go along. Shanda said she didn't have the right clothes on, so Hope volunteered to go inside with her and help her pick out something to change into and Laurie went back to the other girls.

Standing out near the car, Laurie opened the back door, reached into the backseat, and adjusted the blanket over Melinda. She added a few items of clothing and some fast-food bags on top to camouflage her further.

"Hope's bringing her," Laurie said quietly as she adjusted the blanket one last time. Before they knew it, Hope and Shanda came bouncing toward the car. Laurie told Toni to get out of the front passenger's side to let Shanda in the middle.

"Where's Amanda?" Shanda asked as she sandwiched herself between Hope and Toni.

"At The Witches' Castle," Laurie said with a reassuring voice.

"What's she wearing? Does she look cute?" Shanda asked.

Having met Amanda once before, Hope knew enough to make up an outfit that would fit Amanda's style: loose baggy shorts, a baseball cap, basically a "skater" look.

By then, the car was rolling, and they were on their way to Utica, to the "castle." It's a place better known to Utica residents as Mistletoe Falls because of the mistletoe on the property. Once a nice home, today it's just the stone remains. Even in the daylight, sitting up in a wooded hillside in an isolated spot that faces the Ohio River, the place is spooky, with its serpentine walls, foot bridges, and burned-out fireplace. To the girls, it seemed even more ominous that night.

Legend surrounding the castle says that it was once inhabited by nine witches who controlled the town of Utica. It had been burned by townsfolk who tried to destroy the witches. At least, this is the legend Laurie believed, and she was eager to talk about it with others. In fact, Laurie had taken Toni and Hope up to see it just the day before. It was one of the stops they made on the ride down to Melinda's.

Laurie had been going up there for some time. She had taken Melinda and Amanda up there, too. Laurie showed them what she called "the mausoleum" where she believed the nine witches were buried. She also showed them the "dungeon" and an altar-like place where there was an inscription that said something about death. She told them she felt the presence of witches there.

Twisting through the country roads toward Utica, Hope engaged Shanda in further conversation about Amanda. It was a discussion that she knew would cause trouble.

"Do you know Melinda?" Hope asked.

"Yeah."

"Did you know that Amanda and Melinda broke up?"

"Well, I think me and Amanda have been going together for about four months now," Shanda said proudly.

In the backseat, Laurie tapped Melinda under the blanket, giving her the signal to appear. With that, Melinda jumped up, pulled Shanda's hair back, and put the knife to her throat.

"Surprise! I guess you weren't expecting to see me!" Melinda squealed.

"Please don't hurt me!" Shanda yelped and started crying.

"Shut up, bitch!" Melinda told her as she pressed the dull of the knife even harder into Shanda's neck.

"I just want to talk about Amanda. I want you to tell me the truth about Amanda. I'm not going to hurt you, I just want to talk."

Shanda just kept crying.

Melinda had the knife to Shanda's neck for the entire ride to The Witches' Castle as she continued her interrogation.

"Are you and Amanda going together?"

"No!"

"You're lying to me! I just heard you!"

"No, I was just saying that!"

"Did you go to the Harvest Homecoming with her?"

"No! Please don't hurt me, Melinda!"

"You better tell me the truth or I'll slit your throat!"

"I won't talk to Amanda anymore!" Shanda cried.

"Are you and Amanda writing to each other?"

"Yes."

"Did you go to the haunted house with Amanda?"

"Yes."

"Did you and Amanda have sex?"

"Yes."

"You're a liar!"

Shanda was hyperventilating.

"And Amanda knows I'm going to kill you . . . Amanda said she wants you dead just as much as I do!"

By then, they had turned the final corner, and they were at the foot of the castle. All five girls got out of the car and Melinda took one of Shanda's arms, Laurie took the other, and they led her up to the dungeon. Hope and Toni followed closely behind, using lighters to illuminate their path. Once in the dungeon, Laurie produced a couple of pieces of rope from her pocket and tied Shanda's ankles while Melinda tied her wrists. They sat her down on a bench. Hope and Toni kept two lighters going which produced eerie shadows on the fallen stone walls.

Melinda began to mock Shanda's looks, asking why she wore her hair that way, why she wore the shoes she wore. She hated the attitude Shanda had about her looks. She hated that Shanda was somehow trying to copy her.

Hope held the knife now, and was harassing Shanda with it. She made Shanda take off her rings and her Mickey Mouse watch. The watch played music and Hope thought it was fun, so she put it on and pressed the button a few times, laughing at Shanda.

"Doesn't she have pretty hair?" Hope teased.

"Yes, Shanda does have pretty hair, and I'm going to cut it off!" Melinda said.

It was a threat she made more than once.

Laurie pointed to the back of the dark dungeon and told Shanda there were bones buried back there.

"It could be you next," she said with a taunting glance.

Toni went back down to the car with Laurie and returned with a black T-shirt which they tried to set ablaze. It was a black T-shirt with a picture of a yellow smiley face with a bullet in its head. Laurie dowsed it with whiskey and was able to start a small fire.

"That's what you're going to look like, Shanda," Laurie told her.

Shanda couldn't say anything. She was still crying.

All of a sudden, about six cars went by at once and the girls got scared. The castle is private property, and they didn't want to get caught up there. Laurie was afraid people were going to see the flames.

"I know a better place where we can go," Laurie told them, "let's go to this place by my house." Everyone agreed; it was time to get out of The Witches' Castle, and Laurie and Melinda untied Shanda, grabbed hold of her arms, and escorted her back to the car.

Hope was driving, Toni was in the passenger's seat, and Melinda and Laurie had Shanda wedged between them in the back.

"We need gas, we're almost out," Hope said.

But nobody knew where a gas station was.

Shanda told them where she thought there might be an open gas station, Five Star, right near her dad's house. Shanda gave them the directions. Shanda must have felt safer being close to home, perhaps hoping she could recognize somebody and signal for help. But Laurie was one step ahead of her. Just before they pulled in, she covered Shanda with a blanket and she and Melinda stayed in the car to see that Shanda didn't make a move.

Hope pumped the gas, she and Toni went in to pay
for it, and they ran into a couple of good-looking guys in
a blue convertible on their way back. They struck up a
conversation and Toni joked about them taking her
home with them, asking if they were headed toward
Madison. The guys said they weren't. Hope was getting
nervous, thinking Laurie and Melinda might become
suspicious about their being gone so long, so they cut
the conversation short and hightailed it back to the car.

After they took off, however, they realized they didn't
have their bearings. They didn't know how to get back
to Madison. They had to stop at another gas station. At
the second station, Toni got out and called a friend of
hers, Mike, someone she had planned to look up in
Louisville. Toni talked with him for a couple of minutes,
just chitchat. Meanwhile, Hope got directions back to
Jeffersonville, and from there she knew she could find
their way.

It was about an hour's drive on the isolated country
road Route 62, and along the way, Laurie played strange
music, industrial punk music, and the other girls got
spooked because Laurie started to act strange. Laurie
screamed, she cried, she laughed her "Devil" laugh. It was
so unusual for Laurie, all these outbursts, she usually
showed hardly any emotion at all.

Melinda clutched the knife, holding it in full view.
The tip of it reached Toni's back up in the front seat.
Shanda was sobbing quietly.

"I just want to talk to you, Shanda," Melinda said in a
consoling voice. "I'm not going to hurt you."

When the girls arrived in Madison, Laurie directed
Hope to drive down Broad Road, a gravel road that led
just past Laurie's house. It was a heavily wooded area,
sparsely populated and lightly travelled. After they drove
for a few miles, Laurie told Hope to turn down a logging
road. It was actually a dirt path, and barely visible at that,

and Hope drove through the brambles and dirt until they reached a clearing which was used as a garbage dump.

Everybody got out of the car and walked around for a minute. Toni gave Shanda a hug and said she was sorry.

"Tell them not to hurt me," Shanda pleaded.

Toni turned to Melinda and asked her to take Shanda home.

"Shut up!" Melinda's voice boomed.

Toni was frightened. She and Hope got back in the car. They watched Laurie and Melinda make Shanda take off her clothes. Melinda came running back to the car with the items in her hands.

"I'm going to keep them for souvenirs!" Melinda said as she threw the sweatshirt, jeans, and bra in. Melinda grabbed one of Hope's T-shirts and took it for Shanda to wear. Hope took Shanda's white polka-dotted bra and put it on. She and Toni turned up both available radios, the jam box and the one on the car dashboard. They didn't want to listen to what was going on outside but they couldn't help themselves from watching through the windshield.

"Hit her!" Laurie commanded, holding Shanda's hands behind her back to give Melinda more leverage.

"Melinda, help me . . . please stop . . . don't do this to me," Shanda cried, "I'll stay away from Amanda, please . . ."

"Shut the fuck up!" Melinda howled.

Melinda punched Shanda in the stomach and the little girl went down, holding her stomach, gasping for air.

"Please stop! I have asthma! I can't breathe!" Shanda whimpered.

With Laurie egging her on, Melinda took Shanda's head and slammed it into her knee a couple of times. Shanda's mouth started to bleed profusely.

Then Melinda and Laurie each took one of Shanda's arms and Melinda tried to cut Shanda's throat. Melinda tried to use her foot to push the knife into Shanda's neck, but the knife was too dull. At that point Hope jumped out of the car and tried to hold Shanda down. When she got back in the car, Toni asked her why she was helping them. Hope didn't say anything.

When Toni looked back out the window, Laurie was sitting on Shanda's stomach and Melinda was sitting on her legs. Laurie was trying to strangle her but Shanda was still struggling. Melinda got out the rope and handed it to Laurie. She helped Laurie put it around Shanda's neck. They each took hold of it and pulled as tightly as they could until Shanda was unconscious.

A few minutes went by before Laurie came and tapped on the car window and said that Shanda was knocked out. She needed the keys to the trunk. Hope handed them to her, and Laurie asked that the two of them assist but neither girl budged. They watched as Laurie and Melinda opened the trunk and dragged Shanda; when they put her in, there was a loud thud.

Hope started to cry.

"Is she dead?" Hope asked.

"Yeah," Melinda told her.

"Oh, God! Oh, God!" Hope cried hysterically. She floored the gas pedal, driving frantically to get them out of the woods. Along the way, she hit a log or a bump, and it tore the muffler off the car.

"Oh, shit!" Laurie yelled. The car engine roared in the background.

The girls stopped over at Laurie's house. Laurie went into the kitchen, got some Pepsi and brought it up to her bedroom for everybody to drink. Laurie had on a long dark-colored trench coat similar to Melinda's. There was some blood splattered on it and she quickly washed up in the bathroom.

Hope and Toni were lying on the bed; they told Melinda they were tired. They wanted to go to sleep and wake up and find out that this was all just a bad dream. Just about then, Laurie's dog started barking outside and it startled the girls. All of a sudden—it was barely perceptible—they heard Shanda's muffled screams from the trunk.

"I'll take care of it," Laurie told them.

She raced from the house with a small paring knife in her hand which she had taken from her mother's kitchen.

Moments later, Laurie reappeared with more blood on her. Shanda's screams had stopped.

After Laurie washed her hands again, she came back to her room, pulled out a velvet pouch which contained Rune "stones" and poured them out onto the bed. She pulled a book out and began reading Melinda's future. Based on the ancient Rune magic which dates back to pagan Viking times, the stones are inscribed with messages, encoded with occult meaning. For Laurie, the stones were better than Tarot cards.

"Everything's going to be okay," she told Melinda.

Laurie made a quick phone call and the others overheard her saying, "It doesn't matter what I need it for! I just need it!"

When she hung up, she suggested that they all go out "country cruisin'." By then, it was after 2:30 in the morning, and Hope and Toni weren't interested. They didn't want to go and Laurie didn't push the issue.

Laurie grabbed her coat, and she and Melinda took off. Their first stop was the garbage burn pile next to Laurie's house. The girls were arguing about what to do with Shanda, and suddenly they heard kicking and screaming coming from the trunk. Somehow, they quieted her.

Laurie was getting nervous about her neighbors because she saw the lights on in their trailer. She figured they might have heard something, so she left Melinda out there in charge of Shanda and decided to go check out the situation. The people there had a working Coke machine on their front porch, and Laurie knocked and asked for change of a dollar, saying she was thirsty.

Her neighbor thought Laurie looked extremely upset, and he asked her if everything was alright. She explained about her muffler being torn off, saying she was going to get in trouble over it. She bought a Coke and left.

Minutes later, Laurie got into the driver's seat and started off toward Canaan, a nearby town. She suggested that they just stay up and drive around all night so Shanda could die slowly. She took them on isolated country roads, Melinda had no idea where they were. Then Shanda started kicking and screaming again, this time clawing at the insides of the trunk.

"I'll make her quiet," Laurie said as she pulled over, taking the trunk key from the ring, directing Melinda to get into the driver's seat.

Melinda was looking in the rearview mirror, watching Laurie open the trunk, and then she saw Laurie throwing punches and she heard Shanda screaming. There was a struggle going on between them, a lot of commotion. Melinda kept her foot on the pedal to drown it out. Suddenly she heard a thump and Laurie slammed the trunk down and came running back inside the car.

"You should have felt it!" Laurie yelped as she banged a black tire tool down on the dashboard. "It was so cool! I went like this and I could feel her head caving in!"

"Smell it!" Laurie said, and she stuck the tire tool up to Melinda's face.

"That's sick! I don't want to smell it!" Melinda protested. The tool was dripping with blood.

Laurie said she'd take over the driving again and they drove for a while. They were thinking about burning Shanda. They stopped the car again and both went back to the trunk to assess the situation.

As the trunk opened, both girls became startled.

Shanda sat straight up. Melinda could see the whites
of Shanda's eyes; they rolled back up into her head. She
was covered in blood. Her hair wasn't blond anymore . . .
it was red.

"Mommy," they heard her say as they closed the lid.

After that, Shanda wasn't moaning, she wasn't talking;
she was like a zombie. They stopped again and were
going to throw her over the bridge, but before they
could get her out of the trunk, they saw headlights approaching. Melinda threw the knife down and Laurie
quickly slammed the trunk on Shanda.

They continued driving and Shanda started kicking
again but this time they couldn't hear any screaming, all
they heard was gurgling. They stopped and opened the
trunk again and Shanda said "Melinda."

They closed it and kept driving until they heard the
banging again. Laurie went back to the trunk by herself.
When she came back, Melinda asked what happened.

"You've got to see her, she's soaked with blood. She's
red," Laurie yelled.

6/13